M000288400

A LOOK BACK

My Fifty Years Hosting Entertainers, Celebrities, and The Mob

By
Dick Cami

Henderson, Nevada
Ink & Quill Publishers
2018

A Look Back
My Fifty Years Hosting
Entertainers, Celebrities, and The Mob
By
Dick Cami

Line/Content Editor: Janelle Evans
Interior Design: Sherry Angell
Cover: Richard R. Draude

p. cm. — Dick Cami (Biography & Autobiography
Entertainment & Performng Arts)

ISBN: 978-1-941271-32-2/Paperback
ISBN: 978-1-941271-37-7/E-Pub

1. Biography & Autobiography/
   Entertainment & Performng Arts
2. Biography & Autobiography/Business
3. Biography & Autobiography/Rich & Famous

www.iqpublishers.com

Henderson, NV 89002
Printed in the United States of America

1 2 3 4 5 6 7 8 9 10

To Cindy

ACKNOWLEDGEMENTS

My profound thanks to:

All the guests, patrons, front and back of the house staff and entertainers at either of the Peppermint Lounges, Top of the Home or later Cami restaurant incarnations who took this ride with me either as lifelong friends or just ever so briefly. You are all part of my life story.

My parents, Richard and Alba Camillucci, who were my first musical inspirations, and my father-in-law, Johnny Futto, who was my most ardent supporter.

My partner of 26 years at the Top of the Home, Chef Joe Ezbecki, who also had a hand and a say in every restaurant to follow.

My life long friends who were part of so many stories and adventures, great and less than, and who no matter how many times stories are told are the best to sit down with and look back, Dick Kline, Vincent Marchese and Finbarr Nolan.

All those who shared stories, listened and encouraged me to write a book, especially Gregg Sutter who was the first to get me to really seriously attempt writing my stories down and John Henley who not only encouraged my efforts, but also generously shared his knowledge of the publishing process.

Long-time and loyal pal, Vinnie Curto, who introduced me to more recent friend Orlando Spado who put me in touch with Dennis Griffin who after reading and assisting with some early story organization sent my drafts to publisher Jo A. Wilkins.

All of Mystic Publishers, Inc. especially CEO Jo Wilkins for her dedication to a first time author, expert professional guidance and continued personal support. To editor Mary Einfeldt who was the first set of fresh eyes. To editor Janelle Evans who brought her experience and expertise as a published author herself to the final edit and proofing. And, thanks to all those behind the scenes who contributed to making this book not just a reality but, the best it could be.

Wilford Brimley who didn't even slightly hesitate when asked if he would consider writing a forward.

Most of all, in getting this book over the finish line, to my lady, Cindy Aumann, who provided unwavering encouragement and support in every manner imaginable and was with me every word of the way.

Reviews and testimonials

On vacation in Miami I was at the place to be, the Peppermint Lounge, to see and to sit in laying sax with my old friends, The Seven Blends. Finishing my stay I was driving out of the peppermint parking lot one night when I heard my name called out. That's when I was invited to join the BG Ramblers. We were invited back every winter to be the Miami Peppermint's house and. I have to say if it wasn't for the kindness and love from Dick Cami I wouldn't have had the break of my life to travel the world with the Ramblers. Or the opportunity at the Peppermint where we performed with some pretty well known people. Man, what a night it was when the Beatles came in!

Kenny Pimental,
Vocalist and Head Saxophonist, BG Ramblers

From the first story Cami grabs you by the collar and pulls you in as he guides you through a world that most of us have never encountered. This is the work of a master storyteller that you will have a hard time putting down.

Joseph Hacker, A Friend

It's not Dr. Seuss but it's great. The only thing better than reading the book is meeting Dick Cami in person. When Dick told his stories at the Top it was wonderful. You wanted to bring in good friends to hear them and the food was good too. Take time to read this book. Those were great days. I re-lived them and you can too. Where are those places today? I have the best memories... and, think I still owe a bill there.

Shecky Greene, Comedian,
Character Actor but Horse Bettor first

Dick Cami is a storyteller like no other. Whether he is talking Muhammad Ali or the Beatles, Frank Sinatra or Jimmy Hoffa, his words have the power not just to chronicle, but to transport readers and listeners back to any decade."

Jon Varese, Author,
The Spirit Photographer

"I remember the good food and beautiful view but what I recall most fondly and miss the most is the pride, warmth and caring with which my good friends, Sam Kornweisser and Ralph Saggese, NYC Peppermint Lounge managers, introduced me to their friend Dick Cami's Florida estaurant, Top of the Home. As a guest I appreciated the experience of that old-time sincere, welcoming hospitality not felt often enough in today's world."

Joe Scognamillo,
Restaurateur/Owner of fourth generation
Patsy's Italian Restaurant, Mid-town Manhattan, NYC

Top of the Home, was known for fabulous food and elegant ambience, but you were truly fortunate when Dick Cami sat down at your table and shared his stories. Sure to entertain... everyone left with a smile.

Dick Kline,
Music Industry Executive

The Top Of The Home was a place where the who's who would meet. There would be famous singers such as Tony Bennett and others, movie stars, mobsters, judges, politicians and friends of Mr. Cami's. Dick has friends all over the world. I entertained there for a while and can only say, once you meet him you realize there's something special about him. He makes you feel special because he's just a goodhearted real man with great qualities. I've entertained in hundreds of clubs and restaurants but never worked for a better man. We became lifetime friends. This book is about an absolutely brilliant, goodhearted man who values friendship and family and all his memories from 50 years of in this business. This about my great friend Mr. Dick Cami.

Jimmy Sabini

When there is time travel, I'm going back to Dick Cami's "Top of the Home" Hollywood Florida, Christmas Celebration December 1980! Dick has two best friends by his side; John and Tony Bennett, family name Benedetto. The place to see and be seen by the top recording stars and the best recognized actors. Those whose names are known worldwide. Dare I add the elusive mobster? Names you have never heard or read.

Patricia Benedetto, Author of:
The Shadow of His Smile, Brothers Together in Life and song

Forget Will Rogers and Uncle Remus! When it comes to great storytellers nobody does it better than consummate restaurateur and raconteur-extraordinaire than the charming Mr. Dick Cami. Throughout his career he has made friends with both the famous (think Frank Sinatra) to the infamous (how about Meyer Lansky). They all came to dine at his award-winning restaurant Top of the Home in Hollywood, Florida or The Peppermint Lounge in New York City and Miami, the home of the Twist that helped change the history of music in the 1960's. He made friends with them all and they let their hair down and acted naturally, or sometimes badly, when they were around him. And Cami remembers it all. When he tells anecdotes about his experiences with the icons of our society with his down-home wit, he brings them alive as if you are a fly on the wall watching all the action. You can never get tired of hearing Cami tell a story even if you heard it many times before. There's always a new aspect to it. Cami has elevated storytelling to an art form and he paints each picture with spell-bounding keenness that keeps you mesmerized. Cami is a talented writer who is able to transfer these tales successfully to paper. I know this book will be a compelling read and a page-turner that you won't be able to put down.

Alice Fisher Edelman, Publicist and co-author of
How to Survive a Second Marriage

Dick Cami is the friend everyone wishes they had! Some of the greatest memories my wife Joanie and I share are with Dick at The Top Of The Home, his fabulous restaurant, in the Cami home and on trips together. Dick has a great memory. His recollection of noted actors, politicians and famous people from many parts of the world will keep you mesmerized for hours. He is one of the greatest storytellers and entertainers I have ever known. His career spans decades and he has always been a tremendous success. Dick Cami is a loyal and beloved friend. I wish Joanie and I were seeing him tonight at the Top Of The Home.

Donald L. Tucker,
Former Speaker, Florida House of Representatives

FORWARD

My dear friend, Dick Cami, asked me to write a forward to his book. In response I have to say that I'm honored, humbled and delighted to do so.

I've known Dick and considered him a friend for the last thirty years. When we first met I was sent to Miami to do a film. A mutual friend told me that when I got to Florida, there was someone I had to meet. That someone was Dick Cami. Thank you, George, from the bottom of my heart. From that meeting developed a friendship that I have treasured for the past thirty years and still do to this day.

The stories in this book are humorous, very colorful, and most important, they're all true. I have met and come to be friends with many of these colorful characters.

I got to know Angelo Dundee. I got to know Finbarr Nolan. I became good friends with the real guy they call Terry Malloy in "On the Waterfront."

I met Jake Lamotta and many others...too many to name. Hell, I was given the key to Hollywood, Florida!

This book is a real treat. It's a close look at life, perhaps a life that many of us have only seen in the movies.

It's interesting. My personal background is that of a cowboy from the Rocky Mountain West. That's a long way from the "mean streets of NY." But, the men I grew up with, other than the accent, are pretty much the same as those from Dick Cami's background. They all pretty much try to do the right thing.

Thanks, Dick, for your friendship, your example, and for taking the time to share your life in this book.

"When you live in a world of insanity...and find another mind that thinks and speaks as yours does...it's a blessed event, much like Robinson Crusoe finding a footprint in the sand."

If Dick Cami told me that a piss-ant could pull a plow, I'd just hook him up.

Enjoy!

Wilford Brimley

INTRODUCTION

"One could almost see Frank Sinatra suavely sliding into a booth or Shecky Greene wisecracking with the waiter as he orders his favorite dish, stone crabs, or Tom Jones singing Happy Birthday to his son, or Rocky Marciano studying the menu and passing up the 'plum de veau' in favor of roast beef, or Don Shula and Chuck Knoll sharing a bottle of wine and talking football."

Miami Herald review of Top of the Home Restaurant

October 21, 1987

In early 2000, at my last restaurant, Grumpy Dick's Seafood Grill in Plantation, Florida, a guest does a double take and calls me over to his table.

"Aren't you Dick Cami?"

"Yes," I answer with a smile.

He starts telling me about his memories of the Top of the Home. He calls it the Golden Years. We look back together on an era at The Top, the rooftop restaurant of fine dining that I owned for a quarter of a century from 1965-1990, in Hollywood, Florida. This is the book everybody says I should write. It's a collection of vignettes and short stories of some of the incredible experiences I had with famous stars, athletes, politicians, celebrities, and wise guys who were my guests over the years. It showcases a time when guys dated dolls, wise guys didn't go to shrinks, and Florida resorts were the place to see, be seen and, sometimes, hide out. It is a story of some of the people who wrote major chapters in history.

From our first day the elevator doors opened to the Top of the Home restaurant on the 19th floor of the Home Federal Building, we welcomed guests into the opulent gaslight era of Diamond Jim Brady and Lillian Russell. The 6,000 square foot restaurant and bar had red flocked wallpaper, dark mahogany woodwork, dining tables covered in white linen tablecloths surrounded by red velvet chairs, antiques, and accents of gold and black. The fifty-mile panoramic view from Fort Lauderdale to Miami became legendary, as did our tableside preparation of dishes by tuxedoed captains. The bar area pulsed with live entertainment and dancing until two in the morning. Both of our bartenders sang as they poured drinks and were often joined by a well-timed aria from my partner, Chef Joseph Ezbicki, as he exited the kitchen. It was a magical time–a scene that could have been in *Goodfellas*.

Home Federal Bank building with rooftop Top of the Home restaurant on the circle in Hollywood, Florida, 1965-1990. (Dick Cami)

You entered another era when you stepped out of the elevator into the lobby of the Top of the Home. (Dick Cami)

Top of the Home interior with fifty mile panoramic view of South Florida. (Dick Cami)

Newspaper advertisement for Top of the Home, 1986. (Dick Cami)

Tom Jones with Top of the Home partners Chef Joe Ezbecki and Host/Owner Dick Cami in restaurant foyer after dinner celebration for his son's birthday. (Dick Cami)

Top of the Home guests, Tony Bennett and Martha Raye. (Dick Cami)

Dick Cami with Joe Ezbecki in front of the photo memory wall at Grumpy Dick's Seafood Grill, Plantation, Florida, 2006. (Cindy Aumann)

I don't remember exactly when it began, but at some point my guests started inviting me to join their tables. Eventually, it became a ritual for me to sit with them and exchange stories. I entertained everyone from Frank Sinatra to John Q. Public, Meyer Lansky to J. Edgar Hoover. While they enjoyed our exceptional dishes and great wines, we talked. I heard their stories while collecting my own to share.

The stories, however, started long before the doors ever opened on the 19th floor. Before there was ever a Top of the Home, there were the Peppermint Lounges. I was only in my twenties when my father-in-law, Johnny "Johnny Futto" Biello, a major wise guy, gave me a piece of the original Peppermint Lounge in New York City. The club had been taken over as a favor from a fellow wise guy, Sibbey Mamone, when he had to go on the lam. Futto renamed it the Peppermint Lounge, and it opened in 1958 as a bookie front and teenage dive right off Times

Square. By a serendipitous fluke, it became the city's hottest nightspot. It was the first rock and roll nightclub of its kind, having a major impact on the music scene. Teenagers joined by high society types danced the Twist to our house band, Joey Dee and the Starliters. Following the success in New York, I opened a second Peppermint Lounge on The Causeway in Miami Beach, Florida. Miami was the entertainment capital of America during the winter and the perfect place for it.

New York City cabbie minds the pooch while a NYC Peppermint Lounge society patron "Twists the Night Away" inside, 1961. (Dick Cami)

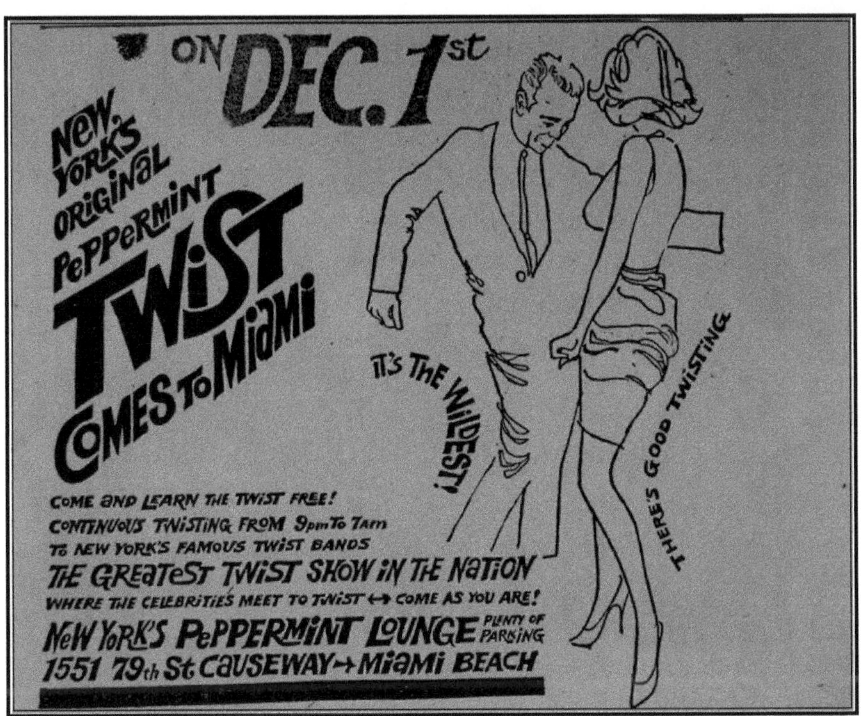

Newspaper ad announcing the opening of the Miami Beach Peppermint Lounge, 1961. (Dick Cami)

Custom designed musical van that made a nightly circuit advertising the Miami Beach Peppermint Lounge, 1962-1964. (Dick Cami)

Twisting to the music of the B.G. Ramblers at the Miami Beach Peppermint Lounge. (Dick Cami)

Dion playing the guitar on the Miami Beach Peppermint Lounge stage. (Dick Cami)

Uncle Scatsy Biele in the kitchen during the nightly Midnight Twist-A-Rama at Miami Beach Peppermint Lounge. (Dick Cami)

Former music partner Vincent Marchese with Dick Cami in front of photo wall of memories at Grumpy Dick's Seafood Grill, Plantation, Florida, 2006. (Cindy Aumann)

As a nightclub guy and restaurateur open to opportunity, I had the pleasure and the headache of promoting countless entertainers, including music legends Tony Bennett, Engelbert Humperdinck, Dean Martin and Julio Iglesias. But it didn't stop at musical acts. I somehow got a hand in the boxing world and even, at one time, promoted Irish touch healer, Finbarr Nolan: the seventh son of a seventh son.

The one thing I never thought I'd do was become a writer. But, you can't be out hosting and table-hopping nearly every night for the best of five decades and not have a collection of stories. I acquired a reputation as a storyteller and received invitations, not just to sit down while my patrons dined, but to come open other restaurants—and bring my stories. Short of that, many conversations ended with the comment, "You should write a book!" My honest reply, in an easily recognizable Bronx accent, was most often, "Write...I don't even talk good." But, eventually, with increasing interest, encouragement, and the advent of the personal computer I did start putting down first some notes, then stories.

In this book, I'll share my fifty years of experiences with you from my days owning and managing the Peppermint Lounges and the Top of the Home, to working with superstars in entertainment and sports and, of course, rubbing elbows with the mob. You will recognize many names. I'll admit that even I was amazed as I was putting this collection together of how many lives intersected across the lines of status, interests, career choices, and generations.

Part Two contains the longer short stories of Mikey the Hat and Favo Allan. While these stories are mostly true, based on actual characters and real events, they have been expanded for clarity and interest. Some names have been omitted or changed to protect both the innocent and the guilty.

A LOOK BACK

Part 1

ENTERTAINERS & CELEBRITIES

CONTENTS

Part 1: Entertainers and Celebrities

ON STAGE:
Conway Twitty, Jerry Lee Lewis, The Regulars, Little Willie John, Mitch Ryder, and Mary Wells

Conway Twitty began his music career in rock and roll. Even though he had a number one Billboard hit with *It's Only Make Believe*, his initial success in that genre faded in the early 60s. He began adding country songs to his act and broke into the country Top Ten with *The Image of Me*. Following that, he teamed up with Loretta Lynn for their first duet, *After the Fire Is Gone*, which became the first of their five straight number one country hits. Twitty's solo career thrived at the same time with a string of Top Ten singles.

Sometime in the seventies, I walked up the steps to Caesar's Palace in Vegas. I saw Conway walking toward me. He'd come a long way from the decade earlier when I booked him as the first headliner at the Miami Beach Peppermint Lounge. His face lit up like a Christmas tree when he saw me. We hugged and brought each other up to date.

He said about working the Peppermint, "It was the best time I can remember working in a club." I walked away a little taller.

In spite of his status as a country music star, he seemed less than confident when he said, "How do you think I'll go over in Vegas?"

"Are you kidding me? You're a star—you'll do great wherever you perform."

"I've never worked here before so I was just wondering."

I thought about that first time he appeared at the Peppermint. He was already a star with his big hit, *It's Only Make Believe*. Most performers, especially those who are already known, tend to be a little reserved the first day or so, but not Conway. He came into the club to rehearse with a big smile on his face and was friendly to everyone, including my incorrigible uncle Scatsy, a small pitbull of a man who just about lived at the joint running the kitchen and service bar among the myriad of other things with a sure hand, fierce loyalty and a well hidden heart of gold.

I noticed a strange thing when Conway did his first set in front of an audience though. He stood alongside the band and not in front of it, like the star of the show normally does. My customers asked their waiters, "Which one is Conway?"

When the set ended and Conway came off stage, I explained what I had observed.

"I'm giving it to you straight," I said. "You're going to have to stand in front of the band so people will know who you are. Stand out front in the middle of the stage and sing your songs—that's what the star of the show is supposed to do."

"Gee, I've never done that before. I always sing with my band."

"Well, you can't do it that way here. If you have intentions of staying in this business you'd better get it right, starting now. I can't believe I'm explaining this to you."

"Okay, I'll try it for a set," he replied without much enthusiasm.

After the next set, a very concerned Conway came off the stage and over to me. "I don't think I can do this," he said. "I was so nervous my behind was twitching like crazy. I'd rather sing all the sets standing with the band."

I couldn't believe what I was hearing. I stared at him for a few seconds and then said, "Okay, do it the way you want. Just make sure they announce you. And mark my words, someday you're gonna have to separate yourself from your band and sing up there on the stage alone."

Conway turned and walked away without another word. When he was gone, Scatsy came sauntering toward me, "What's up with this palooka? He don't wanna do a show?"

"He's gonna do the show, but he's going to do it singing with the band. The band will announce him to the audience so everyone will know who he is. It'll work out all right."

And it did.

The curious thing about Conway was that as nervous as he was being the center of attention on stage, when off the stage, he was all over the club socializing. He really enjoyed meeting people and engaging in conversation with them. Everyone had a good word to say about him.

L-R Joe E. Ross and Burl Ives with Conway Twitty, our first Miami Beach Peppermint Lounge headliner, 1962. (Dick Cami)

After Conway Twitty's appearance at the Peppermint Lounge booking a headline act in addition to our nightly bands became our practice. Jerry Lee Lewis was next up. I didn't know the performer but he shared Conway's manager, whose name had been given to me by Morris Levy. The manager had accurately predicted I would love Conway but warned that Jerry Lee was "a little weird." When Conway was closing out his engagement knowing that Jerry Lee was following him for a two week stint, he advised me that he was a fantastic piano player but would have to have a good baby grand. I knew this beforehand but suggested to Conway that we might play a little joke on Jerry Lee, bringing in a small broken down upright. I wanted Conway's thoughts as I explained to him what their manager had said and I didn't want to truly piss off Jerry Lee, getting off on what could be a very wrong foot.

Conway was all for the joke and encouraged me, saying it would be the funniest thing ever and urged me to really do it. Conway even promised to be there when Jerry Lee came in and suggested he would take any blame for the whole thing.

Over time, having rented many pieces of equipment from Larry's Piano and Organ, I had developed a very good relationship with them. When I walked into their showroom I asked Larry, "What's the biggest and best grand piano you have in the house?"

"The concert grand," Larry answered. "The black one over there...you want it?"

The piano was a beauty and I would have taken it, but I could tell just by looking it would be too big for our stage so I asked about a baby grand. Larry told me that they had just gotten in a Yamaha, the best made, and that it wasn't even out of the crate yet. It was just the ticket and I didn't hesitate in taking it. I then asked if he had a little broken down upright available. His forehead wrinkled up in confusion. Once I explained the set-up to him he said, "What's life without a few laughs? I only wish I could be there to see Jerry Lee's face when he sets eyes on the spinet." I suggested he come over with the crew when they delivered the piano but warned that as soon as the laugh was over they had to be immediately ready to install the baby grand.

A full-on sunny day with just the right amount of coolness in the Miami air welcomed the arrival of Jerry Lee and his band to the Peppermint Lounge. He wore a white and blue striped polo shirt, Caribbean khaki trousers with a fourteen-inch peg cuff, with a sweater over his arm. His famous blond hair was uncombed and waving in all directions. He headed to where we sat and immediately said to Conway, "Hiya, Horse, watcha doin'?"

Conway nodded. "I'm doing okay, Killer. Say hello to the

bosses here. This is Dick Cami and his uncle, Scatsy." After shaking hands, Scatsy excused himself to go over to Nick and Arthur's next door to let Larry know that it was okay to bring in the piano.

When Jerry Lee looked over to the stage and noticed the obvious absence of any piano, I quickly let him know that it was on its way and should be here very shortly. Meanwhile, Larry had left Nick and Arthur's, turned the delivery truck around and pulled up to the back of the Peppermint. Scatsy opened the door to let them in, hollering at the top of his lungs, "Crissake, hurry up! Jerry Lee is already here and has got to rehearse."

The piano, covered in large moving blankets, rolled past Jerry Lee up to center stage. Larry in a grand flourish grabbed the cover and pulled it off. Jerry Lee didn't so much as twitch or show any emotion. He just walked up on stage over to the piano where he positioned himself at the keyboard and with one finger depressed a few successive keys. The out of tune notes bounced all over the empty room. Then he looked over at Conway and said, "You wouldn't have anything to do with this, Horse, would you?" The whole room broke up with laughter as Conway shrugged.

Scatsy turned to Larry and started barking out instructions. "All right, get that piece of shit outta here and bring in the good one."

A flicker of emotion finally showed on Jerry Lee's face. He gave the slightest smile as he looked down at Scatsy. The baby grand came in on its side and was positioned while the band got set up. After everything was in place, Jerry Lee sat down on the piano seat, threw his sweater on top of the piano, spread his hands over the keys and musical magic filled the room. He looked up at me and said, "This will do just fine."

Conway and Jerry Lee couldn't have been more different from one another, total opposites. On stage, Conway was shy about his ability while nothing could hold Jerry Lee back. Yet, as sociable off stage and well liked by all our staff and the public as Conway was, Jerry Lee was unsociable and diffident; ducking into his dressing room as soon as he was finished performing. He would sit there alone, brooding and depressed, doubting his talent and any possibility of future success.

Interestingly enough, country music beckoned to each of them. Conway, perhaps, made the transition more willingly. In talking to Jerry Lee, he expressed his desire to stay at the top of the rock-and-roller heap. I remember when he appeared at the Paramount Theater in New York during the glory days of rock and roll. He drew the biggest crowd to date and that included topping Frank Sinatra. I was glad of Conway's eventual legendary status in country and encouraged Jerry Lee—though I never felt he listened to me much.

Within the last few years, on a personal visit back to New York City, I took in the musical *Million Dollar Quartet* about a Sun Records jam session with Jerry Lee, Carl Perkins, Elvis Presley, and Johnny Cash. Talking to the couple next to me at intermission, I found out, quite by chance, that Jerry Lee was performing the next night at B.B. King's Blues Club. As soon as the box office opened the next day, my lady and I were there getting tickets for that evening.

Jerry Lee Lewis performing at BB King's Blues Club NYC, 2012. (Cindy Aumann)

When we arrived at the club, I sent a note back to Jerry Lee's dressing room just in case there was any chance I might see him after the show. Seated dead center, with a great view of the stage, we struck up a conversation with two guys at our table. They knew Jerry Lee well, and they told me he really didn't like seeing much of anyone these days. As it turned out, I wouldn't be the exception! The years had taken a toll on him, and he had to be helped out on stage to the piano bench by a couple guys on either side of him. Nonetheless, when he hit those first chords with flying fingers, hands, elbows, whatever it took, never hitting a wrong key or missing a beat, there was no mistaking that Jerry Lee was still every bit the unbelievable entertainer I remembered from his early days in the sixties at the Peppermint.

The band perhaps most famous and often associated with the Peppermint Lounge, was our initial and longest playing house band at the New York Peppermint, Joey Dee and the Starliters. They played a brief two weeks at the Miami club before capitalizing on their fame and going on the road. The Miami Peppermint had the unique format of being the only club in the country that featured four bands plus a star attraction nightly performing sets without interruption until our closing at 7 a.m. The Coasters, with Earl "Speedo" Carroll as the lead singer, were regulars at the Peppermint and an all around favorite. Speedo had a distinctly lyrical voice and perfect comedic timing. He was always smiling and laughing, but one night he showed up with misery written all over his face.

I noticed the unusual demeanor right away and took him aside. "Hey, Speedo, what's up? You look like shit."

"I got pain, man." The words had come out barely audible. "I can't believe how I'm hurtin'."

It was a packed-house Friday night about an hour before show time, and Speedo was looking uncertain. I wasn't overly worried because the Coasters were such an individually talented group, I knew even though it would be less without Speedo they would still put on a good show. However, I'd had similar emergencies before so I'd developed contingencies. I called up my friend Dr.

Glassman, who somewhere along the line we had dubbed "The Croaker." Actually, he was anything but. He was more like an old-time house call doc who'd come out anytime, day or night, rain or shine. He was at the Peppermint fifteen minutes after getting my call. "Listen, Doc," I explained, " You gotta give Speedo something. We got three shows ahead tonight."

Barely a half hour later, and just minutes before the show, I see Speedo grinning from ear to ear and flashing me the okay sign.

Just then I heard, "Ladies and gentlemen...the Coasters."

Speedo turned, joined the Coasters as they danced their way onto the stage. He grabbed the mike, did a spin, leaned in, and started singing:

Walk right in...sit right down...and welcome to the Peppermint Lounge.
We got Whitey on the door, Scatsy on the floor,
The cutest bunch of twisters you ever saw,
So...walk right in...

It was maybe their best show ever.

Bobby Borda Band with The Coasters. Speedo far right in dark jacket. (Dick Cami)

A great all-around band is hard to find, but that's exactly what we landed with the B.G. Ramblers. Out of Bowling Green (BG), Ohio, these six all-American kids could double up on various instruments and put on one hell of a show. I hired them on a recommendation that, besides playing rock and roll, they could duplicate all the big bands sounds. The timing couldn't have been more perfect. I had just hired a Broadway choreographer to create a show about popular dances from the beginning of time right up to and including the Twist. We called it *Crazy Crazes*, and it ran for that whole season in Miami Beach.

The show consisted of two male and two female dancers plus Regina Rae, the lead singer, who performed show-stopping tunes between costume changes. The B.G. Ramblers did such a phenomenal job that season, I made a decision to bring them back the following year. But the back story on that brings a practical meaning to the term *photo op*.

Newspaper advertisement for Headliner Hank Ballard and his band The Midnighter's. (Dick Cami)

On their first trip to the States The Beatles pose with the B.G. Ramblers at the Miami Beach Peppermint Lounge, 1964. (Dick Cami)

The NY Peppermint Lounge was a target stop on the Beatles' first trip to America. I got a call that the Beatles were coming down to Miami and wanted to meet Hank Ballard, who they greatly admired and found out was performing at our club. When the Beatles came in, Hank was just finishing a set. The Beatles weren't yet the craze they would become. Initially, Hank balked at the suggestion and convincing him to take a picture with them took considerable arm-twisting. But once that was done, I invited the B.G. Ramblers to step up and also have a picture taken with the Liverpool group. Shyly reticent at first, I got a couple of the members to step forward, the others followed and we got a great picture of the two groups, Beatles and Ramblers.

The following season when we were getting ready to open, I called the B.G. Ramblers to set the date when they would be coming down, but was hit instead with an unexpected confession.

"What dates can you get down here for?" I asked.

"Well, Dick...things have changed for us a little."

"What do you mean?

"Well, we're getting more money now."

"No kidding?" I was happy for them. "What happened, did you guys get a hit record?"

"No...not exactly. You know that picture you made us take with the Beatles. Well, wherever we play now the club owners use the picture and advertise us as the Beatles' favorite band. We're getting double what you paid us." The explanation came out like an apology. "So, I don't know what to do."

"Well, I know," I said,"Stay where you are and God bless ya."

I had no animosity. In fact, I was glad for them...though I couldn't help but be a bit amused as I thought about how I had to coax them into taking the picture. Still, it couldn't have happened to a better bunch of guys.

There's no question that Little Willie John was one of the pioneers of R&B, a rock-and-roll great, and precursor to soul music. He sang with passionate energy in a big voice, even if his stature didn't match. He had hit songs before and after *Fever* was released in 1956, but that was the one he is best remembered for. Even though his version didn't go to the pop charts, it sold an unheard of million copies. The success of that record prompted Peggy Lee to record it. Her famous rendition not only was a pop chart hit, it became her signature song.

Little Willie had problems with his temper and alcohol; a bad combination. He came into the Miami Peppermint countless times broke and looking for a handout. I'd always offer him a meal and usually gave him fifty bucks or so even though I knew he would go right out and buy a bottle. What really got to me was the many times he would come in shoeless, which probably meant he'd been too helpless to prevent his shoes from being stolen on the streets.

I couldn't help but admire his talent and rue his fate. I had acts appearing on stage then that couldn't touch him, and yet he became a totally broken man. A talent who should have had everything ended up dead in prison. I did see that in 1996 he was posthumously, and much deservedly, inducted into the Rock and Roll Hall of Fame.

Vincent "Vinny" Marchese, my music partner and talent manager, called me right away after he cut a demo with a new dynamite artist he felt tremendously sure of. Originally from Detroit, Mitch Ryder had that natural feel for the music. Listening to him, you could almost mistake him for a black musician with all the soul he put into his songs. The demo Mitch cut that day was the top ten hit, *Jenny Take a Ride.* Vinny flew down to Miami Beach and we took the demo over to Steve Alaimo, who at the time was with Henry Stone at Tone Distributors. Henry Stone was a legend in the music business and one of the pioneer producers of the rhythm and blues era that gave us such eminent entertainers as Ray Charles, James Brown, and Sam and Dave.

I left the record with Alaimo but before they made a decision on it, Dynamo Record Company was started and Vinny took it from there. Mitch's second release was another monster smash, *Devil with the Blue Dress On.* What a group! Mitch Ryder and the Detroit Wheels were riding high.

Then the wheels came off.

Vinny wasn't sure, but he suspected that Mitch was doing drugs. He asked me if I had a musician we could put with the group that could give us an inside look. I told him I did. Andy Dio, a talented musician who played for us as a solo act while also attending the University of Miami, took the gig. He could play his trumpet with the best of them. It wasn't long before Vinny found out why Mitch's behavior was so erratic. Not only was he mainlining heroin, but he put other musicians in the group on to the stuff as well.

Both Vinny and I could scarcely believe that a nineteen year old kid earning $400 a week only six or seven months earlier to now making twenty-five thousand a night would throw it all away by getting started in with drugs and alcohol. Things fell apart quickly for Mitch. Vinny couldn't tolerate the ups and downs and there was soon a parting of the ways.

What happens to performers when they hit it big? Why do they resort to drugs and drinking and lose control of their personality? Why do so many of them sink into that hellhole of substance abuse? Can anyone explain this to me? We see it happening in the papers all the time—entertainers who have it all doing the stupidest things in public. I guess some people just can't handle success. Here's another example of what I mean.

Applause, a nightclub I opened in downtown Miami in the Omni Complex, was definitely the biggest and most beautiful club in all of South Florida. It reeked with elegance and cost the drug dealers who first built it well over three million to put it together in 1980. Soon after they opened, the Florida State beverage department closed them down for drug trafficking. I then took it over and reopened it featuring some of the greatest musical dance groups ever, including Tito Puente, Tito Rodriguez, and Willie Chirino.

When the opportunity of booking Mary Wells, a legitimate record act, came to my attention I immediately jumped at the chance. I looked forward to her performance because she was an icon in the rock-and-roll world, and the first rhythm and blues artist out of Detroit for Motown Records in the early sixties. Her recording of *My Guy* is still one of my favorites.

You can imagine how disappointed I was when she came into the audition completely stoned. By now, I'd seen this with other artists that achieved famed, yet it always amazed me. Maybe it was a form of depression. It truly depressed me.

Mary was supposed to come in with a trio to perform with her, but all she had was a tape recorder and a bass player who was more stoned than she was—her boyfriend or whatever. I hesitated letting her go on, but we'd been advertising her appearance for a week and a capacity crowd came in to see her opening night. I knew I'd made a mistake the moment she hit the stage. She was so God-awful bad that it hurt me to see her perform. I've been through other nights like it, and who knows how, but somehow we got through them.

At the end of her show I summoned her to my office. Although I'd booked her in for a week, I paid her off for the one night and told her that she wouldn't be doing any more shows for us. She knew she'd bombed and didn't offer any argument. I had an urge to get into why she had this problem but I've been down that road before with other artists, and frankly, that's why I got out of management. *You're Mary Wells for crissake,* I wanted to tell her. *How can you act this way?*

I didn't really expect to see Mary again and certainly not any time soon, but about three months later, I was in London, England with world-class hustler Terrance Cole, a black friend of mine from Arkansas. We were pursuing a deal with a wealthy Nigerian diplomat that never materialized because the most incredible thing happened. While the diplomat was walking in Soho, someone came up from behind and plunged a hypodermic needle full of drugs into him, then put his unconscious body in a box to be shipped back to Nigeria as freight. It would have been a done deal at Heathrow Airport but for the fact that while tied up in the box waiting to be loaded onto the plane, he came to and started yelling and was quickly discovered—lucky guy. After that he took off on the lam never to be seen again. It was a big story that hit the front page of all the newspapers.

Another good friend in London, Eddie Richardson, had the reputation of being the man to see in town. Several days after the incident with the Nigerian diplomat, Eddie heard I was in town and asked me to join him for the evening at his nightclub in Southeast London. Cole said he would like to go but first he had a dinner engagement with some sheikh, and promised he'd join me right after that. I gave him the address and phone number of the club, just in case he had any difficulty.

Eddie ran the typical nightclub. It was a one floor walk up without much décor. It featured a big bar with plenty of seats around a large dance floor and bandstand. Their house band filled the club with pretty decent renditions of 50's and 60's dance tunes.

I was at the club only a short while when Eddie said there was a phone call for me. I knew it had to be Cole and that there had to be some kind of problem.

"Are you all right there?" Cole asked.

"Of course, I am," I replied. "Come on, I'm waiting for you."

When he finally arrived, he plopped down next to me and relayed the full story. "When I hailed this taxi and gave the driver the address, he stopped and told me to get out—just like that. I figured it was because I was black. Then I hailed another cab and when I gave him the address he also pulled over to the side and told me that he wouldn't take me to this address unless I called first. He further went on to say that he'd been driving a taxi since WWII and this was the first time he'd ever gotten a fare that asked him to take them to that part of town...Southeast London. That's when I called you."

Just as Cole wrapped up his story, the emcee of the club walked on stage. I couldn't believe my ears when he announced that the star of the show that evening was Mary Wells. *My Mary Wells?* Well, I was flabbergasted to say the least. She walked on stage with three beautiful back up singers and I could see that this wasn't the same Mary Wells that I'd let go at my club. She had totally changed—definitely not the wacked-out, stoned wretch that came to work for me that unfortunate night. What a transformation! She was very much the beautiful composed Mary Wells that one would expect to see all decked out in a magnificently custom-designed gown with spangles that glittered with every note she sang. The three exotically dressed dancers she had on stage with her shimmered like stars themselves as they sang backup vocals for her.

Mary put on a fantastic show and as she came off the stage, Cole went over to congratulate her. That's when she saw me. I thought she was going to have a melt down or heart attack. *What did she think I was going to do...tell Eddie about her?* There was no way I would do anything like that. I just played a dead hand and smiled, shaking her hand like we'd never met before, congratulating her on a dynamite show. It was great to be present for a happy ending.

Chapter 2

ON THE FLOOR:
Ginger Rogers, NYC Trouble, Miami Beach Trouble, and More Trouble

The NYC Peppermint was peaking in the early 60's when Ginger Rogers showed up at the door one night to see what everyone was talking about. Like so many celebrities before her, she was somewhat ignored at first by a staff who, surrounded by the stars night after night, didn't much care who was who. Maybe that was part of the fascination that attracted such a wide cross section of people. Accustomed to neither the nonchalance that confronted her, nor being made to wait, she showed a combination of impatience, intolerance and disappointment as she stood in line with her two escorts.

When I first glimpsed her there, I briefly compared her to the other Hollywood beauties who came into the club, trying to decide who was the most beautiful; Arlene Dahl, Loretta Young, Rita Hayworth, Ava Gardner. Some made better guests, such as Elizabeth Taylor who was always gracious, and some, especially those who drank a lot, were not the best behaved, to say the least. I had favorites based on that, but each was stunningly beautiful. Ginger Roger's eyes sparkled and her face matched her screen image. She wore a soft silky sweater with a tight fitted skirt to match, and looked like she could step onto the dance floor and embark on a routine at any moment. Only Fred Astaire was missing.

As soon as I caught our maître d, Fredie Pace's eye, he moved into action pulling her party out of line. "Step aside will ya and let these people through. Hey! Buddy, that means you!" Then he turned to the Turk. "Put this party on a four top."

"Where? We don't have anything open."

Freddie stared him down.

"Ok...Ok. Gimme a minute." The Turk approached the last table he'd sat ringside and nicely told them a mistake had been made and that their table was reserved. The Turk gestured toward the line and said, "Accept my apologies and get back in line. You get the next table and the first round of drinks is on us."

"No way. I'm not moving." The guy was adamant and the Turk, with only so much nice in him, saw that he had to step it up into another gear.

He leaned over and whispered in his ear probably something like, *Lissen a me you cocksucker. If you don't get up from this table, and I mean right now, I'll pick you up and take you out back and beat the shit out of you. So whatta ya say?*

The table was quickly surrendered.

After a round of drinks were brought to the table, the lights dimmed and the show began. The magic of April Stevens and Nino Tempo hypnotized Ginger Rogers. Here were young performers that did everything she didn't. Two rock and roll kids pouring their hearts out, raw and free from pretension. No staging, no script, no retakes—live.

April Stevens stood center stage wearing a beautiful, simple, knee length white dress that showed off her shapely legs. She was lovely and sexy, yet at the same time, appeared unaware of it. Nino Tempo, her handsome brother, stood off to the side with saxophone in hand and a confident look on his face. There was no denying the message from the combination of voice and music.

Ending a ballad, April said, "Ladies and Gentlemen, we have someone with us tonight, one of my idols. I can tell you that in my opinion, besides being the most beautiful, she is the most famous dancer in the world. You've all seen her in films...the glamorous Ginger Rogers."

The audience burst into whistles and shouts. As they applauded, Ginger Rogers stood up to accept the accolades. The drummer's arm extended overhead twirling a drumstick, then in a flash, it slammed down hard on the snare drum. April brought the microphone up to her lips, pointing a finger at Ginger Rogers as the words, *Shake it up Baby,* erupted from her throat. The band kicked in with *Twist and Shout.* And the crowd went crazy.

April Stevens and Nino Tempo backed by the B.G. Ramblers on stage at the Miami Beach Peppermint. (Dick Cami)

On the floor, Big Sal was yet another set of eyes watching over the riff raff off Broadway that might drift into the Peppermint Lounge, particularly in the earlier days. Bruno Sammartino, one of the greatest professional wrestlers of all time, sent over an endless supply of wrestlers to us to work as bouncers. It could be a rough crowd and we weren't interested in competing with the bouts at Madison Square Gardens.

It didn't matter who you knew or what you did, when you entered any of my father-in-law Johnny Futto's clubs you'd better act right. Justice could be harsh and swift. Two New York City patrolmen who had just made detective came to the Peppermint to celebrate. Both men had had too many drinks when one called Josie, the waitress, over. He insulted her in a degrading manner by putting his hand up between her legs and reaching her crotch.

She ran into the kitchen upset and angry. Uncle Scatsy, Johnny's brother and that night's manager, saw her crying and inquired about her predicament. She was reluctant to say what happened but Scatsy finally pumped it out of her. Just as he stepped out of the kitchen he saw the laughing hyenas heading for the men's room. He turned and sent Johnny Superman in to teach them a lesson in manners.

Superman approached the first detective, who was at the urinal, spun him around and stuck a .45 up his nose. "Here's what happens to pricks like you that get smart here with our girls."

He then proceeded to pistol-whip him to the ground and kick him until he was bleeding pretty good. The other detective was so frightened thinking he was going to be next he promptly proceeded to piss all over himself.

"We run a fuckin' respectable joint here," Superman said raising his .45 to strike again.

Big Sal came in and grabbed his wrist. "Whoa, that's enough," he said. "He's had enough."

Big Sal growled to the terrified cops in a low voice. "If you know what's good for ya, you'll both get outta here now."

It was about five in the morning, two hours before closing at the Miami Beach Peppermint. I was at the bar when this detective from Metro Dade came up to me and flashed his identification. It was obvious he'd been drinking. He didn't mince words. He pointed his finger and said in a gruff voice, "Give me 300 bucks out of the register." When I didn't move he repeated the demand.

Thinking it out to a logical conclusion, I didn't say anything. I just walked around him, went behind the bar, positioned myself in front of the register then extended my hands out in front of me, motioning for him to come on. "You want it...come and get it."

He smoldered in silence, not quite sure what to do. Then he turned around and left. It must have been eating at him because a couple of days later he came back to see me early in the evening and apologize for what happened. This time he was sober. I didn't know how to take it, but we eventually became friends.

Years later, he joined the Broward County Sheriff's Office and told me the Peppermint Lounge was always harassed because the law enforcement departments in Florida were racist organizations and didn't like the idea that we often featured black bands and entertainers. It was the south then and that was the way it was. The Jews didn't exactly get good treatment either. In the fifties posted signs stating "No Jews or Dogs Allowed" were not uncommon.

Dale Hawkins, who'd just had the hit record *Susie Q* and at the time was the leader of our house band, was an expert with cowboy six guns. He was giving me some pointers on the art of the quick draw out back in the alley when two policemen approached and arrested me. I was taken into custody and driven to the police station where they fingerprinted and booked me on a charge of assault and battery.

I didn't even know who I'd hit. It dawned on me that a couple of nights back I had thrown a guy out of the Peppermint who was really out of order, a real first class jerk...actually it was his ass that I saved. Many times I intervened in a beef because I knew if the bouncers got their hands on someone like him, the beating would be worse.

Recalling the incident, I remembered it had taken some serious convincing to get him to walk away from the bouncers and leave with me. As soon as we got outside, I let go and started to turn when he threw a sucker punch to my jaw. I returned a forearm shiver from my football days and left him collapsed in the parking lot.

When he came to, his car was waiting and he drove away. I didn't think much of it at the time—just another incident. When Johnny Lomelo, the King of Hearts nightclub owner, heard that I was arrested he came to see me. He advised that it was a mistake to take the charge lightly. "It's a criminal charge, Dick. Those bastards would love to hang your ass."

He put me in touch with a well-known criminal lawyer, Harvey St. Jean. He told me to get all the witnesses I could to testify. So that's what I did. At the trial, the entire courtroom was filled with my witnesses. The judge swore them in all at once then cleared the room. After the witnesses were out of the courtroom, the judge told everyone to sit down. So that's what I did. The judge's face sharpened as he looked at me, "Who told you to sit down?" he barked.

I thought he was kidding…like it was some kind of joke or something.

My lawyer nudged me. "Stand up."

"What for?" I questioned. "Everyone else sat down."

He silently motioned me to get up. "Because the judge said so, that's why."

I'd never heard of this before and I don't know whether it's recorded somewhere or not, but I had to stand throughout my whole trial, which fortunately only took one day. It was a bizarre ordeal but after every witness testified in my defense, I was found not guilty.

Outside the courtroom after the trial, I went up to the guy who pressed charges against me, resisting an urge to hit him again but instead asked, "How the hell could you press charges against me when you know damn well you were so out of order?"

"I didn't want to press charges," he said, wiping cold sweat from his upper lip. "My father told me to do it. He said we could probably make some big money, being you were the owner."

Johnny Lomelo later told me, "It's the south and this happened to you because you hire black acts, Dick." He was probably right.

Chapter 3

Behind the Scenes:

Steve Palmer, Dick Kline, Morris Levy, and Nat Tarnopol with Jackie Wilson

I first met Steve Palmer at the Peppermint Lounge when he asked me if I would entertain the idea of participating in his teenage dances. The plan was to send the acts I had performing at the Peppermint Lounge over to his dance hall called "The Place" and let them do one show for the kids. He had a working relationship with the radio station WFUN where they would advertise my acts and his dances together. "The Coasters, who are now appearing at the Peppermint Lounge, will be at The Place this Friday night." The publicity worked for both of us and became the start of a long-lasting friendship.

Over the years, this developed into us doing promotions together. I'll never forget the first time Steve booked Jimmy Reed on a tour of a half dozen cities in the south. In Tampa, he sold the show to an independent promoter and got seventy-five hundred. Jimmy Reed had a lot of problems with drugs and alcohol and most of the time his wife had to go up on stage and stand behind him to whisper the lyrics in his ear for him to sing. The next show in Tampa went even further than that; Jimmy staggered, taking a wrong step and fell off the stage into the audience.

The promoter became frantic and called Steve, complaining.

When Steve heard what happened, he shouted into the phone, "What...he did the ten thousand dollar show!"

One night coming back from a promotion, travelling down a lonely mountain road in West Virginia, Steve tried to make up for some lost time and went to pass a truck that he had been patiently following for some time. He decided enough was enough and passed the truck. Unfortunately, another truck was coming the other way and hit him head on. The force of the crash sent him flying out of the car and down the side of the mountain.

When he awoke about a half hour later, he was okay. He got up and checked himself out. As he dusted himself off, he noticed that his attaché case was lying right next to him. He picked it up and started to climb back up the mountain to the site of the accident where by now police cars, fire engines, and ambulances were all gathered around the scene, their lights blinking and blazing in the night.

Steve arrived, case in hand, to find everyone milling around looking for the body. Not having success, a state trooper said, "He must be in there somewhere," thinking he was in the flattened car.

Steve, still a little dazed, stood there amongst the bystanders as the search continued, finally saying out loud, "I guess I'll never drive that car again."

A fireman overheard him and whirled around, "What? Is this your car?"

Steve simply blinked and said, "Yeah."

The fireman jumped up and down waving his arms. "Hey! Here he is, here he is!"

It was a miracle Steve survived such a crash. If he had been wearing a seatbelt, he would have been killed.

On another tour through West Virginia about a year later, Steve needed some cash and stopped at a roadside bar to see if they could cash a check. They wouldn't but the attractive server who was just getting off her shift said she would if they could to go to her house where she had the money. Steve followed her to her house, which was right off the highway. He entered with his attaché case in hand but she had something else in mind. She insisted on fixing him a drink. Before he knew what was happening, she started disrobing and coming on to Steve. Suddenly, the sound of car tires crunching on gravel came from the driveway.

"Oh my god," she screamed. "It's my husband. He'll kill you if he finds you here. Quick, hide under the bed."

Steve panicked, but decided his chances were better if he went out the back bedroom window. What he didn't know was that the house was built on a mountain side. Even though the front of the house was level with the street, the back was built on stilts that went down the sloping mountain. Steve, his faithful attaché case in hand, didn't realize this until he had jumped out the back window and went rolling down the mountain side. Again, dusting himself off after he came to a stop, he made the long climb back up the mountain, got into his car, and drove away. Steve never did get the check cashed. Poor Steve and those West Virginia mountains.

The Ardells were the house band at the Peppermint Lounge for the season. An all-American looking band, they sang harmonies similar to The Beatles. It was Steve Palmer who came up with the idea. "If we were to put wigs on these kids and have them sing a Beatles repertoire it would be hard to tell the difference." Steve was right, and here's what happened.

They wore wigs until their hair grew out and practiced relentlessly every day until they had every Beatles song down tight. We got them outfits very similar to the original Beatles and once their hair had grown enough, it was cut in the exact same style as each individual Beatle. Now ready, Steve convinced the promoters in a half dozen South American cities to book them as "The American Beatles." They bought the promotion and when the Ardells flew into the cities the reception they received couldn't have been bigger if they'd been the real Beatles. Every airport had thousands of Beatles fans welcoming them with open arms, screaming and shouting like they were the real thing. The

American Beatles played to packed stadiums at every location and got rave reviews. The tour was a complete success beyond anyone's dream. No one was more surprised than us.

Debut of The ARDells reimagined as The Beatles and ready to tour. (Dick Cami)

Steve had an office at Criteria records. It became a daily ritual for me to go there and spend an hour or two discussing our promotions. One day, Steve told me that Dee Clark was in a studio recording *Raindrops* but they were having a big problem. Dee Clark lisped, so the song came out Raindropssss. It was the silliest thing to hear. They spent the better part of the day working on it and through magical engineering, cleaned up the record. I've often thought if they'd released the version where she lisped it would have sold better. I gotta admit...when I first heard the record I was looking forward to hearing Dee lisp.

Palmer made the rounds of all the clubs, staying on top of the entertainment and music business, always looking for the next trend or up and comer, and picking up bits and pieces of information that might be helpful in his next promotion. He learned a lot just by being around, going around. *Mind your own business* was not his MO.

King of Hearts was a black club with a white owner in Miami's tough Liberty City neighborhood. When Steve Palmer stepped inside the club, he stopped for a moment, sizing up the room's layout. There were tables of various sizes, some held twelve, others simply four or six…no deuces. It was just before show time, almost midnight and the place was packed. A buzz of conversation filled the room, threaded here and there with laughter.

He walked down the aisle between the tables toward owner Johnny Lomelo, who sat at the bar. As he approached, Johnny turned and got up. "Come on Steve…let's go into my office."

As they entered the office, Lomelo swung around to sit in his chair but his belt got caught on the corner of the desk. Steve never expected to see a gun tucked into his pants. Just then, the .45 slipped out from his belt, hit the floor and an explosion sent a bullet back into Lomelo's stomach. Sprawled out on the floor, Lomelo, his eyes instantly glassy and spit dribbling from his mouth, looked up at Palmer. It was a miracle he wasn't killed on the spot.

"Get rid of the gun will ya…" Lomelo's voice was strained. "Take it with ya and throw it away. Get out of here now…go...my guys will call an ambulance."

The door burst open and Lomelo's crew came running in.

Palmer stood there for a moment listening as Lomelo strained to speak then grabbed the gun and walked out. The inside of his mouth was parched and his nerves jangled as he got in his car and headed toward the Peppermint Lounge. It was a dark, overcast night and there wasn't much traffic. When his car reached the middle of the 79th Street Bridge he stopped, got out and walked slowly over to the railing where he leaned over and let the pistol slide out of his hand into the dark waters of Biscayne Bay. *It ain't been a good night,* he thought.

Lomelo survived. I still remember when he contacted me to take a look at his act, Sam and Dave, the original Blues Brothers, who he wanted me to book into the Peppermint. It was before the Civil Rights Act of 1964 and even though they were great, the timing was off given all the grief we were getting from the authorities. I've always regretted having passed on them. Lomelo became quite a political figure, an all around fixer who later moved to the City of Sunrise in Broward County and was their controversial mayor from 1967-1984. For years he was in and out of the headlines, never shy of determined detractors nor gung ho supporters.

One of the wildest parties the radio and record industry ever had was the Disc Jockey Convention hosted by Todd Storz of Storz Radio Stations, at the Americana Hotel in Bal Harbour, Florida. He was making history with his Top 40 format and wanted to share his glory with those who had made it happen in other cities.

I had just moved to Miami and thought how fortunate I was to be able to go to this convention. The first person I met there was Dick Kline. I knew of his reputation and was surprised to see how young he was. He didn't even look out of his teens. For someone that young to have a reputation of being one of the up-and-coming hot record men in the business was quite an accomplishment.

"I just made it here on time," Kline told me. "I've been in upstate Florida seeing radio stations and retail stores for King Records. Got a breakout reaction to the new Five Royals record called *Think*. Looks like King has another smash in the making."

We hit it off right away. He was familiar with a couple of songs that my partner Vinny Marchese and I had done back in New York. It was through him that I got a good inside look at what the record business was really all about. The hottest on-air personalities from across the country were there at the convention to brag about their ratings and party down. Record companies were also there in force. They made the hits but needed the disc jockeys to expose them.

I watched Dick Kline work the room with the biggest music

legends in the industry. Everyone was there from Mitch Miller at Columbia Records, Mo Preskel from Disney, Morris Levy of Roulette Records fame, to Henry Stone and many more. They came to soak up the Miami sun and schmooze with each other as they watched the beach bunnies at the pool. The party was non-stop and the booze flowed as fast as the jocks doing the bunny hop around the pool. There were hookers in the lanai suites and it was twice around the pool for who was next. Dick Kline explained the deal to me but it was unbelievable to see deejay samples traded for a good time. More than records were the hot commodity of the day.

"Hey Dick," I heard Kline call my name. "Come over here. I want you to meet Henry Stone."

Henry smiled and shook my hand. "Dick told me you've got some artists. Let me know if I can help."

"I like to call Henry my 'Soul Poppa.'" Kline forced a little grin. "He is the music man in Miami and the legend I learned from. Henry's a terrific talent scout, producer and record promoter, and whatever the else you want to call him. He's got a distribution company called Tone Distributors. It was Henry here who helped Syd Nathan, the owner of King Records, and his A&R man, Ralph Bass, sign James Brown, producing an endless string of hits. He's the consummate street man in the Indie record business and outsells most major city distributors, because he sells their biggest accounts for less and gets them the product first. He told me, "Send the jocks to dinner, don't take them."

We all laughed. Henry added, "He forgot to tell you that I also told him to keep his pants zipped and his office door opened."

Kline wanted to reminisce. "I met Henry when I first started with King Records. I listened to a hot new release that we had by Little Willie John titled *Heartbreak (It's Hurtin' Me)* and loved it so much that I loaded thirteen hundred copies into the trunk of my car and drove to Budisco, the record one-stop in Miami. I played it for the buyer and he too thought King had another smash, he bought all the records I had in my trunk. As I'm thanking him, in walks Henry Stone, who has the buyer on a-penny-a-record spiff for Tone Distributors product, he's got a smash for them. He plays his record and it turns out to be the same song, *Heartbreak*, but by Jon Thomas on ABC Records. Flustered, the buyer tells Henry they just bought the same song from me, the new kid at King. Henry was fuming, but turned to me smiling and introduced himself. It wasn't long before we became great friends."

Later that evening, I had it arranged to meet Morris Levy. I got the word from Swat Mulligan, alias Dominick Schivoni to say hello. "Don't worry kid, tell him who you are," Swat said. "He'll say hello to ya good after you mention my name."

Morris Levy was the guru of Roulette Records. His big independent label had George Shearing, Chris Conner and other jazz greats on its roster. He hosted a large dinner at the convention with all their big stars performing. As soon you entered the Grand Ballroom, you were confronted by the centerpiece, a huge roasted pig with a big red apple in its mouth. It was something right out of Louis the Fourteenth.

Gorgeous blondes in low-cut dresses and other assorted beauties filled the room as Morris Levy, known as Moishe to his friends, made his grand entrance with two incredibly beautiful women, one on each arm. This was his kingdom and Moishe was the king for the night that went into the wee hours of the morning. Moishe made sure that his guests were treated to a royal event. Chris Conner sang and George Shearing played to the cream of the music industry.

It was the next morning that all who attended would love to forget. Reporter Herb Rau wrote the headline that appeared in that day's The Miami News: "BABES, BOOZE and BRIBES: Little Tin Gods Live it Up." The headline was picked up and carried in every big newspaper across the country. Thus began the infamous "payola investigations."

One night, in 1963, at the Miami Peppermint Lounge, Dick Kline came walking in looking a little down in the mouth about something so I figured I'd kid him and asked, "How's your love life?"

Dick Kline was now the Regional Sales/Promotion Director for London Records. One of the record companies they distributed was Hi Records whose home was Royal Studios in Memphis, Tennessee.

Kline answered, "It's okay, coming in here and seeing the bands remind me of what just happened to me in Memphis, have you had any problems using colored bands here?"

"Are you kidding? Trouble's my middle name. Even though this is Miami Beach it's not like it is back in New York. The police here and the beverage department are still in the Stone Age and run by racist bigots. I will admit it's getting a little better. Slowly, little-by-little, but it's still a rough road if you're colored. Answer me this question: White people go over to Miami Beach to see Nat King Cole perform yet he can't stay or eat in any other hotel except the one he's performing at, isn't that so ridiculous?"

"You don't have to tell me. I just came from Memphis, listen to what just happened to me there."

"Geez...Tennessee. I can just imagine."

"You heard of Willie Mitchell?"

I shrugged "Not sure, what about him?"

"On my visit to Memphis, Willie Mitchell invited me to one of the sessions he was arranging. Besides being a musician, he's an arranger and a producer, and we've become friends. They were recording artist Ace Cannon.

As the session progressed, I watched Willie take the lead in directing all phases of the session, including the artist and engineers. When the day ended I did some homework on Willie's recording credits. Other than credits as an artist and occasional writer, he had no other recognition even though it was totally his direction and arrangements that created a lot of finished sessions.

That night I visited The Manhattan Club in Memphis where The Willie Mitchell Band was performing. At the end of the set, I invited Willie to come and join me at my table. When he came over he whispered to me could I please sit with him in the back since 'coloreds' weren't allowed to sit at a guest's table. This area was strictly reserved for whites only, and that's the way it is in Memphis and for the most part all over the south."

"I know it's like that here too...maybe not that bad though."

Kline continued explaining that he joined Mitchell in the back and that they talked about the session. Kline asked him why hadn't he received any credit for his creative work on any of his past recording sessions. Mitchell looked embarrassed and said that Kline would have to ask Joe Coughi about that. It was evident that Mitchell was in a difficult position when Kline suggested doing so the next morning. Out of mutual respect, the two agreed to go together to approach Coughi. Kline continued, "So here I am, a young New York Jew with an attitude, trying to figure out what was really going on in the world of Memphis music."

A fair and a good businessman, Joe Coughi made his living in the music business. He was a good guy who was a major partner in the largest record store in Memphis, Poplar Tunes & Hi Records. Joe agreed to have a meeting after the store closed. He broke out a bottle of Jack Daniels, put some dimes in the coke machine and that's the way the meeting started.

Kline related what he'd observed and asked how come Willie's name wasn't on any of Hi Records as arranger or producer? Joe's reply was that this is the South and in Memphis you just don't put a colored man's name on the credits. Both of us realized that Joe was just doing what was customary for the day.

Then Kline said that the Jack got him a little buzzed and his well-known cockiness surfaced. "So I told him...Joe, as long as Willie's name isn't on Hi Records I can't give the label my best efforts at promoting it on the radio. If you have to report me to the New York office go ahead but that's the way it's going to be." It was a wonder Kline hadn't been fired.

"Here's the follow up to the story," Kline went on. "Willie Mitchell's new record *2075*— the number of the record now with his name on it—shipped and I went on the road throughout the South telling every black radio station and disc jockey the story."

"You're kidding?"

"No, I'm not. History was made! Willie had his first chart hit, R&B Radio played the grooves off *2075*, and Joe Coughi also made Memphis history by giving Willie his first well-deserved credit."

"What did Willie have to say about it?"

"Oh, he was over the moon."

"What's he doing next?"

"You know how it is, once you get a hit they all seek you out. He told me he's got some new kid that can sing his ass off, by the name of Al Green."

Dick Kline (standing) with Willie Mitchel and his wife, 1964. (Dick Kline)

One of the most significant figures in rock and roll history was Morris "Moishe" Levy. He was a New York character all the way. He owned the World Famous Birdland nightclub and the Roundtable restaurant. He also started Roulette records in 1956. At the start of the Peppermint days he was in trouble. The payola scandal had cost him dearly and in 1961, Moishe settled with his Roulette creditors for ten cents on the dollar. Besides that, Alan Freed, who he single-handedly made into a legend, stupidly ignored his advice and got indicted. Things looked bleak but he had mob partners.

So Moishe went to Swat Mulligan who went to "Fat Tony" Salerno who went to Frankie Carbo who went to his very close friend, and my father-in-law, Johnny Futto to ask if he would give Levy the rights to do a NYC Peppermint Lounge album. Johnny knew I thought we would have a hit for sure if we went with Chubby Checker. But, there were loyalties. The rest is history. Moishe recorded the three million-seller Peppermint Lounge album with our house band Joey Dee and the Starliters which took Levy straight out of bankruptcy.

When Moishe found out we were opening a Peppermint Lounge in Miami Beach he wanted in and a deal was struck with Johnny and Gambino's crew. They got a percentage, but Johnny insisted that Moishe come down to Miami Beach himself and work directly with me in opening the Peppermint Lounge.

Personally, it was the best thing that could have happened to me because up until then my participation with the Peppermint had been only with the music, and later, getting the mutuals and collecting money. Moishe gave me a crash course on nightclubs, from designing the layout, including installing the right sound system, to dealing with the booze.

Levy was known as one of the great guru's of rock-and-roll music, but I can testify that he was also one of the most knowledgeable nightclub and restaurant operators around. We hit it off right away.

We opened and we're jammin'. Business couldn't have been better. Each night when I surveyed the long lines waiting to get in I thought, *Moishe was right. He didn't get where he was by chance!*

One night at the Miami Peppermint, Moishe shared an observation about me. He told me that I stood too close to customers during a beef. "Don't stand right in front of them. You should stand back a little. Remember what happened to my brother."

I hesitated a moment then I jerked backwards...I did remember.

"He used to stand in front of them just like you," Moishe went on, "until he got stabbed tryin' to collect a three dollar check. Poor bastard never knew what hit him."

I let out a breath as it all came back to me. It had been a front-page story.

"Please do me a favor...stand back...all right?"

I found out later that Moishe had bought his sister-in-law a house in North Miami Beach and had been supporting her since the day his brother was murdered. I also heard a rumor that his brother wasn't killed collecting a check, rather it was a case of mistaken identity. They were really after Moishe. Who knows?

A sellout evening at the Peppermint and Jackie Wilson wanted to give them what they'd come for, a lesson in rhythm and blues. They designed the opening number to warm things up and reaffirm to everybody that Jackie Wilson was the R&B King.

The house lights dimmed and the drum started a slow roll that built to a crescendo as we heard the announcer say in confident tones that the audience was in for a special treat tonight. He paused for dramatic effect, slowly turned and looked off stage for Jackie Wilson, "You all know him for the incomparable singer that he is. Ladies and Gentleman, here he is right now, the one and the only...Jackie Wilson!"

Jackie came out of the wings into the spotlight and took the audience through a wild tour of rhythm and blues, from its primitive roots to the hot sexy choruses of the present day. With a great repertoire and constant change of pace, there was something for everyone. Nobody did it better. Jackie had a freak voice with uncanny range. On stage he was part acrobat, contortionist, and musical genius. The man behind that genius was Nat Tarnopol.

Nat Tarnopol not only guided Jackie's career but he was the brains behind Brunswick Records, the company that got Jackie a string of hit records and broke him out of the standard black singer's mold. Jackie was one of the first rhythm and blues singers to appear before all white audiences.

Nat knew that if rhythm and blues was going to be a big part of the future of music, its sound had to be commercialized slightly to suit the taste of the white audience. Wilson was the first artist to make the crossover from rhythm and blues to a pop sound with records like *Lonely Teardrops* and *To Be Loved*. These records made Jackie one of the biggest recording artists of his day, but in reality he never did get the proper credit he deserved. Decca, who owned Brunswick, treated the label as the ugly stepsister. They were underfunded and known as the label, "We'll keep the coloreds on."

I don't believe there has ever been a black singer that influenced future generations of performers more than Jackie Wilson, from James Brown to Michael Jackson and his moonwalk and every soul group in between.

Morris Levy first introduced me to Nat Tarnopol up in New York, and I became friendly with him when he visited me down in Miami. Despite rumors to the contrary, I only knew him as a perfect gentleman. He was always quiet and polite, not like a lot of guys I met in the record industry. One day he called to say that Jackie Wilson was broke and stranded in Miami and asked if I could give him a couple thousand dollars. Of course I did, even though we all knew of Jackie's faults. He was practically a sex maniac, spending exorbitantly on girls.

Vinny Marchese, my early days partner and talent manager, had a little trick he did to pump up our male performers and get the best out of them. Before the show he would scan the audience for the prettiest girls and, if necessary, even tip the maître'd to sit them ringside. Then he would go back stage into the dressing rooms and announce that he just saw the most beautiful girl sitting in the audience. That's exactly what he did this night to Jackie.

Intrigued, Jackie went to take a peek at the audience. He was so taken by the beautiful redhead he spotted that he asked Vinny to bring her back to his dressing room. The next thing he knew, an ambulance arrived and the audience glimpsed Jackie being wheeled out of the club on a gurney. Of course, Jackie's part of the show was cancelled amidst much concern and speculation. What no one saw was the redhead getting into the ambulance first, waiting for Jackie.

Chapter 4

FINBARR NOLAN: THE SEVENTH SON OF A SEVENTH SON

Although psychic powers have been around since the beginning of man, not much is really known about them. Finbarr Nolan is a touch healer, but there is no significant aura about him outside of the fact that he looks a little like the traditional depiction of Jesus Christ. He's a seventh son of a seventh son, and according to Irish folklore, is a person born with special powers. Famous from the moment he was born. Hundreds milled outside of the hospital to see if the seventh child born to Clara Nolan would be a boy—and, so it was.

Healing is the only thing Finbarr has ever done. His first cure came at the age of two when his mother put his little hand on the stomach of her neighbor's baby who had ringworm. Three days later the ringworm dried up and fell off. From there his legend only spread. Even though he was young, his healing powers were sought by the sick from around the world, most of whom paid through voluntary contribution for his services.

As a young adult he was dubbed, "The Well-Heeled Healer." But that publicity got him into trouble with the Irish Tax Department and he made the decision to come to America.

Seventh son of the seventh son, Irish Touch Healer Finbarr Nolan. (Dick Cami)

I was managing the famous Irish singer John MacNally at the time, and he told Finbarr that when he got to the U.S. he should call me. John explained that I kept him working in the best lounges in Las Vegas and other major cities, and that I was an honest guy connected to friends with pug noses that were either called Vinny, Vito, or Rocco. If Finbarr wanted someone to make sure he was treated right in America, I was his man.

My first conversation with Finbarr was a phone call from Ireland before he left. I wasn't expecting it and had no idea who I was speaking with or what his talent was.

"What do you do?" I asked, thinking he was a singer or another entertainer.

"I'm a healer," Finbarr replied.

This must be a joke. My friend Vinny is screwing with me.

"Is that you Vinny? You bastard." I shouted into the receiver.

"No," the soft, gentle voice replied. "I told you, I'm Finbarr Nolan from Ireland."

"Oh, all right, give me your number and I'll call you right back." I all but growled at him through the receiver.

To make sure it wasn't a joke, I called another Irish friend of mine in Dublin to verify this Finbarr Nolan guy was legit. To my surprise, he gave him the highest recommendation and said he was the real deal. "Everyone knows him here in Ireland," he added.

Intrigued, I called Finbarr back to see how and where we could connect. He said he was going to Amsterdam the next month and then coming on to America. I decided to meet him in Amsterdam.

The way Finbarr operated his clinics back then was to tell the people who came to see him they had to visit him at least three times, with a day off in between. If they didn't get some reaction within that time period, he felt that he probably couldn't help them. And, above all, he never made any guarantees or predictions, and always recommended they continue seeing their doctor.

On my very first day in Amsterdam, I saw a crippled woman come off the elevator and go into Finbarr's clinic using a walker. She left the same way after her treatment. On her final visit four days later, I couldn't believe my eyes. She walked off the elevator without her walker or any other assistance. Whatever Finbarr did, it had worked and I considered it a miracle.

I flew back to New York and went to see Tommy Vastola, who was known as "Corky" and also called "The Big Guy" or "The Galoot." Corky was the nephew of Dominick Schivoni, an associate of my father-in-law in the Genovese organized crime family. Corky always had his hands in show business. He owned Queens Booking, which specialized in black artists like Sammy Davis, Jr. and an array of rhythm and blues acts and singers like Gloria Gaynor. My plan, bring Finbarr over, book him into hotels like a show business act, and charge a moderate fee for the touch healing. I figured black folks would be the natural market for this kind of thing, thus my meeting with Corky.

Corky was a tough guy with little appreciation for Finbarr's healing ability—he was more into hurting than healing—but he took on the project. He assigned it to his agent Sol Levine.

I called Finbarr and told him that someone from Queens Booking would be calling him about doing an American tour. Unbeknownst to me, Sol got into trouble for not paying his gambling debts and Corky fired him.

About a month after my meeting with Corky, I got a big surprise when I tuned into Tom Snyder's late-night television show and saw Finbarr as one of his guests. What the hell? I was pissed that Corky didn't even have the courtesy to tell me Finbarr was here. I called him the next day, but he didn't know what I was talking about.

"I fired that prick Sol a few weeks ago," he said. "He must have made his own deal with your guy Finbarr. Dickie, go do what you gotta do with the bastard."

Corky was right. Sol Levine screwed me. He closed the deal with Finbarr while pretending to be still associated with Queens Booking. Believing Queens was acting on my behalf, Finbarr agreed to everything.

I flew up to New York, met up with my former partner,Vinny Marchese, and explained to him what Finbarr did and that I wanted Vinny to take Finbarr out on the road as soon as we found out where he was. I knew there was no one better to do this then Vinny, the original "Broadway Danny Rose."

"It sounds great, I love it." Vinny beamed. "Just like Elmer Gantry, right?"

"What do ya mean Elmer Gantry?" I replied, out of sorts. "Why you think there's a scam here? I'm telling you this guy's legit."

"You mean to tell me this guy just touches people and they get better." Vinny's eyes narrowed.

"Isn't that what I just said." My closed fist pounded the desk. "Hey, I know it's hard to believe but I'm telling you I saw it myself."

"Where did this guy come from?" Vinny asked.

"He just popped out of the woodwork," I replied. "From

Ireland somewhere."

Now I found myself in the ridiculous position of trying to convince Vinny that Finbarr was legitimate. This should have been an indication of the difficult job we had ahead of us.

"So what do we do," Vinny said. "Bust out people or what?"

"Will you stop it with that bullshit," I said. "Get this through your thick, dago skull...this guy's legit."

"If he's so legit, what is he coming to us for?"

I threw up my hands. "That's what I don't know. I thought the same thing myself. Maybe it's because everyone thinks he's a phony that he's forced to deal with guys like us. I don't know." There had to be a way to get him to buy into all this. "You know he's treated royalty?"

"Royalty?" A blank expression remained on Vinny's face. "So? He can treat my sister's haddayacallit...who gives a shit? What royalty anyway?"

"The English. I saw the check. But the problem is they won't endorse him...something about protocol. This guy is famous in Ireland, there's a lot of money to be made legitimately with him. We'll treat him like one of our acts and take him on the road. What's the difference, an act is an act, right?"

"I don't know nuttin' about healing."

"Neither do I. We'll learn together. Whatta ya gotta know? Gimme the money...touch 'em. Gimme the money...touch 'em. Right now we must find where that piece-a-shit Sol is with Finbarr. They're on the road somewhere. I'm going to go up to see Sonny Boy in Brooklyn." I stood up and started toward the door.

"What for?"

"Corky told me he was one of his bookmakers that Sol owed the money to."

Sonny Boy, a Capo in the Genovese family, was a friend of mine. When I explained the situation to him he agreed to help. We had done favors for each other in the past and he was happy to oblige. After I went back to Florida he tracked down Sol within a week and told me Finbarr was working out of a motel outside of Philly in Cherry Hill, and when I was ready he'd send a couple of his boys down there with Vinny to straighten him out.

But Sonny Boy added a warning.

"This Sol is such a good bullshitter. He conned my bookmakers into settling his debt with them by taking a piece of this healer ya got. He painted them a picture to let the ten thousand ride, for twenty five percent of Finbarr's take...my guys agreed."

"What?" I could feel an explosion building up inside me.

"Take it easy." Sonny Boy did his best to calm me down. "Remember these are my boys so here's what we'll do. Of course, the ten's gotta get paid back, but after that's paid back to me...the deal's canceled and Finboard, or whatever his effin' name is, is yours."

"Thanks, Sonny," I said. "And let me assure you if that prick doesn't pay you back, I'll take it out of my profit of Finbarr's earnings."

"I hear ya," Sonny Boy said in a sudden husky voice.

Vinny was foaming at the mouth when I explained this to him. "Why the dirty scumbag," he said. "Where is this Sol now?"

Vinny went to Cherry Hill with two of Sonny Boy's guys, Bad Bart and Sal the Mooch. They could best be described as The Creature of the Black Lagoon and Frankenstein. They walked to the door of Sol's hotel room. Usually these doors were bolted shut from the inside, but on this night, Sol left it unlocked.

"Whatta ya wanna do, knock?" Bad Bart said.

Before Vinny could answer, Sal the Mooch turned the handle and the door opened. Sol got a current of fresh, cool air on his face. The door of his hotel room creaked open and the dimly-lit figures of two big hulks stomped into his room.

"For crissake," Sol said. "Who are you guys?"

Sal the Mooch, not too bright even for a gorilla, flung Sol across the room onto the bed where he laid in shock.

"Close the door." Vinny stepped out from behind them, his face hard and empty. "Well, whatta ya know, Sol Levine, the asshole."

Sol scrambled back up, rubbing a rising bump on the back of his head. Vinny sat down and asked him for an explanation in not so nice terms. Sol quivered and fell down again. Bad Bart grabbed him by his shirt and dragged him up. He stammered and looked to walk out of the room but Bad Bart blocked him.

"Just a minute Buster, I want ten fuckin' grand in cash now," Vinny said "And then you got the balls to sell my friends a piece of Finbarr. Gimme the money now you bullshitter and don't tell me you don't have it. I know you got it 'cause you been on the road."

Sol had only seventy five hundred left and he told Vinny that he buried that in the trunk of his car. Bad Bart and Sal the Mooch went out and took the money to give to Sonny Boy. "Dick will get him the rest," Vinny said.

Now visibly shaken, Sol grabbed his chest and sunk to the floor. Thinking it was a ploy, Vinny pressed on for the rest of the money. Sol's color drained from his face, turning into a corpse before their eyes. Vinny paid no attention and kept pressing him even though his eyes remained open and unseeing. While the Fire Rescue pronounced him dead and hauled him off, Vinny was in the next room with his hands full, trying to convince Finbarr they hadn't killed Sol and that he should come to Florida to see Dick Cami so they can start a tour.

To Finbarr the whole thing was a nightmare. He was tired of Sol Levine and all his bullshit. He was also tired of New York City, where he had been robbed at gunpoint on his first night in America. Swindled by the phony public relation agent Sol got for him and, in general, thoroughly disgusted, he just wanted to go back to Ireland. "I've had enough of America," he said.

"Give it another shot." Vinny pleaded with him. "What do you have to lose?"

"No, I think I should go back to Ireland," Finbarr said. "Since I've been here, I've been swindled, robbed, insulted, called a fraud and now maybe I'm going to be implicated in a murder. I think those are a few valid reasons."

"Why don't ya stop?" Vinny said standing before him with his hands opened. "Whatta ya keep talkin' about murder for."

"Do we look like murderers?" Vinny turned and looked at Bad Bart then at Sal the Mooch. "Don't answer that," he continued. "Lissena me, we gotta go down to Florida and see Dick, he'll treat ya right. He's never screwed anyone in his life."

"He's the one that sent Sol to see me," Finbarr said.

"No, he didn't. He doesn't even know Sol. It's all a big mistake, that's what I'm tryin' ta tell ya. Corky was the one that was supposed to bring you to America—not Sol."

"Who's Corky?" Finbarr asked.

"Corky's, the big guy, The Galoot," Vinny said.

"The Galoot?" Finbarr said politely.

"Corky! Yeah, that's Tommy Vastola," Vinny said now getting down to business. "Finbarr, there'll be a moment or two of confusion, but if we all keep our heads, things are gonna work out."

Vinny went on to explain the story like only he could and finally convinced Finbarr to come down to Florida.

In Florida

"What took you so long to get here?" I said, an annoyed tone to my voice.

Vinny's flustered "Are you kidding me? Ya know what I had to go through to get this fuckin' Finbarr here?"

"With you everything is a federal case," I replied. "I don't wanna hear it."

Once in Florida, I put Finbarr up in an apartment I had in Hallandale. The first thing he did was to go sit in the sun by the pool while he waited for Vinny. But, instead of eleven in the morning, Vinny showed up at three in the afternoon. All the while Finbarr sat out there, taking in the sun. Four hours in the Florida sun in August was enough to give anyone third degree burns, but not Finbarr, he had no burn, no color, no nothing. He didn't look like he had sat in the sun at all. That's when Vinny first learned that Finbarr was from a different bolt of cloth.

The Top of the Home, my fine dining restaurant, catered to an upper class clientele. Located on the top floor of the Home Federal Savings and Loan building on US 1 in downtown Hollywood, Florida from 1965-1990, it was my base of operations. While in the States I made sure Finbarr was there every night so I could introduce him to the local dignitaries, most of whom were initially indifferent. Some were even hostile, but after seeing his results, they changed their opinion.

I applied a little pressure to my friend Joe Viens, who in 1980 was the mayor of the city of Miramar, for his help. He sponsored the first clinic for his people there. Joe thought it would be a good idea for the people of Miramar—but it backfired.

"Everyone gets treated for nothing," Joe Veins said with pride waving his arms from the podium.

But it didn't fly. Some citizens were upset because they thought the city was sponsoring a healer. Poor Joe! He lost the next election because of it. After that we rented a conference room at the Holiday Inn on Hallandale Beach Boulevard and put some ads in the newspapers. Surprisingly, we started to do business.

Miami Herald Write-up

I told Vinny to go to the Miami Herald and see the editor of the Living Today section about writing a human-interest piece on Finbarr. For several days Vinny went to her office but she wouldn't see him.

"The broad won't come outta her office." Vinny was adamant. "What do you want me to do?"

"I'll tell you what I want," I said. "Go there first thing in the morning and wait there all day until she comes out to see you."

"Are you kidding? I'll be there for a week."

"So who cares? You'll be there for three weeks if that's what it takes." On the second day, the editor steamed out of her office and approached Vinny.

"What is it you want to see me about?"

Vinny flashed his million-dollar smile and explained about Finbarr. She invited him back to her office, sat at her desk and buzzed her secretary, "Get me the head of the paranormal department at the University of Miami, please."

The secretary came back in a few minutes, "I have Dr. Jack Kapchen on the phone for you."

"Dr. Kapchen? I'm wondering if you can help me out? I'm

sitting in my office with a man who claims to represent someone that can heal a person simply by touching them. Is that possible?"

"It certainly is," Dr. Kapchen replied. "May I remind you that Jesus was a healer?"

That Sunday we got a front-page story in the Living Today section of the Miami Herald and business took off like a rocket.

The Experiments

If you look in the dictionary for the word "atheist" you'll find heathen, non-believer, and Dick Cami. How I ever ended up with a guy that performed miracles almost on a daily basis was a mystery to me. Anyway…

From the Miami Herald article, which mentioned my name, Dr. Kapchen came to see me at the Top of the Home about conducting some experiments with Finbarr. Of course, I agreed.

"How far can I go with Finbarr?" he asked.

"Listen, Doc," I replied. "You can go as far as you want. This guy is for real. I mean you can't hang him upside down or anything like that but any experiment you want to do is all right with us."

"I can't believe your honesty," the Doctor said. "I once offered to do experiments with Olga Worrall, the famous faith healer," Dr. Kapchen said. "But when I tried to approach her on stage I was gooned off by her bodyguards."

"That's because religion was involved, Doc," I answered. "Finbarr's got nothing to do with religion, and besides, nobody's going to goon you here, Doc, I can assure you."

"Well, that's good to know. What do you know of holy water?" he asked.

I shrugged. "Nothing."

"Maybe we can find out why they call it holy water?" Dr. Kapchen said. The Doctor explained that the first thing he wanted to do was a blind study. The first set of students he sent over put Finbarr's hand in a pail of water, then they went back to the school where another set of students took Finbarr's pail and watered designated plants with its water. A third set of students noted the condition and progress of the plants. The final results were amazing. Finbarr's plants grew three to four times faster than the other plants, but they had moldy spots on them. When the spots were analyzed at Jackson Memorial they were discovered to be penicillium. Unfortunately, Dr. Kapchen never finished the experiments

When I called to get the final results of the experiment, Dr. Kapchen explained that he was putting the project on hold.

When I asked why, he explained."I'm in love and getting married." Kapchen had fallen in love with some German broad and was leaving for Berlin. The unfinished experiments left Vinny jumpy as unfinished sex.

"Doctor Jerkoff's in love." Vinny's loud protestations echoed off the walls. "And he ain't gonna finish the experiments?"

Finbarr said softly, "These things happen."

"Fuck that." Vinny shook his head. "We gotta get this holy water shit in writing from that fat, love starved doctor." Vinny was not in control of his emotions. "If I'd known this I woulda got him a couple of broads."

Dr. Kapchen got married and took off for a year to Germany with Hilda. The marriage fell apart, taking its toll on him, and he went out of circulation for a few years.

A Dr. Wilner saw the write-up in the Miami Herald and came to see me at the Top of the Home. "Dick, is this guy you've got for real?"

"Do ya think I'd be involved with a phony?" I answered. "I don't know how it works Doc but believe me, he's for real." I put it to him. "If you're really interested in healing people why don't you conduct an experiment. I mean an honest to God experiment documented by a real doctor like yourself to show that Finbarr can actually heal people just by touching."

He agreed and I laid out the following experiment. Now that I was a little knowledgeable about healing I suggested what should be done. We took ten patients from the hospital that they had been treating for years without success. Nothing terminal. They were told that a pharmaceutical company had discovered a medicine that might cure their disease but before they could be treated with it they had to come in at least three times with a day off in between to be examined as to the state of their condition.

When the parties came in to be examined, Dr. Wilner told them that Finbarr was his assistant, a doctor from Ireland. During that posed routine examination he asked Finbarr to touch the patient's affected part to see how it felt. This gave Finbarr the chance to do his thing. Out of the ten people one dropped out, but of the other nine, four were greatly improved and two were totally cured. The results of Dr. Wilner's blind study are officially listed in the AMA Medical Journals. Pertaining to the one person who dropped out, when asked why, he replied. "When that doctor from Ireland touched me I got a funny feeling and didn't want to do it anymore."

Next we got booked on Larry King's network radio show. I had known Larry for a long time. He was the emcee for a few concerts I promoted. He believed in Finbarr and was on the air with him for the whole three hours. One caller asked, "If you can heal, why don't you go to Africa and heal all the sick people they have there?"

Larry answered, "What business are you in, sir?"

"I own a motel."

"Well, then why don't you go to Africa and open a motel." Things got good for us after the Larry King show and a lot of people started coming into the clinic. We hired Michelle Dibble, a PR person, to do TV interviews of the people Finbarr cured. She was a beautiful, blond, with a high IQ and a Mensa membership. She was doing a great job for us until one evening she came up to the Top of the Home all shook up with her girl friend, Clara. "Please, Dick, we have to talk to you." They went on to tell me this incredible story.

They had been at a house party in Coral Gables. Unbeknownst to them the owner was a big Columbian drug dealer. They were having a wonderful time but on their way to the bathroom they took a wrong turn and went into a room where a man was gagged and bound to a chair. Michelle's friend, Clara, was the receptionist at a local health club and recognized him as one of its customers. "Oh, hello Mr. Smithson," she said without thinking. "What are you doing here like that?"

"I don't think he's waiting for a bus," Michelle quipped.

Bug eyed, all Smithson could do was mumble through his taped mouth. While they stood there in shock the drug dealers came in and discovered them. I would think under normal conditions that this would be the end of the story but for some reason the drug dealer made them an offer. He gave them ten thousand each and told them to leave town or else. That's when they came up and asked me what they should do?

"You're a Mensa," I said. "And you ask me that?"

"Come on, Dick, don't joke." Michelle was frantic. "What should we do?"

"Keep the ten thousand and run like your ass is on fire. That's what you should do, and the quicker you go the better."

And that's what they did. The last I heard Michelle was a disc jockey in Texas somewhere.

In Tampa

"Whatta you mean Finbarr's in jail?" I said.

"I'm telling you," Vinny's voice was raspy. "They took him away in handcuffs right outta the motel in the middle of him touching someone. These are bad people here in Tampa. I'm serious."

"What was he arrested for?" I smelled something fishy.

"For not having a Certificate of Occupancy."

There was a moment of silence while I digested what Vinny said. "What? Are you kidding me? Nobody's ever arrested for that."

"Well, he was. Another first for Finbarr Nolan. They took him away in handcuffs."

I immediately called Henry Gonzalez, a major lawyer in Tampa. Santo Trafficante introduced me to him years ago and we became close. I explained what happened and he laughed. "They don't arrest people for not having a Certificate of Occupancy."

"That's what I said, but they did Finbarr."

"If they did it's got to be the first time that's ever happened in this country."

Henry Gonzalez called me right back and told me I was right. "They thought he was a phony." He couldn't hold back his laughter. "All you have to do is pay a hundred dollar fine and he'll be released. It's harassment that's all. Even if he were for real he'd be in for trouble around here."

It was music to my ears.

"Poor Finbarr," Vinny said. "The saddest thing I ever saw was them taking him away in handcuffs. Ridiculous. The poor bastard is so honest, it hurts ya."

Later that month, Santo Trafficante came to see me at the Top of the Home with Henry Gonzalez.

"There's a whole other world out there," Santo said. "We're not talking hundreds, not thousands, we're talking millions of people should believe in this healer you got. I know I do. I saw it when I was a kid, a friend of my father's, he was from Catania—the son-of-a-bitch had hands of magic that cured people."

"You're kidding." I took a long look at Henry. "See, I told you."

"I believe it now," Henry said quietly and stared off in the distance.

In Atlanta

After a local radio show, Vinny retrieved a message at the hotel desk to call Augie of the Atlanta Hawks. It seemed their star player, Tree Rollins, had a bad knee injury and couldn't play.

"See this bone forming in the front here," Augie said pointing to Rollins knee. "During practice somehow it moved out of its proper place."

"So you're sayin'." Vinny added his two cents, recapping the situation in his own medical terms. "When he got clunked on the knee the whole thing went kablooey."

Augie waved a hand. "Something like that."

After three treatments from Finbarr, Tree Rollins was playing again. He stated on TV during an interview that the reason he was playing again was because a healer treated him. He even named Finbarr Nolan. Vinny tried to get a written statement from the

Atlanta Hawks but they wouldn't give him one. We didn't even charge them and they gave Finbarr an autographed basketball signed by Tree Rollins that said, "Thanks a lot for your help."

"That's all you got? A freakin' basketball?" I couldn't believe a pro team would be such cheapskates.

Vinny straightened up. "These assholes are so afraid to acknowledge that Finbarr cured Rollins because maybe they thought we were gonna hit them with a big bill or somethin'."

It became clear to me now. Of course, all the people who came to see Finbarr wanted to be cured but they were reluctant to give him the credit.

Canadian Handicap

"Son-of-a-bitch." Carl Vengeloff breathed in deeply. "I can't catch a break with Poverty Boy. I finally got him entered into the Canadian Handicap and now he's got a sore back. We can't even put a saddle on 'em."

Carl, a wealthy horse owner, was having dinner at the Top of the Home with Jackie Mason, the comedian. The Canadian Handicap had a purse of seventy-five thousand dollars, and Carl admitted he was lucky to get Poverty Boy entered in the race. There was no question the horse was in over his head, but on top of that, he had acquired a sore back after a workout and probably would be scratched. Carl was disgusted and gave a philosophical shrug.

"Aw, what can you do, that's fate I guess?"

"I'll tell you what fate is." I pointed a finger. "Let my healer touch Poverty Boy. He's good with animals and ya might have a shot."

I didn't even know what I was talking about but I thought if Finbarr could cure humans why couldn't he cure animals too. Why should horses be different? Besides if it worked, it would open up a whole new territory. Jackie Mason added his view in his well-known Yiddish accent. "All he does is touch...Vot could it hoirt?"

Finbarr went to the stable at Gulfstream Racetrack and treated Poverty Boy three times. Not only did the saddle go back on, but that Saturday when the Canadian Handicap went off, Poverty Boy came in third in a photo finish. Whatta ya know, another miracle.

Kentucky Derby

Gene Stevens, the ever-popular editor of the racetrack magazine Post Time, knew about Poverty Boy and approached me.

"You know Jorge Velasquez took a bad fall?"

"I heard."

"Pretty bad," Stevens said. "Hurt his back, he can hardly walk and cancelled out of the Kentucky Derby. He was supposed to ride Pleasant Colony."

"That's too bad." I could see where this was headed.

"Finbarr that healer, the one you sponsor, you think he can help him?" Stevens asked.

"I don't want to bullshit ya, with injuries like that Finbarr feels they should heal by themselves. He hasn't had too much success with broken bones but you never know."

"Velasquez didn't break any bones. They're just dislocated."

"If you want to give it a shot bring him over."

Finbarr treated Velasquez three times and three weeks later he re-entered the Kentucky Derby. He rode Pleasant Colony to a Kentucky Derby victory then he went on to win the Preakness Stakes. He missed winning the Triple Crown by just a few inches, finishing third to Summing in the Belmont Stakes.

The Drug Dealer

Vinny and I stood under the awning of the hotel as pouring rain filled up the parking lot like a lake. No one expected the big stretch limo that pulled up in front of us to have Renaldo Ruiz, Miami's biggest drug dealer inside.

"Renaldo's in a lot of pain," Jose Zampas said. "He can't walk."

Jose was a Cuban connection I had who was the bagman and enforcer for Renaldo.

"Renaldo's gotta know that there's no guarantees here," I said. "I don't wanna be a bullshitter with him, the way he gets excited and everything. I don't want any misunderstanding here with him."

"He knows," Jose said. "I explained everything to him."

Renaldo was let in through the side door in his wheelchair to a private room where Finbarr treated his bullet-riddled body.

"My God, Dick," Vinny said when he saw Renaldo. "That guy's in bad shape. Are those bullet wounds? Who is he?"

"I don't know," I replied. "He just paid a little extra for a private session."

After two more treatments, Renaldo drove away watching his back.He was up and about shortly thereafter. He was happy about Finbarr, but not about what he learned about his drug business. What bothered him most now were the reactions of the Columbians when he laid down the terms of his ultimatum.

Renaldo believed that Paco was in agreement. That was a mistake. No one remembered exactly what happened just that Paco had his men gun down Renaldo—this time for good.

"Isn't this the fellow we treated?" Finbarr said holding up the newspaper showing a front-page picture of the murdered Cuban drug kingpin, Renaldo Ruiz.

"Naw, I don't think so," I said.

"Mmmm, I don't know," Finbarr quietly murmured.

Finbarr came to speak to me alone and told me he was thinking about going back to Ireland to marry the girl he had once loved. Caroline had resurfaced as a flight attendant for Aer Lingus, the Irish airline. On a layover in America she'd contacted Finbarr and the romance rekindled. I'd met Caroline and she was a wonderful person.

Finbarr had decided that life for him would be better and less complicated back in Ireland, married to Caroline and raising a family. This news came at the time as the South American tour I had been getting ready to launch for him. The funny thing was, even though it was hard for me and Vinny to take, I always knew that fame and fortune were not the important things to Finbarr; Caroline and a quiet family life were. Years later that's exactly the way it worked out. Finbarr Nolan, one of the most extraordinary men in the world, is still married with two sons living quietly today in Dublin.

On Caribbean cruise with Caroline and Finbarr Nolan, 2009. (Cindy Aumann)

Chapter 5

Tony Roma and Other Adventures

Soon after he sold his interest in the Montreal Playboy Club, Tony Roma and his wife, Beverly Bronfman of the Seagram's Whiskey Bronfmans, moved to Hollywood, Florida and became frequent guests at The Top of the Home.

I'd known Tony for many years, but with him in Florida we began going deep-sea fishing two or three times a week and became even closer. Prior to opening up his rib joints, Tony once asked me to go polar bear hunting with him in Alaska. He said Beverly had given him a single shot, custom made, Weatherby rifle he was itching to try it out.

Hunting was his first love, but it wasn't mine. In fact, I'd never been hunting and I refused to go with him. Tony kept trying, but I told him there was no way I was going hunting for polar bears. Those cuddly little things could rip your arm off in a heartbeat.

When Tony got back from his hunting trip he came to me all excited. "Boy, you should have been with us, Dick. What an adventure you missed."

"Really?"

"You bet, and I'll never forget it. We were in my guide's ski plane when we spotted a polar bear on an iceberg. We landed on the opposite side of the berg, grabbed our rifles and started out to get the bear. It was so damn cold that we wore two of everything and spread Vaseline under our fleece neck warmers to keep our skin from freezing. I swear it was as cold as I'd ever been.

As we came up behind that bear, the guide told me to load and fire. I did, but all I got was a click—the gun misfired. The bear turned and started coming toward us. The guide hollered at me to reload and fire. I dropped the bear dead about twenty feet from us. It was a close call, but it got worse."

As harrowing as his story of the confrontation with the bear was, the rest of the story got even crazier. He told me that while the guide was skinning the bear, his knife slipped and he stabbed himself in the leg, causing a deep wound. Tony knew enough to apply a scarf as a tourniquet to stop the bleeding, then finished skinning the bear himself. He then put the skin in the plane and helped the guide in, who by this time wasn't looking very good.

The pilot/guide got the engine started and the plane in the air. However, they weren't in the air very long before he started slipping in and out of consciousness. When he flew into a cloudbank, Tony realized he might have to take over and asked the pilot to tell him how to keep the plane in the air.

However, the guy stayed awake long enough to bank the plane hard to the right. The clouds broke and the mountainside of the coast filled the windshield right before a rough landing. They were alive and on the ground.

"Unbelievable." I shook my head in amazement. "This is the adventure you wanted me to be with you on? You should get your head examined."

He laughed. "That's the past. I've got a new trip I want to go on."

I thought he must be kidding.

"No," he continued. "I'm serious. I'm going to Lago Enriquillo, a landlocked lake located below sea level in the Dominican Republic, where they have the largest crocodiles in the world. I wanna shoot one over twenty feet long. Come with me, it'll be a kick."

"You know, Tony," I said. "I'm probably the luckiest guy in the world not to have gone polar bear hunting with you. And there's no way I'm going to tempt fate by going with you on a crocodile hunt."

Tony went—and got a twenty-two foot monster.

The idea for his original and famous Tony Roma's Ribs restaurant was actually born of a conversation one night at The Top. When he first opened in 1972 , every wall of his place was decorated with his stuffed animal trophies, including the polar bear. People walked in and went right back out when they saw the decor. Tony finally realized that most people were not thrilled about eating while surrounded by dead animals. Once removed, his business took off. The rest of the story is restaurant history.

Angelo Dundee, Muhammad Ali's trainer, put me and my pal Bill Johnson in touch with Gerrie Coetzee, a heavyweight contender from South Africa who Angelo thought had the potential to be a world champion. We went to Johannesburg to sign Coetzee to a bout in the States, but there had been a mix-up in the dates. Coetzee was out of town and wouldn't be back for a week.

With time to kill, someone suggested we go on a safari. It sounded exciting, so we booked a guide and flew to Kruger National Park the next day. It happened I had brought along my Nikon with a 500mm lens for long distance shots, and I was intent on getting pictures of as many wild animals as possible.

I asked our guide, who could easily have doubled for Stewart Granger, "What was the greatest animal you ever saw?"

"Actually, I haven't seen it yet," he said. "But my dream is to one day go to the northwest corner of South Africa, between Botswana and Namibia, and see the legendary lion I've always heard about. He supposedly has the most magnificent mane of any lion ever."

His story really grabbed us. The next day we took off on the four hundred mile drive to where the lion with the super mane hung out. We hired a local guide who made it clear that this particular lion was rarely seen. Nevertheless, we climbed into his Land Rover and set out into the bush.

I had barely gotten my Nikon out of its case and adjusted the lens, when we came around a curve in the road and there was the lion, sitting on a knoll right in front of us. He was the most magnificent lion I'd ever seen in person or on film. His legendary mane was all that our guide in Kruger had claimed and more.

I recovered from my awe and quickly brought up my camera. I was able to snap one picture before our presence and the click of the camera scared him away. But I think that one picture is truly worth a thousand words.

So here it is. Take a look and see if you agree that you've never seen another lion like this one.

(Dick Cami)

After getting a photo of the lion with the super mane, I became hooked on getting pictures of wild animals. I learned during a subsequent trip to Africa's Kruger National Park, there are close-calls and then there are calls that are too close. This is a story about a call that went way beyond too close—way, way beyond.

My friend Bill and I had an excellent guide and I let him know that I thought lions were magnificent animals to photograph. "You think we'll come across any lions?"

"Probably." He shrugged.

Full to the brim with excitement, we took off in his open Land Rover the next morning. I sat in the front seat with my camera ready. As the morning progressed we saw very few animals, practically none. I was beginning to feel like it was a wasted day when the guide stopped and recommended that we walk up to the top of a knoll to see if there were any animals. We went up single file, the guide first, Bill second, and I brought up the rear.

As I walked under the limb of a large tree the sleeve of my jacket got caught on a thorny vine. I stopped and blurted out, "Damn it," as I tried to untangle myself.

The guide turned around to see what the commotion was. When I looked up at him, the expression of horror on his face told me something was very wrong. His eyes were bulging out of their sockets and his mouth hung open. His arms were outstretched in panic mode. "Snake!"

Snake? I looked all around me but didn't see anything. My sleeve came loose and I stood there bewildered, trying to figure out what was going on. Then I heard the guide's footsteps whiz by me with Bill right behind him. I figured that I'd better follow them. We all ran as fast as we could. When we stopped the guide explained what he'd seen.

A snake had been on the limb of the tree I had stood under while my jacket was snagged. It wasn't just any snake. It was a lethal Black Mamba, about twelve feet long, stretched out to get some sun on a large branch right over my head. I didn't see it because I looked everywhere but up. My shout disturbed it and it slid down the tree. The guide said it was the closest call he'd ever had with a Black Mamba.

He went on to say, "They're the most dangerous when sunning themselves and usually bite whatever disturbs them. That he didn't bite you is almost a miracle. You can consider yourself a very lucky man."

He added that they usually travel in pairs, so another one was probably lurking nearby.

When we got back to Johannesburg, I bought a book on African animals written by the zookeeper of the Frankfurt Zoo. He wrote that the Black Mamba is the largest and most dangerous poisonous snake in all of Africa. One bite can kill a water buffalo that weighs a ton. No wonder the guide ran away like his ass was on fire.

I knew I had been a very lucky man, and sleep didn't come easy for me that night.

My next adventure took place much closer to home. I had only been fishing once when I decided to buy a twenty-four foot sport fishing boat with a tower. There was a dock behind the Peppermint in Florida where I kept it moored. I loved fishing, but with so little experience, I bought a book called All About Fishing to help me learn about the sport. On my first trip taking the boat out to go fishing in the gulfstream I took Scatsy and Ray Peterson, who was currently appearing at the Peppermint Lounge, with me. Neither of them had ever been fishing before.

The day shimmered sunny and beautiful, and the ocean was calm. We spent a good chunk of time struggling to hook up our lines. We finally got them trolling as we approached the edge of the gulfstream. It wasn't long before Ray spotted a fin sticking out of the water about a hundred yards out from us. I headed right for it and made a pass, but nothing happened. I tried it a couple more times and still got nothing. I thought the fish was dead. Finally, I edged the boat right next to the fish and was surprised to see that it was about the same size as the boat.

Scatsy yelled at Ray, gesturing toward his gear. "Try to hook it with your rod."

"This little thing?" Ray lifted the rod in disbelief. "You kidding me?"

"Go ahead, give it a try and let's see what happens."

"I'm afraid to...it might eat me alive."

"Ahiish." Scatsy gave him an exaggerated eye-roll.

I didn't know what kind of fish it was so I yelled to Scatsy to give me the book on fishing, in there were full descriptions of every fish. I told Scatsy to go to the bow while I scanned the book for something useful. "Does the fish have a big bill?"

"Yes," Scatsy yelled back. "And a damn big one too."

"Does he have a big eye?"

"You ain't kiddin' a big son-of-a-bitch eye...geez."

"Does he have a mark on the front of his belly?

"You ain't lyin'. I mean a big mark."

"Holy shit, it's a giant black marlin." I kept reading. "This fish has been known to sink fishing vessels when disturbed while sunning itself." I dropped the book, grabbed for the drive gear and slammed it into forward, speeding off as fast as I could. I looked back, watching the fin get smaller and smaller. Lucky me, again.

Scatsy Biele on left with Ray Petersen on a later and more successful fishing trip! (Dick Cami)

Chapter 6

Las Vegas

In 1966, Vinny Marchese and I agreed to manage Lenny Welch, a black singer who was coming into his own. Lenny wanted to get a gig in Las Vegas. There weren't many black acts working there at the time. Nat King Cole, Sammy Davis, Jr. and Ella Fitzgerald were among the few headliners. The fabulous Treniers were filling the lounges, but building white audiences was a time-consuming job for black entertainers. Even Lenny's big hit, "Since I Fell for You," hadn't generated a demand for him in Vegas, and the big venues weren't beating down his door.

When Lenny first came to our office on 60th Street and Central Park West in New York, he made a good impression. He had an athletic build, a handsome face and a beautiful smile that showed a great set of white teeth. His voice left little doubt that he could belt out some incredible love songs.

Vinny got right to the point. "There are two kinds of entertainers—the ones that have a great recording voice and the others who do a great live show. Which one are you?"

Lenny thought for a few seconds and said, "I'm pretty sure I'm both, and I think I'd go over well in Las Vegas."

Lenny and Vinny sat staring at each other in silence for several seconds until Vinny broke the ice. "Yeah, okay. We'll see."

Las Vegas proved to be tough to crack. We got Lenny a few good bookings, but nothing like the headlining shows he dreamed of. Finally, in 1969 Lenny stood in front of Vinny's desk, expectantly. Vinny leaned back in his chair and looked up at him. "We got the lounge at Caesar's Palace in Vegas," he said. "I'm flying out there to firm up the dates."

It was like an historic moment for Lenny. He extended his hand. "You did it! That's exactly what I wanted."

"We've gotta work on your act," Vinny said. "We opened the door, but now it's up to you to deliver a killer show."

"I don't know how to thank you," Lenny said, taking great gulps of air in his excitement. "Man, you really came through for me."

Vinny smiled. "Maybe you got it because you deserve it."

What Lenny didn't know was that I was close with Jimmy Hoffa and asked him to set up an appointment for Vinny to see Davie Victorson, the entertainment director for Caesar's Palace.

Hoffa told me that when he contacted Victorson he said, "When you're talking to Marchese, remember that he's a friend of mine." I would hear that line used again at a later meeting and came to know it as a standard Hoffa used to apply gentle pressure.

Victorson, who was a pretty sharp guy answered, "You can bet on that Mr. Hoffa. I'm sure we'll work something out."

Tom Jones was all the rage in 1969 and was scheduled to appear in Vegas at the International. His music director, Johnny Spence, told me that Jones admired Lenny Welch so much that he insisted on meeting him when he came to America. I got right on the phone and called Vinny who was in Vegas with Lenny.

"Listen," I said. "Tom Jones is going to be in Vegas and wants to meet Lenny. Take him to Jones's show when it opens and then go backstage and introduce yourselves to Johnny Spence. Mention my name he'll bring you in to meet Jones."

Vinny more than knew his way around a nightclub, practically being weaned into show business at the Town and Country in Brooklyn. He tipped the maître d' the right amount and got a ringside table. Sitting at the next table to them was none other than Elvis Presley and his wife. According to Vinny, the atmosphere was electric.

The lights dimmed and Johnny Spence struck up the band. Tom Jones walked out on the stage and performed a great opening number. At the finish, he spotted Lenny and walked to the edge of the stage overlooking Lenny's table.

Jones turned to the audience and said, "Ladies and Gentlemen, when I first came to America I asked to see Lenny Welch. Lo and behold, here he is sitting right in front of me now."

Jones reached down and shook Lenny's hand.

"What an honor and what a country." Then he began to sing, a cappella, "Breaking Up Is Hard To Do" which was Lenny's biggest hit.

A hush settled over the room. Vinny said everything came to a standstill while Jones sang. There was no talking—not even a whisper. It was so quiet you could have heard a pin drop. After Jones finished the song the room exploded in applause like a bomb went off. It was an unbelievable moment, especially with Elvis sitting nearby.

When Vinny called and told me about it I asked, "Did ya get a picture of them together?"

"No—I got so excited I forgot."

"Did ya get a picture of Lenny and Elvis?"

"No," Vinny said sheepishly.

Disappointed, I asked, "Did ya get a picture of your mother-in-law's balls?"

"Yes, I did get a shot of those."

"Balls my ass," I said, and hung up.

In the early 1970s, things were going all right for me. I was managing singer John MacNally, "The Tenor of Ireland," among others. He sang like a racehorse could run, and got a standing ovation every time he performed. Buddy Hackett told me confidentially, "If you quote me I'll deny it, but MacNally is the best damn singer that ever opened for me."

Henri Lewin, the Executive Vice President of Hilton Hotels, was a stern sort of character who spoke with a heavy German accent. He was managing the Hilton in San Francisco when he told Barron Hilton that they should buy the Flamingo in Las Vegas and get into the casino business. From there he went to the International Hilton off the Vegas Strip.

Another interesting guy at the time was Rudy Tham. Rudy, who among other things, was the Fire Commissioner of San Francisco that always went out of his way to park his car by a fire hydrant. He also was the President of Teamsters Joint Council 7. This local had the Hilton Hotel in San Francisco—run by Henri Lewin—under contract.

Rudy surrounded himself with goons to do the heavy work when necessary. Two of them were each about six-foot-five and weighed close to three hundred pounds. One looked like Godzilla and the other like the Creature from the Black Lagoon—easy to see why they were successful when it came to getting the job done. Rudy had set up an appointment for his friend and mine, labor leader Bill Johnson and me to meet with Henri to discuss booking MacNally in Vegas.

A strange thing happened on the flight from San Francisco to Las Vegas for that meeting. Bill noticed a gentleman sitting across the aisle from us dressed like royalty and maybe beyond. Never before had we seen anyone dressed so immaculately—starched French cuffs with the most beautiful cuff links that had the initials "HL" inset with diamonds. His tie was made of silk with a stunning diamond stickpin. I had a premonition. I'll bet you that's Henri Lewin sitting across the aisle.

As we departed the plane, a limo pulled up and "HL" walked over to it. The driver put his luggage in the trunk, and Bill and I approached. Bill cleared his throat, maybe to get his attention, or maybe because he was nervous. "Are you Henri Lewin?"

"Yes, I am," he said, standing stiffly.

"Well," Bill said, "we have an appointment with you at your hotel in an hour."

"Yes, I know." Instead of offering us a ride, Henri turned

around, got into his limo and took off.

Bill and I caught a cab to the Hilton International and got to Henri's office right on time for our appointment. After waiting twenty minutes Henri came out and explained he was late because he was trying to get Jimmy Hoffa on the phone, but was having difficulty getting a hold of his number.

"If you want his number Bill will give it to you," I said.

Henri stopped dead in his tracks. "You know Jimmy Hoffa?"

"Yes, we do. Here's his number." Bill rattled it off.

We entered Henri's office. He sat down behind his huge desk and dialed Hoffa's number on his speakerphone. When Hoffa answered we could hear him clearly.

"Hello. Who is this?"

"Mr. Hoffa, it's Henri."

"Henri who?"

"Henri Lewin."

"Oh, hello, Henri, what can I do for you?"

"I'm sitting here with a friend of yours."

"Who's that?"

Without mentioning any names, Henri motioned to Bill to speak up.

"Hi, Jimmy, how are you doing?"

"Hey, Bill, Josephine and I were talking about you yesterday. Maybe we could meet up at the Top for some of Dick's great shrimp pasta. What are you doing with Henri?"

"I'm here with Dick to see about booking some acts into his hotels here."

"Let me speak to Henri."

The change in Henri's tone with us, from casual condescension to respectful, was notable. "Yes, Mr. Hoffa?"

Hoffa used his typical line, applying just the right amount of pressure. "Henri, do me a favor. When you talk with those guys, pretend they're me."

Hoffa hung up and Henri booked MacNally into the International Hilton.

People think that show business in America and Europe operates in the same way—they don't, especially when it comes to music. There are singers, musicians, composers and producers that cross paths covering each other's material in different languages and styles, and then re-release songs in their own country under different names.

Claude Francois, a recording star in France, took a song that was a minor hit in America, gave it his own rendition and called it "Belles Belles Belles." It sold two million records and made him an overnight star in France. After that he knocked out one hit after another.

Ironically, his successful formula of taking American rock-and-roll hits and adapting them for the French market reversed itself when he wrote "Comme d'Habitude." Claude's agent got Paul Anka to write the English lyrics to the song, which became a legendary hit for Frank Sinatra, called "My Way." The music attorney who put the deal together was Walter Hofer, from New York City. He was also my attorney and did all my concert contracts.

In February 1977 Walter called me to say that Claude Francois was coming to Hollywood, Florida and staying at the Diplomat. He was sending him to my restaurant, Top of the Home, for dinner and wanted me to hold the check for him.

At the time, I had never even heard of Claude, but Walter filled me in and had also told Claude about me. He knew I'd had the Peppermint Lounge and was fascinated with the whole Twist saga. He had an outgoing personality and was easy to be with. We spent the major part of the evening bouncing stories off each other.

Toward the end of the night he told me how disgusted he was with Paul Anka. He had just come from Las Vegas where Anka was performing and, for some reason, Anka snubbed him and wouldn't even see him.

"Who does he think he is?" Claude ranted in his heavy French accent. "I go all the way to Las Vegas and he doesn't have time to see me? Why? Is he too big a putain d'étoile?"

I drove him back to the hotel and he made me promise that

if I came to France I would call him. As he got out of the car he said, "I'll be back next year. In case I don't see you first over in my country, I'll see you here."

The year went by and Walter called to tell me that Francois had died. I was shocked. "What happened?" I raked a hand through my hair in disbelief.

"He was taking a bath in his apartment outside of Paris when he looked up and saw that the light fixture on the wall was a little crooked. He got up to straighten it out and when he touched it he was electrocuted."

"Does Anka know?"

"Why? Were they close?"

"Never mind, I was only kidding."

Marvin Gaye wanted to headline a big room at a major hotel in Las Vegas. At the time he was a giant star but only known to black audiences. He'd recently worked the Miami Stadium in front of 28,000 people—all black—yet he approached me to work in Vegas. Why? Because he knew we were the connection he needed to succeed there. Previously Gaye had asked me to make hotel arrangements for him and his show in Miami.

"How many rooms you need?"

"Well, we've got 28 people that travel with the show."

I called Charlie Ferrara, the General Manager of the Sonesta Beach Hotel in Key Biscayne, and he gave him all the villas they had. After they settled in I went over to see Marvin Gaye in his villa.

"Why do you want to work Vegas?" I asked.

"I'm older now and I want to sing to the same people that Jerry Vale sings to," he said in a serious tone.

At the time, Jerry Vale could fill a room in Vegas, but not Marvin Gaye. Gaye wanted this so much that he was willing to let us have part of his management if we could put him in a main room of a major hotel there. The trouble was Vegas wasn't ready for black rhythm and blues headliners and wasn't particularly interested in drawing black people to Vegas, afraid it would chase white customers away. The timing was wrong.

Gaye heard what we did for Lenny Welch but it was a different story with Lenny, because even though he was black, he was a white act with the same potential as Nat or Sammy. His recording voice testified to that. Lenny came to Vinny after he had his first hit record. It's the same old story, another one hit recording wonder going nowhere.

Vinny's perception of what Lenny needed was correct. We'd have to fuse the two…a hit record with an act that can do a stand up show for white audiences in Vegas. I told Vinny, "Don't worry about Vegas. You get him another hit record and I'll open the door for him there." And that's what happened.

Vinny went to the director of McCann-Erickson ad agency, who did all the Coca-Cola commercials and had the idea of having Lenny record Neil Sedaka's bubble-gum hit, "Breaking Up is Hard to Do" as a ballad with a plush arrangement of strings and just the right sensuous beat. Arranged by Hugo Winterhalter, it became a #1 hit. As successful as this strategy was for Welch, and try as we did, we never could get any traction for Marvin Gaye. Nobody wanted Marvin Gaye in Vegas then. Today only a few people know Jerry Vale, and while Lenny Welch has held his own, Marvin Gaye is the most famous…go figure.

Jimmy Grippo, a headline act in Las Vegas at Caesar's Palace, was a magician and friend of my father-in-law, Johnny Futto. I first met him when Johnny brought me over to his apartment in South Miami. We were all going to lunch at Pumpernick's, but beforehand, at Johnny's urging, Jimmy spread out a deck of cards on the table before me. He then walked to the far side of the room, casually folded his arms across his chest and told me to look at one card and silently repeat it over and over in my mind. As I am thinking Jack of hearts...Jack of hearts...Jack of hearts.

Jimmy says out loud, "Jack of hearts."

While I'm still in disbelief, he then has me gather up the deck and throw it against the wall where all cards slip to the floor except for the Jack of hearts, which sticks to the wall. It was as mysterious to me then as it is every time I have seen anyone do it since.

After lunch at Pumpernicks, we make our way to the parking

lot where former Middleweight Champion of the World, Solly Grieger, is the lot attendant. His eyes light up as he sees us and calls out a greeting to both Johnny and Jimmy. Grippo extends his arm high into the air and a quarter appears between his fanned out fingers. "This is for you, Solly...naw...wait a minute," he says. "That is not enough." He flips his hand once and there's a half dollar in place of the quarter and with another flip a silver dollar appears. "Naw." Grippo persists. "Still not enough." Solly's smile continues to get larger and larger, like the money. In the end Grippo hands over 2 silver dollars.

Sometime later Grippo was hired by NASA to hypnotize the first astronauts scheduled to go into space to help them overcome claustrophobia in the constricted confines of the space capsule. Hypnotism was his specialty, and Futto always thought that was how he pulled off all his tricks. I didn't see it.

When he took his act to Las Vegas, appearing at Caesar's in the Bacchanal Room, he got a reputation for astonishing people from all over the world with his magic. One night at the restaurant, a customer just back from Vegas told me that he saw Jimmy perform a dinner show. That night Elizabeth Taylor and Richard Burton were having dinner when Grippo approached and convinced Elizabeth Taylor to take off her incredible and well-publicized diamond ring, a gift from Burton. Grippo never touched it but rather had Taylor wrap it in a piece of flash paper, put it in an ashtray where a match was put to it. Whoop.... nothing left but ashes. At that precise moment, with Elizabeth too stunned to yet react, a waiter walked by with a fresh loaf of warm bread on his tray. Grippo summoned him over, had him put the tray on the table and commanded him to open the bread. There in the middle of the loaf is the ring!

That story was told to me well before the majority of people had a cell phone in their pocket and could bring up such events on the internet. Curious what might be on the internet about Grippo, I looked him up. From what I read it appears not just his magic but many aspects of his life were, and still remain, a bit mysterious. I didn't find the incident about Elizabeth Taylor, but did find a similar account of a ring belonging to Aristotle Onassis.

Chapter 7

Engelbert Humperdinck

In another joint venture with a longtime friend from way back to my Freeport High School days, Bill Johnson and I were interested in promoting Tom Jones, who at the time was the hottest entertainer in the world. His manager, Gordon Mills, agreed but insisted that we first promote another artist he wanted to bring to America. "He'll do great," Mills insisted. "Engelbert Humperdinck has got a hit record going for him now, 'Please Release Me' is a smash."

We researched the possibility and agreed we could make a go of it even though his price was fifty thousand for one concert. That was a lot of money back in '68. Maple Leaf Gardens, a venue which sat about twenty thousand people, fit our needs perfectly. William Morris provided the opening acts. The Primo's, a singing family, started things off. The mother was the drummer, the father the piano player, and the five kids all sang. The comic and emcee was New York comedian Alan Drake.

I made arrangements for Humperdinck to stay at the Skyline Hotel. Humperdinck insisted that we call him Enge. He was a nice fellow and we all got along good. After dinner at the hotel, we had two limos standing by to take us to the concert. When we got to the Maple Leaf Gardens the concert was just about to get underway when someone backstage said to me, "Lloyd Greenfield is on the phone and wants to talk with you." Lloyd was William Morris' man and he'd just had dinner with us back at the hotel. I was surprised. He was supposed to get into the limo behind us with Enge. I answered the phone and Greenfield told me that Enge had lost his voice. This is precisely what a promoter never wants to hear.

"What?" I shouted into the phone. "Well, what are you doing about it?"

"He's up in his room and we're waiting for a doctor."

"Forget about that," I said. "Get him over here to the Gardens right now. We'll have a doctor here for him."

I slammed down the phone and went to Harold Ballard, the owner of the Gardens, who called a throat specialist to make an emergency visit. When Enge got there the doctor was ready to examine him. His first impression was that he'd be all right after a little oxygen was sprayed down his throat. By now the concert had started and the Primo's were out on stage opening the show. I grabbed Drake, the comic, and told him when he went on next after the Primo's to only do twenty minutes.

"Twenty minutes?" Drake's face twisted up in frustration. "My act is thirty-five minutes."

"Yeah, well, forget about that. Only do twenty then bring Enge out."

Drake was disappointed and tried to argue but to no avail.

In the dressing room I was disappointed to find out the doctor had not gotten Enge's voice back yet and we needed more time. So I went back to the wings just when Drake had finished his act, doing his first walk off to the applause of the packed house. Grabbing his arm I said, "Go back out there and do another half hour...Enge ain't ready yet."

"What? Are you kidding—I just did all my best jokes."

"I know, but we need more time."

Drake went back out and a half hour later after telling boring, humorless jokes the restless audience had started screaming for Humperdinck. I signaled to Drake to call for an intermission.

Now it's a half hour later and Humperdinck still has no

voice. The audience was upset, having been charged more to see Humperdinck than any other performer ever in the history of concerts in Canada—a single ticket was $15 dollars. The Russian Ballet had just played there and that ticket was $12. The audience started hollering in unison. "Humperdinck! Humperdinck! Humperdinck!" Fourteen thousand people were shouting—possibly the largest chorus ever in the world. Enge still didn't have his voice back so I went to Ballard and asked, "What do we do about refunds in a situation like this?"

"I don't know," Ballard answered. "I've been with the Maple Leaf Gardens for forty years and we've never had anything like this ever happen before."

By some miracle Enge thought his voice was strong enough to go out and do a show, so Bill tells Drake to go out and announce him. When the audience sees Drake coming out again they think he's going to do another set and they start booing. Drake stood at the mike but couldn't be heard over the crowd so he just threw his hands down and walked off stage. That's when Enge walked out. It sounded like a bomb went off they were so happy to see him. The applause lasted for over five minutes. If there's something to the old show business adage of coming on stage late, this certainly was it.

Enge got through the show to a standing ovation but the reviews were less than admirable. The Toronto Star review read:

Last night at the Maple Leaf Gardens we witnessed what we thought was the worst act in show business, The Primo's. Nobody could convince us that there was an act worst than this...that is until the comedian came on...then we realized that was the worst act in show business. The headliner Engelbert Humperdinck finally appeared and had a way with a lyric but his range was D above middle C...that's one note.

I was so happy to get through the night and realized that reviews mean little if everyone loved the concert.

Chapter 8

S-S-Stutterin' Joe Cohen

Of all the Damon Runyonesque characters I've met, stutterin' Joe Cohen was without a doubt the most unique. He was a great supporter of the Peppermint Lounge as well as the Top of the Home. I have so many stories to tell about him that they could fill an entire book on their own.

The best way for me to describe Joe Cohen is to recount what happened when I tried to reach him years ago up at the Drake Hotel in New York City via a person-to-person operator. Initially the operator at the Drake said he was taking his calls at Le Mistral, the French restaurant. The operator called there but the hostess came back a few minutes later saying, "There ezz no Mr. Cohen in zee restaurant."

I butted in knowing better. "Operator, may I describe Mr. Cohen to the hostess?"

"Certainly," she replied.

"Hello, ma'm...he's about sixty-five-years-old and looks like the Penguin out of Batman comics. He's got a goiter coming out of the side of his neck the size of a grapefruit, his right arm dangles at an angle from an accident and he'll be holding a big cigar at the end of his fingers. Now where he's sitting will be like a disaster area. There'll be cigar butts and ashes, breadcrumbs, spilled drinks and wine stains, plus bits of food all over the table and the floor around it. Also, he's probably with a twenty year old Chinese girl—oh, and on top of that, he stutters.

It only took the hostess a second before I heard her say, "Oh, yes Mr. Cohen, zee telephone for you."

Joe Cohen moved from New York to Chicago when he was a kid. One of his first business ventures was a retail store. He got wind that Sears was opening a big new department store projected to cover an entire city block. But before they finalized their plans, Cohen took a lease on one corner of the proposed location. Sears approached him but there wasn't enough money in it for him to sell. He had a plan in mind and he needed just that location.

When Sears opened Cohen painted his storefront the same color as theirs and put a sign over his front door that read, "Main Entrance." He got away with this because his corporation was registered as Main Entrance Inc.

Sears opened before the Christmas holiday season and customers came pouring into Joe's joint. He told me that's when he realized people would spend more money when using credit rather than cash. When a customer would present their Sears card he would explain to them, "S-s-sorry, t-t-this is the c-c-cash only department."

Within a short time Sears approached him again with an offer to buy him out. Joe wasn't anxious to sell because he had a gimmick going with someone in the sales tax department—he didn't pay any. Between selling his products for just over costs and not paying any sales tax he did all right. However, when Sears offered a ridiculously high price, he couldn't refuse.

Joe was going out with a girl in the chorus line at the Chez Paree nightclub in Chicago when she received an offer and moved to New York to work at the Copacabana. Joe went back to New York with her.

One night she asked Joe if her girlfriend and date could join them for dinner. Joe didn't care. The guy was simply introduced as Howard. They had a nice dinner and since the guy was dressed shabbily with sneakers, without even thinking about it, Joe picked up the check.

The guy got a kick out of Joe Cohen and his stories, and it became a ritual for them to have dinner together in the Copa lounge before the show without the girls. The guy loved the little Chinese steak they served. One of the owners Julie Podel cornered Joe one night and asked him, "You know who that guy is you're eating dinner with every night?"

"No...w-who is he?"

"Howard Hughes. One of the richest men in America."

"W-w-what? The f-f-fuckin' bum don't go for a quarter."

The next night at the Copa lounge while having their steak Joe said, "H-H-Howard, I would like to ask you for a loan of ten thousand for my b-b-business. I've got little problem to work out but I can pay you back before too long."

Howard put down his knife and fork and as he left the table said, "Could you excuse me a minute, Joe?" That was the last time, Joe, the girlfriend, or the Copa ever saw Howard Hughes. Until, a few years later when Joe was in Vegas at the Desert Inn and spotted Howard Hughes waiting in line to get into a show. He went to the maître d', his friend Jimmy Mac, and told him who was in his line. Jimmy answered, "I know. Screw him. I lent him twenty bucks last week and he still hasn't paid me back."

Bill Johnson's first date with airline flight attendant Jennifer was a disaster. He realized he hadn't acted properly and wanted to make it up to her with a second date but she wasn't having it. It was a year before she finally relented and called him while down in Miami Beach on a layover, agreeing to have dinner with him.

Johnson was overjoyed, but he foresaw a problem. He already had dinner arrangements with Gus Zappas and Joe Cohen and both were bringing dates, ladies of the evening, of course. He didn't want to lose Jennifer again and knew, especially with these guys, there could be a lot of cursing at the table. So he went to them before hand and made them promise. "No cursing, because the girl I'm bringing doesn't go for any of that—she's a lady."

They weren't too happy about it, but reluctantly agreed.

Joe Cohen promptly said, "Who the h-h-hell is she...Q-Q-Queen of England?"

Sometimes things don't go exactly as planned and this was one of those times. In Joe Sonken's restaurant, after everyone ordered, Joe Cohen went up to the bar to get a cigar and bumped into a friend. They had a drink and became engaged in a long conversation. Meanwhile, the food came and everyone ate while Cohen's steak grew cold on the table. Bill, known to be a big eater, finished his dish and figuring Cohen had left, plunged his fork into his steak, put it on his plate and ate it. By the time Joe came back the table had just been cleared, and he said, "W-W-Where's my s-s-steak?"

No one answered, so he called the waiter over. "W-W-Where's my s-s-steak?"

The waiter looked confused. Cohen started to get angry. Normally at a moment like this he would have cursed the waiter out but remembering his promise to Bill he just yelled, "G-G-Get me the C-C-Captain."

The Captain promptly arrived at the table and Joe Cohen again asked, "W-W-Where's my s-s-steak?"

The Captain, all wringing hands and worried glances said, "Did you order one, Mr. Cohen?"

At this point Joe was so twisted it was all he could do to keep his self-control and not curse. Steam practically came out of his ears. "G-G-Get me the g-g-goddamn m-m-maître d'."

The Captain went and gave the maître d' an update on the problem and they both came back to the table. By this time Joe Cohen had had it.

"Good evening, Mr. Cohen," the maître d' said. "May I help you?"

"Good evening, m-m-my ass. Where's my s-s-steak?"

The maître d' made a fatal error in telling him he didn't order one. That was it—school was out.

Joe Cohen stood, put his finger up by the maître d's nose and shouted in his face. "W-W-Why you dirty b-b-bastard, don't t-t-tell me I didn't order a f-f-f...s-s-steak."

Whereas, Bill shouted back at him, "Hey, Joe you promised

you wouldn't curse."

"Yeah, well f-f-f...youse and the s-s-ship yas came in on."

"Stop it, Joe," Gus said. "Bill's with a lady."

Then Gus's girl became angry, stood up and started screaming at him. "So, what am I? A tramp?"

The other girl, also furious, started cursing and it went on and around like that. The only one that wasn't upset was Jennifer. She saw the situation for what it was, and was pleased that Bill had at least tried to make an effort on her part.

Later that night, after the fiasco was over, I met Bill at the Place for Steak where he related what a miserable evening it had been.

"I've got an idea," he said.

I followed Bill to a payphone. It was now 4 a.m. He dialed the Eden Roc Hotel where Joe Cohen was staying and asked the operator to ring his room.

After five rings, Cohen answered in a deep, groggy voice. "H-H-Hello?"

"Mr. Cohen?" Bill disguised his voice.

"Y-Y-Yes."

"This is the kitchen at Joe Sonken's. We found your steak."

Joe Cohen exploded. "F-F-F-...youse...Y-Y-You d-d-dirty r-r-rotten..."

We hung up before the string of curse words ended.

Everything worked out for Bill and Jennifer who ended up getting married and I was the best man.

This next story is very crude and has racial overtones, but it's dead true. It's what a restaurateur has to endure when dealing with characters like Joe Cohen.

A high society woman from Palm Beach, who was Paul Getty's ex-daughter-in-law and now married into the automobile Dodge family, came to the Top of the Home to see me because someone told her I was a friend of stand-up comedian Shecky Greene. She had just bought a horse named Shecky Greene and wanted the real Shecky to know that the horse would be in good hands. During the racing season at Gulfstream, she came in about once a week, usually early.

One evening when she was there with her husband, I saw the maître d' seat Joe Cohen, who was alone, a few tables over from them. This was going to be trouble, and I knew it. It was early and the restaurant wasn't crowded yet. I worried that they'd see him eating and lose their appetite. I was bouncing between the two tables when she beckoned me over. "Why don't you invite that lonely old man you were sitting with to join us at our table?"

Talk about a recipe for a disaster. "No, no...no...no that's all right, he likes to eat alone."

A few seconds later the maître d' called me away from their table. When I returned I couldn't believe what I saw. Joe Cohen was sitting with them finishing the rest of his dinner. I quickly joined them, figuring to be the moderator to keep Joe from embarrassing himself, and the couple from being embarrassed.

"So, I see you've met the great Joe Cohen," I said trying to make the best out of a potentially disastrous situation. "You know Mr. Cohen has been around the horn a few times and knows a lot of interesting people."

"Oh, really?" the society lady perked up. "Did you ever meet Ava Gardner?"

By this time, Joe had had a large goiter removed from his neck and couldn't talk, so he had this little pad and pencil he carried around to write on. Well, Joe wrote worse than he spoke. He had very little knowledge of English grammar and misspelled practically every word, but that didn't stop him—oh, no. When he heard "Ava Gardner" his eyes went wide and his arm reached out for his pad as he made room by spreading the dishes in front of him out of the way to write. In doing so he spilled his glass of wine and her glass of water. Oh Boy...here it comes. His head went down in intense concentration as he wrote what we all expected would be a serious and noteworthy comment about Ava. When Joe finished he handed the note to her.

After she read it, her head reared back so fast in laughter that it hit the glass window she sat in front of with a big bang. I picked up the note. It read, *Yeah, I met her in a ni**er whorehouse in Chicago.*

When we visited Bill Johnson, who was now a labor leader in Toronto, Joe Cohen decided the best way to spend his time there would be to throw back a few drinks. Even though he was already half in the bag, we decided to go see Robert Goulet, appearing at the Royal York Hotel. Their fabulous maître d', Louie Genetta, put us right up front in the middle at a ringside table. Joining us were some business friends of Bill's from Montreal. It didn't take long before I knew it was a mistake to bring Joe. The first thing he did was fall asleep at the table. As a gag, Bill said that Joe was Dr. Cohen, a brain surgeon from New York, and was very tired from operating all day. Then, as Goulet performed, in a sense Joe performed along with him—almost like a duet. When Goulet sang, "If ever I should leave you…."

Joe, sleeping at the table, answered with a loud snore. "ZZZZZ...."

Then Goulet sang, "It wouldn't be in springtime..."

And Joe came back in again. "ZZZZZZZZZZZZZZZ…"

"Joe," I whispered nudging his arm. "Wake up, will ya?"

It went on like that for the rest of the show. The next morning at the airport, we ran across the gentlemen from Montreal. They waved and said, "Good operating today, Doctor Cohen."

Joe turned to me looking confused. "W-W-What the h-h-hell... do they m-m-mean by that?"

"Dammed if I know." I shrugged.

I was in New York City down in the lobby of the Warwick Hotel talking to Joe E. Lewis, waiting for stuttering Joe Cohen to arrive. As soon as he came in he said, "There's a g-g-great new d-d-deli over on forty s-s-seventh, let's g-g-go there for l-l-lunch."

Off we went. Now if there is one thing you want to avoid in life, it's going to lunch with Joe Cohen, but if you can't help it, you should definitely not sit across the table from him, because it's even money you'll get hit with the food flying out of his mouth.

The deli was crowded and Joe ordered tuna fish salad on rye, which I knew right off the bat would be a problem. It didn't take long for the food to arrive. Joe picked up half of his sandwich with his pincher-claw fingers. He looked at the huge tuna fish salad portion between two meager slices of rye bread, staring at it intently until his mouth shot open as he lunged forward, taking a big bite in the middle. Tuna salad flew out of each side of the sandwich in arcs, landing on the table on either side of his plate. Joe paid no attention to this and continued eating. The same thing happened when he bit into the other half of the sandwich. When finished there were four globs of tuna fish salad on the table, surrounding an empty plate.

As a finale to this wonderful lunch, Joe took his false teeth out and washed them in his water glass.

"For cryin' out loud, Joe," I said. "Are you crazy?"

"What about?" Joe continued swishing his teeth around.

"I'm talking about the waitress who just walked by and saw your teeth in the glass."

"Who the h-h-hell cares ab-b-bout her?" he said.

"Her? What about me? What am I, chopped liver?"

"I love chopped liver." He smacked his gums, and popped the teeth back in.

Just then, a vision flashed before my eyes—of him ordering a chopped liver sandwich—please.

Chapter 9

Frank Howard, Chuck & Don, and Charlie Noto

Day-to-day, I never knew what I'd have to face at the Top of the Home and, eventually, nothing came as a surprise. I don't want to say every situation known to man but something close to that would fit the picture.

Frank Howard retired as head coach of the Clemson Tigers after more than thirty years. He had one of the best records of any college football coach in the country. In 1969 he coached that South team in the Orange Bowl in Miami. It was the last game Clemson's revered Coach Howard ever coached. Unbeknownst to me, one of the Budweiser salesmen played at Clemson and he arranged to host a celebratory dinner party at my restaurant for Coach Howard and his guests after the game.

During the course of the busy evening, the salesman waved me over to the table for an introduction. As soon as I arrived he stood proudly and said, "Dick, this is Frank Howard, my famous coach when I played at Clemson."

Coach Howard stood up to shake my hand and I almost fainted. It took all I had to put on a happy smile, pretending that I'd only heard of him. "Wow...the great Frank Howard," I said in disbelief. "You have no idea what a surprise it is to meet you Coach. Welcome to the Top of the Home."

He nodded, we chatted briefly and I congratulated him on

the game. Little did anyone know that I was a former archrival Gamecock from the University of South Carolina. For those who don't know what that means I'll try to explain, but I'll never be able to put the true feeling of it into words. It's like a Mongoose and Cobra on steroids. The dislike between the Clemson Tigers and the South Carolina Gamecocks was, and still is, infamous. More than a dislike—it is a loathing, an abomination, a feeling of malice of the biggest proportions. Whenever we played each other it went way beyond a grudge—way, way beyond. We could lose every game of the season but if we beat Clemson, it was a winning season to every Gamecock fan in America.

I didn't want to ruin the coach's dinner party so I decided to wait to tell him who I was on his way out. But to my surprise, when the party left, the coach and his wife decided to go into our lounge, have a drink, and listen to the music. I saw this as my opportunity. I could see he was in a good mood as I approached him sitting at a window table near the bandstand. When he saw me he stood outstretching his hand, which I grabbed and shook vigorously. "We had a right fine meal here, son." Coach Howard smiled. "I'll be talkin' about your restaurant when I get back home. It was wonderful."

"Thanks, Coach," I said. "Coach, there's something I've been meaning to tell you."

"There is...and what's that, son?"

The words just flew out of my mouth with no pause to think. "I'm a Gamecock!" I let my gaze linger.

Shocked couldn't describe the look on Coach Howard's face. He stood there like someone hit him with a bat, then took a step backwards and said sternly, "What'd you say, boy?"

"I said I played football at South Carolina."

"Damn you did." His eyes flashed in disbelief. "What's your name, boy?"

"I use Dick Cami now but at Carolina I played under my real name, Camillucci."

"Camillucci? Well, I'll be damned." He spun around to his wife who was sitting, looking out the window. "Edna," he called out and she turned to look up at him. "You hear what this som-na-bitch just told me?"

"What's that, dear?" She said in a soft pleasant voice, looking at him.

"He said he was a Gamecock."

"Whaaat?" Her mouth hung open, truly puzzled.

Coach Howard grabbed me around the waist and high-hipped me, lifting my feet off the floor.

"I'm gonna throw this som-na-bitch right out the winda here." He growled like an angry tiger, but a smile teased at the corner of his mouth.

After he put me down I joined them at their table.

"I suppose this seems odd to you, Coach, and a little ironic," I said. "But, I always admired you and if I knew you were coming I would have baked a special cake for you."

He shot up straight in his chair. "It woulda been one hell of a cake to fit an occasion like this."

It was a great pleasure and honor to talk with Coach Howard. Funny how I felt close to him and the thought of playing at Clemson crossed my mind. I knew it would have been an honor if I had. He was one of the greatest coaches of all time.

The Pittsburgh Steelers were scheduled to play in the Super Bowl in Miami in 1976 and again in 1979. The night before the first such Super Bowl, Miami head coach, Don Shula and his wife Dorothy came to the Top of the Home along with Chuck Knoll, the head coach of the Steelers, and his wife for dinner. Don waved me over and introduced me saying, "Chuck is a wine expert and we'd like to show him we have fine wines down here in South Florida."

It was like giving me the ball when it's fourth and goal to win the Super Bowl. After they ordered, Chef Joe Ezbicki recommended we give them a bottle of Le Montrachet, a white burgundy, with the appetizers of Crab Cakes, and a bottle of Romanee Conti, a red burgundy with the entrées that included our Russian Breast of Capon and Chateaubriand Bouquetiere. The two wines provided to accompany their dishes were some of the finest, rarest, and most expensive wines in the world.

In those days our business was seasonal and we closed

in the summer for several months. I would go to Europe and visit vineyards, mostly in France and Italy. Via an introduction from Mel Dick of Southern Wine and Spirits, I was allowed to personally walk the vineyards of Montrachet and Romanee Conti in Burgundy, France, and was lucky enough to purchase a couple of cases of these rare allocations.

To say that Romanee Conti is rare does not do it justice. Some proclaim you should drink it bare headed and kneeling, but who's going to ask Shula and Knoll to do that?

After the meal Coach Shula invited me to join them at their table. I figured I would discuss wines with Coach Knoll but he leaned in and very seriously said, "I'm not familiar with these wines, although I thought they were very good."

After my jaw came up off the floor I said, "Maybe I misunderstood, but I thought Coach Shula said you were a wine expert?"

"Only in American wines," he answered.

In 1979 the Pittsburgh Steelers returned to Miami for another Super Bowl appearance. This time when the two coaches came in for dinner, I was ready. Mel Dick, head of Southern Wines, sent me two bottles of rare California estate bottled wine, each in a hand carved wooden box. One was a Chardonnay from Cakebread Cellars and the other was a select Cabernet from Caymus Vineyards. Now Coach Knoll smiled, which shows that rare wines only mean something to the person who knows about them.

I had a similar experience with Charlie Noto. He was a character right out of the Godfather movie and Carlo Gambino's closest friend. They'd been in the can together. Noto was dining alone and asked me to join him. I told the captain to bring a bottle of Chateau Petrus '64, my compliments. I choose Petrus because it was one of the better wines of France. The captain went through the ritual of opening the wine and showed Charlie the label. I could see he wasn't familiar with the wine so I decided to give him a little history lesson.

A little long winded, I went on to tell him about the Appellation

Controlee, France's system of grading wines. Then I went into the story of Napoleon and how when he led his troops into battle and they marched past this vineyard, he stopped his army and from his horse pointed to the vineyard and shouted, "This is what we are fighting for."

There was a silence as Charlie reflected, then he looked at me and said, "Maw, go where ya gotta go and pour the fuckin' wine."

Chapter 10

John Scali, J. Edgar Hoover, Wilford Brimley, and Don Ameche

Prior to John Scali becoming the U.S. Ambassador to the United Nations, he was one of President Nixon's chief advisors and the one that set up Nixon's famous trip to China. In charge of everything, he worked out of the Nixon winter White House in Key Biscayne. A friend of my mine recommended the Top of the Home to him and he dined with us several times a week. Although he was one of the busiest men in the government, he always came to the Top alone. At his request, I spent many an hour sitting with him and listening to his stories. The historic visit between the superpowers of the United States and China was a frequent topic.

Scali was in charge as liaison for this trip and went to China several times, making the arrangements for Nixon's arrival. One of the things Scali said he was apprehensive about was that once inside China, President Nixon's security and transportation would only be in the hands of the Chinese. This would be the first time a president ever flew in another country's plane and not in Air Force One. When Scali questioned the security of the president and discussed the absence of security guards on rooftops for the motor parade in Peking, Scali was assured, "There will not be any problems. This is not the United States."

On Scali's first trip, he said he witnessed an operation where they wheeled out a patient, laid him out on an operating table, stuck long needles in him and proceeded to cut his chest open like a chicken. They then took clippers and cut out his diseased lung. All of this happened while the patient was awake and being fed tangerines as he looked on at his own operation. After they sewed his chest up he got up off the table and walked away.

I could hardly believe my ears. "What do they call that?"

"It's called acupuncture."

"How long have they been doing that?"

"Oh, for about two thousand years." Scali smiled broadly.

Another night when he was in I said, "If you're in the mood for something special, Chef Ezbicki made some stuffed Cornish hens, they're small but delicious."

"No, thanks," he said. "I've had my fill of small birds for awhile."

I gave him a quizzical look and he asked me to sit down and went on to explain the statement. They had just gotten back from Nixon's trip to China. Scali was in charge of all protocol. The first face-to-face meeting of the leaders took place at a State dinner in China's Great Dining Hall. It was a well-publicized event. The whole world was watching and Scali made sure that everyone in the Presidential party understood the importance of not embarrassing anyone at the meeting. He briefed the team about the possibility of encountering some strange foods. "We must eat everything." He was adamant. "Even if it's something you don't like. It's important that no one's insulted. Does everyone understand this? Make sure you eat everything they put on our plates—it's imperative."

Scali went on to describe the service. "It was incredible," he said. "They had five servers for every guest. You can imagine the service was beyond description. They had one server for the water, one for the wine, another for other beverages and on and on. When I heard a slight clunk on my plate I turned and saw that the appetizer server had put a glazed hummingbird on my plate. I stiffened ever so slightly and shuddered in revulsion at what I saw: the eyes, the little beak and the tiny little hairy feet all set in aspic. I realized there was no way I could contradict my own orders. I had to set the example, so I summoned up all the courage I had in my body and in one swoop put the little hummingbird in my mouth, chewed and swallowed it in one gulp. My eyes were still closed, fighting off demons, when I heard another clunk. When I opened my eyes I saw that the server had put another one on my plate, probably thinking I'd enjoyed it so much."

Scali smiled. "You have no idea what I would have given then for the little Cornish hen you're talking about."

John Monahan was the manager of the Diplomat Hotel for its first ten years. He was known as America's host, and was one of the best hotel men in the business. I never met a man who knew more people.

One evening a guest at the restaurant asked me if I knew a John Monahan. "Of course," I answered. "Why do you ask?"

"We were in Egypt," she said. "I was sitting on a camel with my husband when the Bedouin camel driver, who had a turban on his head and a patch over one eye, asked where we were from. When I answered Hollywood, Florida, he stopped the camel, looked up at us and asked if we knew his good friend, John Monahan." See? The guy knew everyone.

Clyde Tolson, FBI Director, J. Edgar Hoover's associate, called John Monahan and asked where they would all be going to dinner that evening.

"The Top of the Home," Monahan answered.

"Would you call our field office and clear that for me?" he asked.

Monahan did and obviously the Top of the Home received clearance because he came to dinner that evening with Tolson and Hoover. During the course of the dinner, Monahan asked me to join them at their table and I did. I thought it was interesting that the Director, who was more than cordial, probed me about a dish that wasn't on our menu. He asked if I knew how to make a classic French omelet. I thought about taking the fifth for a joke. It was a very interesting question because at one time, long ago, when Chef Joe and I were talking food he mentioned that rarely did any American chef know how to make an authentic French omelet and he went on to tell me how it was made. When I quickly explained the recipe to the Director I could see he was truly impressed.

Just then the maître d' called me over to the side. I could see he was anxious.

"You'll never believe who just walked in and is insisting to be seated at W-2." This was the table right next to where the Director sat.

"Who?" I asked.

"Jimmy Blue Eyes"

"Let me talk to him."

I approached Jimmy and told him that sitting next to the table he wanted was J. Edgar Hoover. Jimmy came in a lot but in all those times I'd never seen him smile, not once. But, after he heard what I had to say, he broke out in a big, wide grin.

"Put me over on the other side, out of the way, right?"

"Absolutely," I said to one of the more notorious members of the Mafia Genovese Family

I had a friend, a drama instructor in New York City, who called to let me know that a buddy of his would be in Miami to make a movie. He had told him to be sure to go into the Top and ask for me. He told me that he was a flat-out cowboy but a good actor and a just great guy.

Not too many of my customers walked off the elevator wearing a cowboy hat, so I figured it to be him. Wilford Brimley was in town for his first major movie role in *Absence of Malice.* Reviewing the menu, he pointed to one of the dishes. "What's in the shrimp pasta sauce? I'm diabetic." When I told him the main ingredient was heavy cream he said, "I can have heavy cream. So that's what I'll order."

As we talked, I asked about the movie and found out it starred Paul Newman with Sally Field. Earlier I had been in the lounge with good friend and customer Lorraine Varesse who I knew to be a Paul Newman fan—a fanatic Paul Newman fan. Eventually

I brought her over to the table and introduced Brimley. When he found out what a big Newman fan she was he invited her to the shooting location and offered to introduce her to him. When she regained her composure she got the particulars of where and when to be to meet her idol and returned to her party.

After she left, I asked Wilford, "So, what kind of guy is Newman?"

"I don't know. I haven't met him." He politely nodded.

What...this is my kind of guy, I thought.

Any one of my school buddies or either of my sons can tell you that I ran my Don Ameche joke into the ground.

"Who was the actor that played Alexander Graham Bell in the movie?" I'd ask.

"That was Don Ameche."

"What's the last name?" I'd ask.

"Ameche."

"Well, scratch yourself." I'd say.

I got more laughs out of that joke than I can remember. I still use it today.

One evening here comes Wilford Brimley with the whole cast of *Cocoon II*, and a hand extends out in front of me as a deep, rich voice says, "Hello, I'm Don Ameche."

What to do? My natural reaction was to say, "What's your last name?" But, to tell you the truth I was too much in awe of this great actor.

Brimley told me Ameche was a wine connoisseur so I went down to our cellar and brought up two bottles each of my best white and red wines. I offered them with my compliments because I figured that was the least I could do from all the pleasure I'd received from using his name.

Here's the kick. Ameche took the wine tasting ritual from the sublime to the ridiculous. After our captain opened the bottle and poured a sip in his glass for tasting, Ameche held it up to the light to see the color, stared at it for what seemed like an eternity before swirling it in the glass then swirling it again about ten more times and waiting another eternity before he held it up to the light to determine the wine's body by seeing how the rivulets clung to the side of the glass. All this done while the whole table of Gwen Verdon, Wilford Brimley, Hume Cronyn, and his wife Jessica Tandy watched.

Now for the final stages of the tasting ceremony, Ameche put the glass to his lips, ever so slowly sipping the wine then made gurgling sounds, then gargling sounds, then rinsing sounds like when you brush your teeth. I looked over at Brimley and saw his eyes roll to the ceiling. Is this guy for real?

Ameche performed in ceremonial manner what the serious elite tasters of France do at their wine tasting competitions. It was a ceremony, indeed, which actually everyone got a big kick out of.

Ameche finally swallowed the wine and smacked his lips for what seemed like another eternity before finally turning to the captain saying, "Wonderful!"

Geez. I felt like I passed a test.

The whole process was repeated with the red.

Chapter 11

The Bennett Brothers, Johnny and Tony

Johnny Bennett was my good friend. If you thought his brother Tony was the only singer in his family—wait until you read this.

During the depression, Johnny grew up as Giovanni Benedetto. Nicknamed "Little Caruso," he was only eight years old when he began singing at private events in his Queens neighborhood. When his mother took him to see the great Italian tenor Beniamino Gigli in *La Giaconda* at the Metropolitan Opera house, Little Giovanni knew what to expect because he had listened to all his records. They walked in and Giovanni asked his mother if he could have a soda. As they headed toward the concession stand, she heard Gigli starting to sing. This was the music Mama Benedetto loved. When she leaned over to tell Giovanni to listen she was surprised he wasn't there. She quickly went inside the auditorium to see people in the front row backing away in their seats from the power of Gigli's voice, and there in the back was Giovanni standing tall, drawn in by it all.

Mama Benedetto knew her son had something special and took extra jobs to pay for voice lessons from Guiseppe La Puma, an opera trained singer from Italy who taught out of his home. When La Puma was giving him training in solfeggio, he soon discovered that Giovanni had a natural God-given voice that never sang off key and could hit any combination of high notes without effort.

As young as Giovanni was, La Puma believed that one-day he would be a famous singer and diligently taught him many of the popular operatic arias. He rendered each lyric with such clear and crisp precision that experts believed they were listening to a trained opera singer from a music school in Italy rather than suspecting it was some little kid from Queens, New York.

Giovanni's younger brother, Tony, was called Ninni as a boy and could also sing but their mother recognized his talent as more in drawing. She arranged for him to take art lessons. As Giovanni grew, his reputation spread throughout the neighborhood, creating a demand for him to sing at functions for such diverse people as the Vanderbilts, and Frank Costello, the famous Mafioso—whose wife Loretta particularly loved Giovanni and made sure he performed at all her occasions. These functions were a blessing for the family because it enabled Giovanni to bring home small sums of much needed money.

A friend of the family, Mrs. Quinlen, took an interest in Giovanni. When she found out it was the last day of auditions for Mayor LaGuardia's favorite project, the New York City Boys' Choir, she hurriedly made arrangements to bring Giovanni into the city to his office. After the Mayor heard Giovanni sing, *Un' Aura Amorosa* from Cosi Fan Tutti, he banged his hand down on the desk hard and said, "This boy sings too good. I'm taking him to our new radio station W.N.Y.C. His voice must be heard."

On another occasion Mr. Petri, the head of the Metropolitan Opera's choir, accompanied Giovanni's performance at Frank Costello's anniversary party on a Sunday afternoon in January of 1931.

That night, Mama offered second helpings before clearing the dishes. To everyone's surprise she then placed a big bowl of ice cream out on the table. Baby Sister stood up. "Mama's got some good news to tell everyone."

This surprised Papa because his little girl, Baby Sister, hardly ever spoke. "Yes." Mama beamed with satisfaction. "Our Giovanni sang at Frank Costello's party today."

Papa's face almost hit the floor—he couldn't believe his ears. "Mio Johnny?"

"Si...and Mr. Petri, himself, wants to take our Giovanni down to the Metropolitan Opera House for an audition."

Little Tony shouted out, "Can I go with ya, Giovanni?"

"Sure, I don't care." He smiled.

"Me too." Baby Sister's eyes reflected her mother's fierce Calabrian pride.

"You let-a this happen without me know-a no-thing?" Papa said.

"First of all, I no let anything happen." Mama snapped back. "From what Mrs. Quinlen tells-a me, Mr. Petri dida the favor, and got Giovanni there."

"Mr. Petri? Managia America! You mean Big Nose Petri? You gotta the Mafia in ona this now? You shoulda tell me first?"

"What Biga Nose?" This Mr. Petri, he's a no Big-a Nose. He's-a from the Metropolitan Opera House and remember Papa, no one is gonna mess this up for our Giovanni!" Mama's eyes became darts. "No one, no Mr. Big-a Nose, no Mafioso, no Black-a the Hand and no you—a capito?"

Mama ironed the rest of the blue serge suit and hung it over the door. Giovanni noticed the pleats in his pants were starched crisp like iron and appreciated his mother's attention. Everyone was dressed like they were going to church. Papa motioned for Giovanni to come closer, "Are you all right…how you feel-a?" He had asked this twice before and both times Johnny answered, "Fine."

Giovanni turned and there was Mama standing in the hallway by the door. She lifted a hand. "It's-a time to go." Giovanni didn't even know what it was for—a job or what? He didn't care. He only knew by the way his mother and his teacher Mr. La Puma were excited that it must be something good.

The entrance of the Opera House was packed. People stood and sat scattered throughout the floor. Giovanni and his family followed Mr. La Puma who seemed to know where he was going. *Are all these people here to audition?* Giovanni thought. They ended up in a large room where he saw a mish mash of confused people:

one playing the piano, others vocalizing, and it all appeared to be in such disorder that Giovanni put his hand to his mouth and giggled. He felt a slight twinge when he heard his name being called out to step forward. "Will Giovanni Benedetto come up, please?" the Maestro said.

"Here we are, Maestro," Mr. La Puma said. "I am his teacher."

"What will the boy be singing?"

"'Pour Mon Ame,' from *La Fille du Regiment.*"

The Maestro's mouth twitched, he straightened up in amazement then took another look at little Giovanni. "Surely you jest?"

"We are not here to jest, Maestro," La Puma answered in a sharp commanding tone.

"All right...all right." The Maestro waved off his comments.

"I will be accompanying him, if you please," La Puma said.

The Maestro looked at the fire in La Puma's face. "Fine."

The room was cleared. Only the organizers of the Met were left who took their places waiting to hear the new audition. Giovanni came up and put his hand on the corner of the grand piano. He had never seen such a big beautiful piano before—it distracted him for a moment as he paused to admire its grandeur then with a calm authority he turned, cocked an eyebrow and gestured to Mr. La Puma who placed his hands on the keys and started to play.

They all agreed it was a great performance. "It is in the boy's voice," the Maestro stated. "It's his golden timbre that will be his enduring legacy."

It was here that destiny determined Giovanni Benedetto would go on to become the youngest person ever to solo at the Metropolitan Opera House at the age of thirteen. He was accepted and worked with some of the most famous celebrities of the time, including an appearance on Al Jolson's *Shell Châteaux* program on NBC, and with the Vincent Lopez Orchestra live at the Astor Grill Room.

As he got older he went from cute to good-looking and although he wasn't big, his frame was lean and strong and made a good appearance. Girls were especially drawn to his open personality. He gained popularity as a singer in his late teens and started headlining in all the local nightclubs in and around the city as Giovanni Benedetto. He also earned extra money singing on demo records for songwriters. Meanwhile, Tony who had grown up taking art lessons from a very prestigious art teacher in Greenwich Village, was also singing.

The war not only interrupted both their careers but ultimately changed their lives as well. When Giovanni came out of the service he resumed his singing career as Johnny Bennett. When Tony was discharged, he not only resumed his art lessons but also expressed a desire to sing. Johnny was smart and knew Tony was not exactly an *adorno* on the Manhattan scene, but he nevertheless had the temperament to appreciate he was in a position to help his brother prosper in his singing career and encouraged him on many occasions. On one occasion in particular, Johnny was too busy to do a demo so he asked Tony to fill in for him. The song the publisher gave Tony to sing on the demo was, *Boulevard of Broken Dreams.* It came off very good.

Sometime later, Tony quit art school. When the publisher took the demo of *Boulevard of Broken Dreams* to Columbia records, the A&R executive there, Mitch Miller, liked Tony's voice so much that they signed him up and released the record under the name Tony Bennett. The record made a good showing on all the charts, which subsequently lead to Tony recording *Because of You,* which went to number one and became a hit around the world.

Recognizing Tony's natural artistic ability, his art teacher called and asked him to come back, claiming his talent was too valuable to waste. But by then singing had become his future, and a legendary career his destiny.

Johnny maintained a steadfast faithfulness to his brother and didn't engage in any type of competition. He retired from singing a year later and worked many avenues to help advance his brother's career.

From the stage, Johnny went into legitimate businesses and married. He never harbored any bitterness or wasted time being disappointed in who he was. He measured up to the image he wanted to project and was successful. He was pleased that Tony, hit it big.

You have to wonder, what would have happened if Johnny had been the one to record the demo, *Boulevard of Broken Dreams* instead of Tony?

The art teacher wasn't wrong. One night at the Top of the Home I joined Tony and his brother Johnny at the table and noticed Tony was drawing in pencil on a little 3x5 white pad. He sketched a man's head and asked me what I thought of it.

"Very good," I said. "Who is it?"

Tony pointed two tables away. "That fellow there."

I looked, and there was a guest that looked exactly like Tony's drawing. "Wow, that's great," I said. "You want me to give it to him."

"Oh, no," Tony answered. "Someday I'm going to do a book called *Faces*."

Dick Cami with Top of the Home guests—brothers, John and Tony Bennett. (Patricia Benedetto)

I always felt good when I saw Robert Bleemer's name on the reservation list because he always brought the most interesting people with him when he came to Top of the Home, like Yolanda and John Kluge of Metro-Media, Jim Steward of Lone Star Cement, and Sam Spiegel who produced *Bridge of the River Kwai, Lawrence of Arabia,* and *On the Waterfront.* One time when Bleemer was in with Spiegel, I fantasized how interesting it would have been if Barney Baker—Jimmy Hoffa's ambassador of violence and a Top patron, who was the figure Bud Schulberg patterned Marlon Brando's part after in his movie—had been in that night. Knowing Barney, I believe he would have tried to shake Spiegel down for a few bucks, or at the very least given him his dinner bill.

A talented and top interior designer, Bleemer was very social with a natural gift of gab and could always be counted on for a good time. He was one of the first guys I met when I came to Florida. When we opened the Peppermint Lounge in Miami Beach he was a regular. I called him Bobby.

I had seen him move up the ladder working for every famous design firm in Florida until finally achieving great success in a partnership with his own interior design studio. He did all the big jobs including the Fontainebleau Hotel. The man was a hard working, and after many years, a classic "overnight" success.

This one particular evening, he came in with Ralph Levitz from Levitz furniture. They were a party of eight or ten and the first thing Bobby did was take me aside and tell me he was Levitz's guest. He wanted me to know this because he didn't want me to pick up the check, which I always did when he ate in the restaurant in reciprocity for all the things he had done for me. He was the best.

It was a Saturday night and we were jammed. It was one of those nights when everything was going great. A restaurant is a funny business, when it runs smoothly it's like a symphony, something to be enjoyed and admired. That's the kind of night we had going.

Then I saw Bobby waving me over to the table with a concerned look on his face. "What's up?" I asked.

"Dick, I don't know how to tell you this," he said. "But one of the things I always loved about what you do here is the live music. How come you went to recorded music? I think you're hurting yourself." *I Left my Heart in San Francisco* could be heard in the background.

I wasn't offended, as I knew Bobby only had my best interest at heart. I told him to step into the lounge and take a look-see. Bobby got up and silently made his way to the lounge while I turned to Levitz and answered his question about the stone crabs. "Yes, that's right, they only take one claw and throw the body back." By the time I finished explaining how the stone crab regenerates a new claw, Bobby was back at the table with a big smile on his face saying loud enough for everyone at the table to hear, "Son-of-a-bitch, Tony Bennett's singing in the lounge."

Billy Daniels, Frank Sinatra, and Tom Jones

After Johnny Futto introduced me to showman extraordinaire Billy Daniels in the late fifties, we became good friends. Daniels was a remarkable human being who paved the way for black entertainers in the early years. He had a profound philosophy on life which he interpreted through songs. *Old Black Magic* was his big hit. He was an exceptionally good-looking man who was involved in every situation that could ever happen between a man and a woman, including shootings, stabbings, and beatings.

Toward the end of one evening at the Top, a large table of regulars sat exchanging stories, one after another, when Billy Daniels held us all at attention. As an unknown performing in Harlem nightclubs, he often attracted beautiful women who wanted to sit ringside. After the show and a few drinks, he was in one such beauty's apartment—a five-story walk-up not far from where he was appearing. It didn't take long for them to get down to business. In the middle of their passionate lovemaking he heard a key slide into the lock of the front door.

"Oh, my God..." She gasped. "My husband's home."

"Your husband!" Billy's heart sank.

He didn't have time to assess his predicament so he instinctively pulled on his pants, bolted out the bedroom window onto the fire escape, scampered up to the roof, and continued running to the other side of the building. Tenement buildings in Harlem were built right next to each other only separated by an alley of about five feet. When he got to the ledge of the first building he heard her husband in pursuit and had no choice but to jump over the alley to the other building. He did this successfully, jumping from one building to the next, but the last try didn't go as well. He stumbled and didn't make it to the other side, falling between the buildings.

Washday saved his life. He fell from one story to another, hitting the clothes lines strung between the buildings. They broke his fall right up until he landed on the pavement. Unbelievably unharmed, he was able to continue running, stopping just long enough to turn around and see the husband on the roof shaking his fist. That old black magic indeed.

About this time my maître d' came over to whisper a phone message he'd just received. Billy Daniels was sitting right next to me and overheard the news that Frankie Dio had just died. He shot straight up in his chair and shrieked, like it was the final high note of an opera. "Frankie Dio died!" He then collapsed into his arms on the table and sobbed like a baby. I had no idea they even knew each other.

Frankie Dio had mob connections. I met him when he put in the cigarette vending machines at the Peppermint. A variety of stories about Frankie followed, some of them were humorous, a few were serious. Many at the table felt that Frankie was tougher than his brother Johnny—a New York mobster famous for trying to kill a noted newspaper columnist. After a few cognacs, Billy came out of his depression.

Billy never lost his sense of humor. At the end of the evening before he stepped into the elevator he turned to me and said, "Dickie, let me leave you with these words of wisdom: when in Harlem, never stop a running man to ask directions."

Despite my father-in-law's loathing of Frank Sinatra, I had a more mixed view after frequently hosting him at the Top of the

Home. I don't remember him ever at the Peppermint, but he was well known with his Rat Pack friends throughout the Miami area. He appreciated good food and characterized the Top as having the best south of New York. I was surprised the first time he came to the Top that my maître'd was the opposite of delighted when I asked him to exclusively tend to Frank. Frank's reputation for bad behavior was legendary and my maître d' had witnessed it firsthand. I too knew many of the stories and included some of those in Peppermint Twist, a book I collaborated on with John Johnson and Joel Selvin. Despite his reputation, Sinatra was always a gentleman at my place.

A dear friend of mine, Harold Blitzer, was a survivor of the Jewish horror of WWII. He shared a story with me of one of his first experiences living in this country in the late fifties. A waiter at the famous Riviera nightclub in New Jersey, Blitzer was working the night of Frank Sinatra's comeback appearance. It was Frank's first concert after making the movie *From Here to Eternity*. It was commonly thought that Frank had lost his singing voice and his career was in the toilet.

"I saw a great moment take place in the nightclub that night," Blitzer began. "I guess it could be called a happening. Every guest had come to see if Frank could sing again—the place was packed. I never saw such excitement in any room before or since. Everyone was anxiously waiting for Sinatra to take the stage, including all of us on the wait staff. Captains to busboys, we all jockeyed to make sure we would be on the floor when Sinatra stepped out."

Blitzer explained that the kitchen was underneath the showroom and to bring the dirty dishes to the dishwashing area you had to go down a hall of winding steps. But that night they didn't, rather trays of dirty dishes flew out the side windows to save time and ensure staff would be on hand for Frank's entrance.

I was told that the emcee's booming voice matched the moment as he introduced Sinatra. "Ladies and gentlemen, here on stage...the moment we've been waiting for...New Jersey's very own and the only...Mr. Frank Sinatra."

The sound of the big band blasting out his opening number emphasized the excitement in the air. Frank slowly walked out onto the stage with a solemn face and cautiously took hold of the mike. Now the band vamped and when Frank opened his mouth the notes of the first four bars floated soft and beautiful into the room. Then, just before he was going to hit a high note, he waved off the band. The audience sat frozen and silent. Frank, the master of timing, put his lips to the mike and said with a smile and twinkling eye, "I bet you guys thought I couldn't sing anymore, eh?"

Blitzer told me at that moment, Frank plunged his hand down giving the downbeat to continue and the room detonated with an explosion of applause. Hoops and hollers could be heard all the way across the Hudson to New York City.

I remember my father, a voice teacher to so many stars, telling me about Sinatra's comeback, but it was years before I actually met anyone who had been there.

When Frank Sinatra came to New York City he would give Charlie Zito a call and have him set up a table in his apartment with fresh bread and Italian cold cuts. The imported cold cuts were pretty much all the same but there was only one bread. At Zito's bakery on Greenwich Village's Bleeker Street, about eight guys in the cellar spent their shift turning out loaves, one size, white or whole wheat baked in a coal oven. It only stayed fresh for a day—on the second you could use it for a weapon. That's how stale it got overnight, but that first day? Forgetaboutit.

Charlie Zito married comedienne Judy Tremaine. They were the perfect example of opposites attract. Charlie was very quiet, hardly uttering a word, and Judy? Well Judy was a gregarious, no holds barred, buxom, middle-aged Mae West type.

One time when Frank Sinatra performed at New York City's Carnegie Hall, he gave Charlie a pair of front row tickets. Frank was a master of timing and so was Judy. In the middle of one of his tender love ballads, he paused a moment for effect before he sang the next line, and Judy stood up and shouted, "I love you, Frank."

Her words ricocheted off every wall in Carnegie Hall, bringing a strange hush over the crowd. Nobody knew how to react. Frank, himself, was so startled that he jumped back as she went on. "I'll leave Charlie for you."

Now looking over the stage lights as he made out Judy, Frank smiled and said, "Thanks for the warning."

This brought the house down.

When Sinatra passed away, Charlie called me crying into the phone. "He's gone, Dick...Frank's gone. Can you believe it?" Charlie himself died a couple of years later. When I spoke to Judy I was sad to hear the landlord wanted so much rent that the family didn't renew the lease and Zito's, the best ever bakery, closed its doors. Our world now less two legends.

I went to see Tom Jones perform at the Deauville Hotel in Miami Beach. Before the show, I ran into Johnny Spence, Jones' musical conductor, and agreed to have coffee with him after the show. As usual Jones gave a magnificent performance. Also, as had became usual during his shows, the women were standing, hollering, and tossing all manner of sundries, including lingerie, up onto the stage. One beauty threw her hotel key, which landed right at Tom Jones' feet. He leaned over, picked it up, smiled, and nonchalantly flipped it over to Johnny Spence who, without missing a beat, put it in his top pocket and continued conducting. After the show, when Johnny and I were in the coffee shop, I asked him if he gave the key to Jones. "Oh no!" he said then reached in and took the key out of his pocket. It was from a hotel room in Puerto Rico. Things aren't always what they seem.

Chapter 13

Bill Hodgson, Don Aronow, and The Sheik

Bill Hodgson was a combination of George Steinbrenner and Howard Hughes, but unlike Hughes he liked to socialize. He was a hotel magnate out of Toronto who owned the Skyline Hotel chain, one of the top one hundred hotel companies in the world, stretching from Toronto to London, England. The Skyline in London was the tall round building that once stood by Harrod's. Among other things he owned were a string of winning racehorses and the Toronto Argonauts. More than all of that, he was one of the nicest men I ever met. A true gentleman and a frequent customer at the Top of the Home.

In Hodgson's early years he was a noted boat racer, and remained a steadfast boat enthusiast. He had recently purchased a one hundred and twenty foot luxury yacht, but needed a captain to pilot it from Miami up to Toronto. He interviewed some prospects and called me about one in particular. The last boat he'd piloted was for Dave Iacovetti, a noted wiseguy. Hodgson contacted me, figuring that I might know him. I told Hodgson as a matter of fact I did know Dave.

Iacovetti was part of the Gambino family and also a good friend of Frank Sinatra. Hodgson wanted me to contact Iacovetti and verify the captain's qualifications.

"The captain I'm considering is Max Stillwell," Hodgson

said. "I was wondering what kind of recommendation your friend would give him. I need a captain to take the yacht back to Toronto."

I told him no problem, but when I contacted Iacovetti and gave him the name of the captain he told me in no uncertain terms to tell my friend to forgetaboutit—the man's a drunk.

I passed this information on to Hodgson who thanked me. I thought that would be the end of it, but a week later Hodgson called me back stating that he was still having trouble getting a captain that was willing to sail up to Toronto. He wondered if it would be possible for Iacovetti to personally talk to the captain and let him know how important this was. It would be like a mission for a short period of time. He thought that for just one trip, it might be all right.

Iacovetti said he would do it but there would be no guarantees.

On the way to Toronto, the yacht piloted by Captain Stillwell went down at 3 a.m. off Cape Hatteras. The only people on board were Hodgson's girl, a mate, and the captain. By some miracle they all survived. When the news of the sinking broke, everyone assumed Hodgson was on it and it was reported that he had drowned. Fortunately, he was in Toronto at the time at a business conference. I was in Los Angeles when Iacovetti reached me at my hotel and told me about the disaster. "Jesus, somebody told me you were on your friend's yacht when it went down. I'm glad you're all right. I told ya that damn captain was no good."

Hodgson flew down there immediately and hired a helicopter to survey the damage to the half-submerged boat. Once back in Toronto, Hodgson called to tell me that Iacovetti was right.

When Moishe Levy invited me to lunch and introduced me to Don Aronow, nobody had ever heard of him. Moishe met Aronow when he was developing housing projects in New Jersey and connected him with the right people to make sure he had no labor problems. Moishe had all the connections to do that. He was a big earner for the mob in other areas outside of the music business, including the electrical workers union in New York City.

When I first met Aronow, I was surprised to see how young he looked to be retired. He had a friendly personality and at lunch our conversation covered a whole myriad of subjects. Eventually Don told us that he had just bought an awning company that specialized in canvas tops for boats. It was strictly a toy for him. I was surprised he mentioned boats and expressed my interest in buying one. We had a big dock in back of the Miami Beach Peppermint and my one experience fishing had me...well, "hooked."

"Don't buy one yet," Don's eyes shifted to me. "I'm just going into the boat building business. Buy one from me."

"Why not. You have something I can look at?"

"Sure I've got a prototype model I can show you. We're not in production yet but we will be shortly. What kind of boating will you do?"

"Strictly fishing."

"You're going to love what I designed. Let's go tomorrow."

We met up the next day and drove up to Challenger Marina on 135th and Biscayne Boulevard. When I saw Don's prototype I almost fell off the dock. I don't know what the dimensions were but the boat looked like it only had a six-foot beam and was about forty foot long, like a needle. It had a cockpit that sat just two people. "Who's going to fish in this?" I asked.

"Don't let it scare you." Don smiled. "This is just a sample of the bow's design which will be awesome." He assured me it would be totally adequate for fishing.

I ordered one partly because I was impressed and partly because I was too embarrassed to say no.

"What's the name of your boat company?"

"I've been thinking of calling it *Donzi*."

The boat arrived about three months later and was maybe the first *Donzi* Don sold. I can tell you this, he knew what he was doing. Other boat companies he started were the Cigarette, Formula, Magnum, and others. When he took me on a test ride with him on his first Magnum, it accelerated at such a high rate of speed I had to hold on just to stay in the boat. Without free hands to keep my pants up against the wind from the increasing speed, they dropped. Afterwards he revealed that he was getting fearful about the high speeds the boat racers were trying for, predicting the possibility of not just accidents but deaths.

Years later I had dinner with Don and a blonde beauty on his arm. He asked me to recount some stories from the old days, which I gladly did, then I asked him how Moishe was. I thought he was joking when he told me that they weren't talking anymore. Although it was not true, Moishe thought Don had been sleeping with his wife. Don sounded sad that he couldn't convince Moishe otherwise. One thing's for sure, they never talked again.

Aronow was riding high and doing well in the boat business. He won races, sold one company after another and started new ones. He'd really found his niche. He made the best and fastest boats around and they were in high demand. It seemed the more he charged the more he sold. He sold to drug dealers and DEA alike, sheiks and royalty, too. I knew that President Lyndon Johnson had purchased more than one Donzi, which I read on Wikipedia he raced on his Texas ranch with the secret service agents. When the first President Bush bought an *Aronow* boat it was all over the papers about the two of them going on the shakedown cruise.

He also made a lot of deals that were not just for the boats. I am not mentioning names or details because I don't really know, but a mutual friend of ours told me about one deal that had gone very bad.

This particular deal involved one of the boat companies. It was structured such that a pair of buyers gave Aronow two all-cash payments of $250,000 and got portions of the income while Don continued to run the company.

On the first payment, he was accidently paid three hundred thousand instead of the actual two-fifty agreed upon amount. Don counted it and realized he had been overpaid but never said anything. He did tell our mutual friend about the overpayment and was advised to be careful.

"Don't tell me," Don said. "I was in the room where they keep the cash. There's so much cash there, they don't know what they have."

Shortly thereafter one of the buyers discovered the overpayment and told his partner that Don had never offered to return the surplus to them. Additionally the buyer alleged that they were not getting the full amount of profit due to them from the business as per their agreement. Skeptical, the partner asked for proof saying, "This cocksucker's got so much money why would he fuck with us? Let's give him another chance."

They decided to make a second overpayment to see what would happen. At about the same time, the receipts were suspected of being short again. When Don was confronted about the shortfalls he denied everything, totally underestimating his buyers' concern or reach.

Because mutual friends vouched for Don's honesty, they agreed to wait, giving him more time to say something about the second overpayment. No mention was ever made and the partners eventually decided they had waited long enough.

One day Don came out of an office and got into his car. A car pulled up next to him and when he rolled down his window, Aronow was uzzied on the spot. It was a front-page story and everyone was certain that he'd been offed by drug dealers for divulging names connected with the purchase of his boats—but I never thought that was the real reason.

Munther Bilbeisi, a Jordanian Arab, came to the Top of the Home for dinner with a Sheik friend of his that wanted to buy the Eden Roc Miami Beach Hotel. His lawyers were having difficulties securing the purchase because the hotel was in bankruptcy court at the time. The very Arab-looking Sheik explained his problem.

"I may be able to help," I told the Sheik.

He was very nice and as they left I escorted him and his lady to the elevator. When we got there the Sheik's lady asked him, "Do you have money for the car keep?"

The Sheik then turned to me and said, "When I drive the Rolls I tip two dollars and when I drive the Lincoln I tip a dollar." He turned back to his lady friend and said, "Which car are we driving tonight?"

"The Lincoln," she replied.

He turned and asked me, "Can I borrow a dollar?"

It was the first time I had a billionaire ask for a buck.

I was pretty confident I could help the Sheik because I knew Ed Houston, the Federal Bankruptcy Judge, very well. A meeting was arranged at my restaurant with all involved parties and the deal was struck. The Sheik bought the Eden Roc out of bankruptcy court for ten million dollars—like it was the buy of the century. I was still out the dollar for parking.

In the meantime, the Sheik bought a one hundred and ninety-five foot yacht. That's pretty big considering a military destroyer is only one hundred and sixty five feet long. It wasn't in tiptop shape and the Sheik asked Munther to get it fixed up for him. It took about three months to complete before the Sheik could sail off to Europe.

When Munther handed the Sheik the repair bill of six hundred and fifty thousand dollars he couldn't believe it and refused to pay. This sent Munther into a tailspin—he was completely floored that the Sheik refused to reimburse him and was certain the money he put out for repairs was lost. Knowing Munther, I'm sure he padded the bills pretty good but I'm also sure it cost him a small fortune.

"You know, Munther," I said. "This is America. If someone owes you money you can take them to court to get payment."

Munther couldn't believe what he was hearing but asked me to get him a lawyer. My lawyer put one of the men in his office right on the case. By the end of the year Munther won, collecting his six hundred and fifty thousand plus court costs. He was so over the moon with what the lawyer had been able to do that he convinced him to quit my lawyer's office and open up his own practice near him in Boca Raton.

Chapter 14

Dinah Washington, Hedy Lamarr, Liberace, Joe E. Lewis, Yogi Berra, and James Cagney

I happened to be standing outside the Miami Peppermint when Dinah Washington drove up. As soon as she stepped from the car I immediately recognized her. She won a Grammy in 1959 for *What a Diff'rence a Day Makes* and her distinctive singing style that combined music genres had always been a favorite of mine. I walked over, introduced myself, and she asked if Morris Levy was around.

"Unfortunately, he isn't," I responded. "But, come on in and I'll try to locate him for you."

She nodded and I ushered her into the club to a table on the balcony, along with the two other people in her party who happened to be white. At that time in Miami, black people were not allowed into all-white clubs. A scene of me explaining to beverage agents that she was an entertainer on Roulette Records flashed through my mind.

During the course of the evening, she seemed to enjoy the entertainers but when the Ronettes went on she had an obvious reaction. After the Ronettes got off stage, Ronnie headed to the ladies room and Dinah got up and followed her. I didn't find out until years later that Dinah had offered to help Ronnie obtain a record contract as a solo act. She wanted Ronnie to go out on her own, as a single. Ronnie, committed to the Ronettes, wasn't interested. Dinah was only one of many people who saw the potential Ronnie had for stardom.

At backstage reunion after Ronnie Spector's one woman show, Beyond the Beehive, Dick congratulates Ronnie with Dion on her right, Eddie Money on her left, her husband, Jonathan Greenfield, in the background and unidentified patron in foreground, NYC, 2014. (Cindy Aumann)

Ernie Sloan was a fascinating man. Born and raised by American parents living in China, he could speak about five different languages. During WWII he was a spy for the OSS and a Japanese POW held in China until the war ended. From there he went to Los Angeles where he opened a restaurant and rubbed elbows with a lot of famous people, including Hedy Lamarr. Years later he moved to Miami and wrote a book called *Behind the Velvet Rope*. That's when we became friends.

He called to tell me that Hedy Lamarr was destitute and living in North Bay Village. "The poor woman has nothing," he said.

This was hard for me to believe. "You're talking about Hedy Lamarr, the famous actress?" I asked.

"Yes, Dick," Sloan said. "I am talking about Hedy Lamarr and you came to mind. Maybe there's a possibility you could help her out?"

At the time I was doing a lot of charity work—concerts and things.

"Does she have all her onions?" I asked.

"Oh, yes, she certainly does," Sloan said and genuinely meant it. "How about if we meet her and you can see for yourself."

Ernie was an honest person but if I was going to put myself out on a limb I had to make sure she was into being helped. Ernie set up a luncheon date. Before we went to pick her up I called Al Miniaci and told him Hedy Lamarr was broke, living in Miami, and would he like to sponsor a five hundred dollar a plate charity dinner for her.

"Yeah," he said cheerfully. "Of course."

Right off the bat I knew that would be about twenty-five thousand for her. Then Gloria Estefan's husband agreed to give her two thousand a week if she would function as a promoter for the new club he was about to open on South Beach. So with just a couple of phone calls I got a solid reaction to my requests to help her.

When we got to her apartment and rang her doorbell, there was no answer. We waited awhile and knocked on the door again. Still no answer. I suggested to Ernie that we go have lunch and come back later. When we returned and rang the bell, still no answer. We went back to Sloan's apartment with him all down in the mouth about everything. Then, as I'm telling him not to worry about it, the phone rang and it was Hedy Lamarr. He got all excited talking to her, then handed the phone off to me.

I immediately recognized her accent. She was very pleasant and went on to explain how she was a different kind of woman. *Whatever that meant.* At the time, I guessed, to her the standard rules of behavior didn't apply. I could feel that Hollywood BS coming at me through the phone, so I told her that I understood and she should call us when she was ready to meet. I really wasn't interested now because to me, she was unreliable. I could just imagine having a big function and her not showing up. I didn't want any part of a deal like that and told Ernie he should also forget about her. What a shame, about a year after that she was arrested for shoplifting. However, this was not the whole of her story.

Sometime later I had a call from Sloan who told me with a heavy dose of excitement in his voice that Hedy Lamarr didn't have anything to worry about now. He'd heard that her first husband had left her the royalties to a patent that was the forerunner of some modern day technology, including Wi-Fi. Always a sucker for a happy ending, I passed this story on more than once. It was only way later that I saw a very different account on, of course, the internet!

A legendary beauty, it would not be surprising that in her lifetime she got very little recognition for her substantial brains. Apparently she was a natural problem solver. I saw her characterized as everything from a tinkerer to a lifelong inventor. It seems she was always trying to come up with a better mousetrap, some more successful than others. The most significant had nothing to do with her first husband but rather was a full collaboration with composer George Antheil, with whom she produced and patented an application for "frequency hopping technology" that reportedly today is a concept integral to the functioning of our cell phones, GPS, and multiple military communication systems. It seems that with both incredible beauty and brains she was, indeed, as she herself said a "different kind of woman."

Both from the Bronx, my dear friend Lou Paciocco and I had known each other for years. He produced a review, *La Cage Aux Folles*, at the Sunrise Theater in Sunrise, Florida at the same time Liberace appeared in the theater's main room. During an interview of Liberace in the lobby, he spotted Lou and told the reporters, "What are you interviewing me for?" Then he pointed to Lou saying, "There's the fellow with all the stories."

Liberace knew what he was talking about. During his years owning and operating La Cage, the hottest nightclub in Los Angeles, Lou probably knew more celebrities socially than anyone else in Hollywood. That night, Liberace and Lou came to the Top of the Home. I had never met Liberace before but Frank Bunetta, the director of The Jackie Gleason Show, had told me that of all the guests they had on the show, the nicest ever was Liberace.

After meeting Liberace, I saw it could be true. A true gentleman, he was without question one of the most polite and considerate people I have ever known. I moved to step in to protect him from being bothered by other restaurant patrons hoping for an autograph. But, Liberace signaled it was okay and never seemed anything but gracious that night as so many female fans stopped at his table. Each time he smiled graciously, put his knife and fork down, and stood up to greet his admirer.

He also had a great sense of humor and shared this story with Lou and me. He had recently put his Malibu home on the market. Out of respect for the privacy of any future buyer, he directed that any advertisement should leave out his name as the owner. It took him awhile but it was eventually sold for about $400,000, which was an okay price at the time.

Not much more than a week later, Liberace saw a notice in the paper stating that the very same house identified as his former residence had just been resold for $600,000!

On a subsequent visit to Lou in Los Angeles he told me that Liberace often teased saying, "Let's go back to the Top of the Home where we can get a great plate of pasta."

Another one of the nicest guys you'd ever meet, Joe E. Lewis, was maybe the most underrated nightclub comic of all time. He was the comic's comic. Very few people except us old-timers know about him today, but back then he headlined every top nightclub in America. In his later years, he only worked a few select cities. Miami Beach was one of his favorites. That's when he'd come to the Top of the Home and I'd sit and listen to him recount stories about the old days. He started working in Florida headlining clubs for Meyer Lansky in the early speakeasies. His routine was going to the racetrack during the day and performing at night.

He used to say, "I don't drink from a glass...I use a funnel." As a first hand witness I can tell you that's a bit of an exaggeration, but not far off. At the Top of the Home when he ordered his first drink, a Scotch and soda, he also ordered that we keep his glass filled.

Joe E. would sit at a table at the Top of the Home looking out the window telling his stories—stories about where he lived, where he worked, where he played, and about the many love affairs he'd had. Besides women he loved the horses. Money flew out of his hands.

In his later days he needed someone to take care of him so I got Betty Strausberger to watch over him. She was one of the original Gleason girls on Jackie's TV show and she did a great job as a live-in caretaker, watching out for all his needs until it was the end of the road for poor Joe E.

Some of his best one-liners:

My heart is as sound as a Cuban dollar.

I drink to forget I drink.

I distrust camels or anyone else that can go a week without a drink.

Whenever someone asks me if I want water with my Scotch, I say I'm thirsty not dirty.

A man is never drunk if he can lie on the floor without holding on.

I always wake up at the crack of ice.

I'm still chasing girls but I don't know why.

Show me a friend in need and I'll show you a pest.

I don't like money actually but it quiets my nerves.

Show me a man with very little money and I'll show you a bum.

There's only one thing that money can't buy and that's poverty.

And on and on...

Speaking of nice guys...

Yogi Berra, a Top regular, came in one night with his wife and some friends for dinner. During the course of the meal he motioned for me to join him at his table.

"Who you votin' for," he said.

"I dunno." I shrugged.

"Vote for Ford."

His wife jumped in, saying, "What the hell do you know about politics?"

To which Yogi screwed up his face and said, "Whatta ya mean I played golf wit Ford. He loves At-leets."

Then they both looked at me. "Well, that's good enough for me," I said.

Yogi smiled and turned to his wife. "See."

I felt like I was in a segment of the Honeymooners.

Yogi Berra was a true original. So when he passed away I couldn't help but remember with a smile his quote, "I gotta go to their funerals. If I don't who will come to mine?"

On a recent Fourth of July after watching James Cagney in *Yankee Doodle Dandy*, a holiday tradition of mine, I thought about the following story from the Top.

When I answered the phone at the restaurant, the caller asked for Dick Cami. "That's me," I said.

"I'm Jimmy Cagney's manager and we'd like to make a reservation for dinner this evening."

"Really?" I was surprised to hear that he was in town. "What time?"

"There'll be four of us and we'll be there at eight. Are you from Boston?" He asked.

"No, I'm not."

"Somebody told me you were. That's where I'm from but I'll be looking forward to meeting you anyway."

"What's your name?" I asked.

"Walter Jennings," he replied.

I went into the bar where Charlie Noto was sipping his drink. "I just got the strangest phone call from Jimmy Cagney's manager," I said. "They'll be here in a little while for dinner."

"Yeah... I saw him at the track today," Charlie said.

So it's true, I thought.

I knew a little about Jimmy Cagney because when I was a

kid I would go to my father's voice studio on weekends in the Mayfair Bryant building on Times Square and 47th st. Manny's Dance Studio was on the seventh floor of the same building. Their claim to fame was that James Cagney learned to dance there as a chorus boy before he became an actor—the walls were filled with pictures of him dancing in all sorts of outfits, leotards and all. I heard so much about him there that I felt I knew him.

When the party entered the lobby, I noticed one of the guests was in his 50's and looked distinguished in a conservative style custom-made suit. He had a familiar smile—it was Jimmy Cagney, but with a broken nose. I was surprised at his over-the-top friendliness, it went against all the stories I had heard about him being quiet and reserved. But here at the Top of the Home he acted so outgoing, he even did "you dirty rat" imitations of himself to other patrons. He asked me to show him around the restaurant where told me he was thinking of moving to the area and buying some land, and could I recommend some good locations. I told him he should get something on one of the islands down off of Miami Beach. Before going in for dinner, he was in the lounge having a drink when I noticed something I couldn't believe. Even though this guy looked like Jimmy Cagney I knew it wasn't him. He was seated and I noticed his ankles were thin—so very thin that they could never belong to a dancer. The pictures I remembered of Cagney's legs were thick like an athlete's, no skinny weenie ankles for sure. I didn't know who this guy was but for sure he wasn't Cagney.

Before I left I told my maître'd, no matter what the circumstances don't extend any credit to the Cagney party. Only take cash or a bonafide credit card. I was firm on that and issued a warning to Scatsy about the suspicious Cagney. "I don't know what game he's playing but we're not going to be a part of any of it."

The next day I was told everything went well with the Cagney party. They enjoyed their dinner and paid with a bonafide credit card. Imagine my surprise when I saw a picture two days later in the Hollywood Sun-Tattler of the Mayor of Hollywood giving the key to the city to this phony Cagney. I freaked out—it was a front page story, picture and all. I called Hal Pearl who had a column in the Tattler and he believed I was wrong because his sister knew that Cagney had broken his nose in his last film and heard he was in Florida. Even more unbelievable, the next day on the front page of the Miami Herald there was a picture of Mayor Chuck Hall giving the key to the city of Miami Beach to Cagney. I mean come on...what the hell was going on?

This all came to an end a month or so later when a syndicated story in the Wall Street Journal described how a man resembling Jimmy Cagney went to South Florida and was lionized by its major cities and even given keys to the cities. A friend of Cagney's who lived in Miami exposed the story when he saw Cagney's picture in the paper and called him wondering why he hadn't contacted him when he was in town. Cagney told him this was old news. There were many stories circulating that there was this character going around posing as him. Evidently, the man was independently wealthy and wasn't swindling anybody. All he wanted was the publicity, which he got plenty of.

I guess the moral of the story is: if you're getting an autograph make sure you check the guy's ankles.

Chapter 15

Belle Barth, A Day At The Races, Mr. Nails and Lashes, & Sheriff Joe

On a cloudless evening, Moishe and his new bride, Jean Glassell, held their wedding reception at her mansion in Miami Beach. The massive home sat right on the ocean due north of the Eden Roc Hotel. Naturally, we were all invited to the beautiful, catered to the hilt, affair. As if by design, stars glittered in the night sky and the Miami breeze drifted across the dance floor. The food and all the accompaniments were catered by first rate chefs, and the entertainment was the best. First to entertain were the Bari Sisters. They performed an excellent show, followed by risqué comedienne Belle Barth who topped off the evening—what a show.

I first met Belle in the Peppermint Lounge. Sidney Rosenthal, the night manager, before he took me over to meet her asked, "Dick, you know Belle Barth, don't you?"

"No, I've never had the pleasure. Who is she?"

"She a friend of Johnny's, an entertainer. I'm going to introduce you."

Sidney neglected to tell me that she was a blue comedienne, maybe one of the dirtiest in the country. She sat at the bar having a drink when I approached. Of course, it was all a set-up. Right after I am introduced Belle turned to the side and lifted her dress halfway up her thigh, exposing panty hose, something I'd never seen before. They were purple. Without any "hellos" or "how are yas" she asked me, "How ya like my purple stockings?"

"Very nice," I quipped mildly shocked.

"Yeah, thanks, and besides that, they hide my f**kin' varicose veins."

Everyone laughed. My jaw dropped because it was the first time I'd ever heard a woman curse like that—*welcome to the real world,* I thought. Back in those days you hardly heard a male comic curse on stage let alone a female

Blue comedienne, Belle Barth, dancing at the Miami Beach Peppermint Lounge to the music of Etta James' band, The Kinfolks. (Dick Cami)

Now a year later at Moishe's wedding, Belle got up to sing and I wondered if she was going to do an off-color number, which I couldn't imagine because there were little children there. She was belting out a song, nice and clean like, when some young kids in the wedding party started dancing like little jerks and making fun on the stage in front of her. Belle pushed the mike to the side so no one could hear and told them, "Get off the floor you little pr**ks before I rip your f**kin' balls off and shove them up your ass!" She then came back on the beat to finish the song in her own style as the little brats ran off never to be seen again that evening.

Here's a reason why no one should own a racehorse. The minute I entered Hialeah Racetrack, Petey Cacheech, the horse trainer, looked at me and yelled out, "Thank God."

"Thank God what?"

"Winnick is putting down a horse today to be claimed." Petey replied. "I don't know what the deal is, maybe they're lying to the owners. But this I do know, that horse has great potential. And what's even more incredible, they're letting it go for only fifteen thousand. Those bastards...who do they think they're kidding? Only fifteen grand? They know what they're doing and probably got someone in the mix to put up the claim money. I tell you this is the buy of the century. We can't lose."

"Whatta ya mean we?"

"Dick, I want you to put up the fifteen thousand and claim this horse. I'm telling you we won't lose a dime and can make a fortune."

One thing I knew for sure was that Petey wasn't a liar. I saw the excitement in his face and said, "Okay."

He brought me over to the racing office where I officially put in a claim for fifteen thousand dollars for the horse Muy Picante in the third race at Hialeah.

The day was bright and sunny at Hialeah, which at the time was one of the most beautiful tracks in the country. There were only nine horses in the race and when the bell went off, Muy Picante lunged out into first place and went straight to the rail. Coming into the first turn he had the lead by a head and it looked like the jockey Velasquez was holding him back but as they came into the stretch it was obvious he was going to win it running wire to wire. Then, leading by two lengths, the unspeakable happened, Muy Picante stepped into a hole and everyone in the stands heard a loud crack when his leg split in two forcing him to go down. A strange numbness quickly engulfed me and my eyebrows climbed an inch. Unfortunately, he had to be put down.

There were two other people who put in claims for Muy Picante. They determine the winner by throwing the dice and the highest number won the horse. You guessed it. The only time I ever won anything throwing dice was a dead horse. I thought about telling them to save me the head just in case but, then again, I figured they wouldn't get it. So there went my fifteen thousand escaroles, bye bye.

They say horse racing is the sport of kings. Well, you should be a king to own one. They've got that right. I say it's the sport that makes hundredaires out of millionaires.

Charlie Judge felt reborn the moment he met Sonia. She was about thirty years younger than Charlie, but that didn't seem to bother either of them. In fact, Charlie, who had been around the block quite a few times, had never been so completely and unexpectedly disarmed by a woman. She enabled him to love again, inspired hope for the future and opened his eyes to a new business venture. When Charlie first met Sonia she lived in Toronto, working in a beauty salon where an Asian co-worker perfected a method of putting artificial nails on the hands of nail biters. She did such a good job that you couldn't tell they weren't real.

Charlie came down from Toronto to see me at the Top of the Home to propose the idea of opening a nail salon in South Florida. I sat at Charlie's table and he started pitching the deal to me without fear of humiliation or judgment. He volunteered more information than I wanted to hear. "A nail shop in Miami will knock 'em dead," he said. "All we need is ten thousand dollars to get things started."

Before I could reply, the Captain arrived at the table to collect Charlie's order. "I'll have the baked American red snapper." Looking at Sonia, he suggested one of our signature dishes, the boneless stuffed breast of capon.

Sonia nodded in approval then added, "Can we have a Caesar salad?"

"Of course." Charlie smiled. "They make it tableside here from scratch."

Turning back to me Charlie asked, "What do you think of the idea?"

I shrugged and signaled to the Captain. "Bring a bottle of Chianti Classico, my compliments, after the Caesar."

"This can't miss," Charlie continued. "Remember there won't be any competition." Today, with shops on so many corners and artificial nails on so many hands, it's hard to remember back then when there weren't such shops in the States, or at least in our area of the States. When Charlie paused all I could say was that it sounded all right. I lowered my eyes in thought. Sonia looked at me kindly and also cast her eyes down and fell silent. Soon Charlie was talking again, but now the more information he volunteered, the more I wanted to hear.

Somehow, I began to come around to the idea and could see this being a big business. Finally, I said, "Okay Charlie, I'm in. I'll give you the money and we'll be partners. I'll set the whole thing up with a corporation—a bank account and everything. What do you want to call it?"

"We were thinking Mr. Nails might be a catchy name."

Charlie was no stranger to Miami, he had lived here before. Within a few weeks he and Sonia moved down. Charlie picked a location in Coral Gables. Sonia expanded the concept to also include doing artificial eyelashes so we expanded the shop name to Mr. Nails and Lashes.

We opened for business without any fanfare or advertising on Charlie's conviction that the business, four chairs in front and a larger area for pedicures in back, would take off like a rocket.

Well, it didn't work out that way. After a week I went down to see Charlie at the shop.

"We ain't doin' too good." He gestured to the empty salon.

"What happened to all those ladies you said would be swarming in?"

Sonia, direct and to the point, said, "Publicity! In a word, we need publicity. Nobody knows we exist. With the right publicity they'll be breaking down the doors."

It became clear to me that Sonia was right. Charlie and Sonia had every reason to be optimistic and I now had complete confidence in the concept and the Coral Gables location. The shop looked great, the potential was there and like Sonia said, "All we need is a little publicity."

As I sat in my restaurant an idea of how to get that publicity came to me. John McDermott, a good Top customer, was the number three guy at the Miami Herald. I thought if I could light a fire under his ass I might save my ten thousand. Before the week was out, McDermott came to the Top of the Home where I put it to him honestly. "Jack, I just started a business that I think deserves a write up in the Living Today section of the Herald. It's a first, a real human interest story about something women need."

I went on to explain all I knew about artificial nails and the first question he asked threw me a little. "Can it be done on a man?"

"Of course," I said without hesitation or knowing what the hell I was talking about.

"I've got an idea," McDermott said. "The person that supplies all the paper the Herald uses, has a son who is a chronic nail biter. The nails on his fingers are nubs. Do you think they can put a set of nails on him?

"Absolutely, without question," I replied.

"All right then," McDermott said. "Give me the details and tell your people that we'll be sending him down with someone to do a story."

And that's exactly what happened. I told Charlie to look out for a guy that would be coming down from the Herald to have his nails done.

"A guy?" Charlie said. "We never did a guy before."

"What's the difference," I said. "A finger's a finger ain't it?"

"I guess?" Charlie shrugged. "We did do a big black guy's toe once. He had a size eighteen foot."

"How did it come out?"

"Beautiful."

The chronic nail biter showed up at the nail shop with a reporter and a photographer from the Herald to document them putting a set of nails on his fingers. It worked out better than anyone thought. The nail biter got us a full page and a half story in the Living Today Women's section of the Miami Herald. It was like what happened to the Peppermint Lounge all over again. Crowds of women nail biters descended on Mr. Nails and Lashes. There was no way we could handle all the business but Charlie and Sonia did the best they could.

We decided that the second shop we opened would be a little bigger and better. It was a great location, part of a row of stores in a little plaza in North Miami Beach right on Dixie Highway. The shop next to us was a noted jewelry store. An odd thing happened the night before we were to open. I was at the Top of the Home at about one in the morning when I got a phone call from the North Miami Beach Police saying that I'd better come down to the location. The jewelry store next door was just blown up and there might be damage done to our property. Geez... nothing goes easy with me, I thought. Luckily there was only minor damage and we opened as planned. It went on to become the most profitable location in a soon-to-be chain. By the time we sold the business, we had eight shops throughout Dade and Broward counties.

I had always heard what a wonderful place Phoenix would be for my kind of restaurant. So I went there, found a great location, and opened Seafood Central in Scottsdale, a suburb of Phoenix. I really didn't know anyone there but my sons and I looked forward to a change from Miami life. Boy was there a change! It's a desert town with purple mountains and plenty of year round heat. There's something to say about western hospitality.

On opening day we advertised, "Six oysters for 99 cents." Well that was it. We were so jammed the lines went out the door and around the parking lot. We couldn't shuck the oysters fast enough, so I jumped in to help the shuckers. As I was popping oysters open I felt someone tug at my arm. I turned around and this medium-sized man with angry eyes said, "You know me?"

"No," I replied.

He went off the wall almost in a shout. "You don't know me?"

My first reaction was, *Is this guy kidding?* But then I felt he probably had a bad oyster so I decided to kibitz with him, "No, I don't know ya," I replied. "But just don't just stand there like a mope. Can't you see I'm in the weeds? Grab a knife and help us shuck some oysters."

Oysters were a signature feature at the Cami restaurants. Dick with sons Rich on his right, John on his left. (Florida Sun Sentinel)

Well, it was like I slapped the schoolyard bully. His eyes went wide and in a high shrill voice he said, "I can't, I'm the sheriff."

When he said that it triggered a memory of an interview I'd heard on the car radio about the sheriff who bragged his prisoners wore pink underwear. I only remembered his first name. "Is your name Joe?"

"Yeah," he answered.

"Oh, for God's sake." Luckily a table cleared in the crowded dining room and I sat him and his wife right away. I tried to pick up his check but he wouldn't have it. "What's your name?" he asked.

"Dick Cami," I replied.

Sheriff Arpaio ordered our signature shrimp pasta dish and loved it. I remember him going at it like it was his last meal on earth, then all of a sudden he stops halfway through. "Can't you make this without the shrimp in it?" He asked.

I was amazed at the question. "No," I said. "That wouldn't be shrimp pasta."

"I know that! I'm allergic to shrimp but I love the pasta."

Then I noticed he was only eating the pasta. After that he became a regular customer, coming in about two or three times a week for dinner, always with his wife.

Joe Arpaio's first claim to fame was the French Connection. He was the DEA agent in Turkey where the story originated. After retiring from the Drug Enforcement Agency, he moved to Phoenix. When he saw how the Sheriff of Maricopa County was operating it made him sick. He decided to run for the office and was elected. I will say this; there is no one quite like Joe Arpaio. Brusque, abrupt, and always getting right to the point with his rapid machine gun, staccato style of talking, he is probably the most frank human alive.

When the Super Bowl came to Phoenix in 1996, Dick Schaap, the noted TV sports announcer, held a party at Seafood Central and I invited Sheriff Joe. The night of the affair I saw Arpaio walking at a brisk pace out of the parking lot toward our outdoor patio where the function was being held. He pointed a finger at me as he went by and barked in his signature manner. "I want you to know I came off the dais to be here."

I introduced him to Schaap, and while they talked, I saw Bill Clark who was the producer of the then hot TV show, NYPD Blue. Bill had come in from Los Angeles. He was a retired police captain from New York City and frequented my Top of the Home restaurant. I asked him if he would like to meet the sheriff of our county. "Why, who is he?" he asked.

"He's the guy with the pink underwear."

"Is that here?"

"Yeah." I stifled a laugh. "He's selling them now for ten bucks apiece. I bought a dozen myself. It all goes to a good cause, Joe Arpaio's Posse."

"Sure, I'd like to met him," Clark said.

Sheriff Joe was eating a bowl of no-shrimp shrimp pasta when I introduced him to Bill Clark. Thinking he would be impressed, I was surprised when he said in a gruff voice without looking up, "I never let my prisoners watch your show."

Stunned was not the word. Bill's head reared back. All he could do was ask, "Why not?"

"Too violent." Sheriff Joe came up from the linguini, "Too violent. The only TV shows I let my prisoners watch are portions of CNN, Newt Gingrich, and Donald Duck. That's it."

A few days later when Sheriff Joe came into Seafood Central I asked him why was he so rough on Bill Clark. "He wasn't the real producer of NYPD Blue was he?"

"He most certainly is."

"Well, then maybe he'll be interested in doing a show about me."

After a moment of hesitation I answered, "You want me to be your manager?"

It was one of the few times I ever saw him smile.

Chapter 16

Boxing Tales

Long ago in the boxing world, there were three men who stood out as corner men for Champions: Frank Sylvestro, Ray Arsel, and Whitey Bimstein. Sylvestro had a fighter named Tommy Mills who seemed destined to be a champion. Mills had it all; he was a tough, aggressive fighter with an undefeated record of 18 straight knockouts, more than half of them in the first round. After he had ten victories under his belt, the promoters got him main event fights in Boston Garden. All of a sudden the hammer dropped. It was discovered that Mills was only fifteen years old. Most people didn't believe it. Not only did Mills look like he was twenty, he acted like it. The Boston Boxing Commission gave Sylvestro a two-year suspension. It was a scandal that would have left most corner men devastated, but not Sylvestro. He did what any normal hustler would do. He changed his name to Sully Emmett and moved out of the Boston area to work smaller venues in and around New York City. Although Sully eventually worked the corner of nineteen world champions, the one fighter he never stopped talking about was my friend Bill Johnson.

Freeport, Long Island had a long reputation as a tough town. It wasn't a question of whether there would be a fight on the weekend, but when and where it would be. It was the town where promoters sent their people to get fighters for their undercards.

They knew no matter who they got, it would be a good fight with a Freeporter in the ring. In this hive of weekend bouts, Sully first met Bill Johnson and subsequently became his trainer and advisor. By the age of 16 under Sully's direction and fighting the right opponents, Johnson had a featherweight record of 16 and 0 with 14 KO's.

Sully came out to Freeport to pick up Bill Johnson and take him over to the Stanley Arena in Connecticut to be on the undercard. The promoters there knew Johnson was an outstanding young fighter with a good reputation, and that this fight would be a good opportunity for him. The main event featured a heavyweight bout between Tim McHolt and Jasper Wiggins. Wiggins was ranked number six in the world, and McHolt was an undefeated up-and-comer with a distinguished record of 25 and 0 with 19 KO's. Spectators lined up early, packing the place to the rafters, anticipating a great card.

Just before the main event, Johnson was scheduled to fight an eight rounder. Sully told him in no uncertain terms that it wouldn't be an easy fight. He was facing Tony "Tiny" Grasso, a tough featherweight who also had an undefeated record of 18 and 0 with 16 knockouts. Johnson took it all in but wasn't worried. Johnson would fight anyone at any weight anywhere, he didn't care. He mentally prepared himself for each fight. In his dressing room before the Tiny Grasso fight, Sully made Johnson do a series of exercises that loosened him up, producing a nice sweat. A series of stretches, bends and turns, prepared Johnson for the first round and when he stepped into the ring, he was ready to go.

Now when Grasso got into the ring, the first thing Sully noticed was that his trunks were up very high on his chest. When they met in the middle of the ring for instructions Sully shouted to the referee, "Come on, Ref. This bum's trunks are up too high. Bring 'em down by his belly button."

For some reason the referee ignored Sully's plea. When the bell struck for the first round the fighters came out of their corners circling each other with caution. Johnson threw a few well-placed jabs followed up by a series of combination punches to the body. Each time the referee warned Johnson to keep his punches up. The bell ended the first round and as Johnson came back to his corner Sully shouted another reminder to the referee that the bum's trunks were too high.

After Sully took the mouthpiece out of Johnson' mouth, he leaned down in close and gave him instructions. "Lissena me... ya gotta hit this bum in the allsbay—ya get me? Go out there and step to ya right and throw a left hook right down low into his allsbay."

Johnson knew what Sully meant. He got up off his stool and went out for the second round. After a tough volley of encounters where Johnson bobbed and weaved, he was repeatedly warned by the referee to keep his punches up. Johnson went back to his corner not having heeded Sully's advice.

As Johnson sat on his stool Sully swiped the water off his sponge across his face in a violent splash. "What did I tell ya? This bum don't get it," Sully said. "Lissena me, this next round will ya make sure ya hit this bum in the allsbay. Ya get me now?"

Johnson went out for the third round but it wasn't his style to fight dirty and hit his opponent using low blows. So again, he neglected to take Sully's advice and had another tough round trying to keep his punches up. At the end of the round when Johnson retreated to his corner Sully was fuming. Sully proceeded to tell him in no uncertain terms as soon as he flopped down into the stool. "Lissena me if you don't hit this bum in the allsbay this round when you come back to the corner I ain't gonna be here...I'm a goner...ya know what I mean? You hoo... bye bye—ya get me! So ya better do what I tells ya if ya don't want my name to be Walker, and you're gonna second yourself then."

Johnson got the point. He reluctantly went out for the fourth round and when he confronted Grasso in the middle of the ring, Sully's words still pounded in his head. The first thing he did was sidestep to the right, drop his left hand low and proceed to deliver the most ferocious combination of a left hook and uppercut right into Grasso's allsbay. Grasso doubled over and went down to the canvas writhing in pain. He could barely get up and resume fighting. All Johnson got was another warning from the ref. "I'm not gonna warn you again, keep your punches up."

After that, Grasso wasn't quite the same and Johnson went on to win the bout. Sully was right, sometimes ya gotta do what ya gotta do. It's amazing what'll happen to you if you keep your trunks up too high.

Sully Emmett epitomized the typical fight trainer. He was 4'11" with every other tooth missing, always smoking a big stogie cigar, and dressed in a comical mismatch of colors and patterns. He was the perfect model for a movie character and just what Sylvester Stallone immortalized when he cast his movie *Rocky*.

Keeper of the 5th Street Gym, Sully Emmett with his characteristic smile and ever present cigar. (Kenny Klingman)

Sully even had a vernacular all his own...words and references that Damon Runyon would envy. A "beauty" was a dollar, a "briazad" was a girl, a "Dixie" was a cigar, and an unskilled fighter a "tomato can." When he ordered a boneless snapper in my restaurant he would say to the server, "Gimme the fish, no pins."

On and on Sully went with many more including "mudturtle," his name for a black fighter. For some reason black fighters were never insulted when Sully called them that, and that included Muhammad Ali. Sully's loyalty was legendary. If he liked a fighter, he would go to the ends of the earth to protect him.

A promoter asked Sully to get him a lightweight for a four round fight. "How much?" Sully asked.

"A hundred bucks but the guy better be a good fighter." The promoter warned him.

"Don't worry about it, I got just the right mudturtle for ya."

Now Sully grabbed a black lightweight fighter and told him, "I got a four rounder for ya, ya get me? All ya gotta do is go in there and do a Dixie doodle for a few rounds—you'll be fightin' a statue. Ya get me? Now there's a hundred bucks in it for us. You get seventy bucks and I get thirty."

The black fighter looked up, "Shiiiit, why the hell is you getting thirty for?"

"Lissen a me, ya mudturtle. It's my reputation you'll be ruinin'."

This colorful character, Sully, only knew the world of boxing. Long after his days with Freeport fighters I brought him down from New York to watch over a boxer I had at the time from London, Billy Williams.

The first time I heard of Billy Williams, Albert Dimes, the boss of Soho, called me from London to say that Angelo Dundee, best known as Muhammad Ali's trainer had agreed to train Williams to represent Great Britain in the heavyweight division for the Olympics. He wanted to know if I would set him up with a place to stay while he trained.

My first impression of him at the Miami airport was that he looked light. He had to be under two hundred pounds. "Are you a heavyweight?" I asked.

Defensive as all hell he said in a huff, "I am a heavyweight."

Billy was just a cockney kid from east London, maybe about nineteen or so, and I saw right away that he was a character, not shy about letting you know his opinion on practically anything. A bit whacky and a virtual non-stop talking machine, yet there was something about him that was very likeable.

Billy trained every day in the Fifth Street gym where Cassius Clay (Muhammad Ali) also trained. He trained hard and sparred with the best of them, but in time, trainer Angelo Dundee decided that Billy shouldn't be entered in the Olympics. He thought the American entrant, Duane Bobick, would be too much for him. Bobick was bigger, older, and vastly more experienced. You can't imagine how this twisted Billy. Now by chance, Bobick came to Miami Beach for an exhibition fight and it was all we could do to keep Billy from engaging Bobick in a street fight. Billy taunted Bobick constantly to spar with him, but it all fell on deaf ears. Shortly thereafter, I put brokenhearted Billy on a plane back to England. Oddly enough, we would all miss Billy.

A few months later, Albert Dimes called me up. "Let's be partners with Billy Williams. I spoke to Angelo and he thinks the kid has some potential and has agreed to train him. Let me send him back and put him in your hands and who knows, we might have a champ one day."

I told Albert that he had a deal but the truth of the matter was, I knew by now that Billy would take more looking after than I could personally manage. I thought back to my Freeport days and remembered Sully Emmett. As wild as Billy was, and even though I knew Sully would be at least in his sixties by now, I knew it would be good match. I envisioned Sully providing 'round the clock supervision and knew he could also lend a hand with Billy's training.

I knew Sully was somewhere up in New York City. The problem was where. Phone calls to the gyms in New York as to his whereabouts came up empty and I didn't have any other ideas, until by chance I mentioned to Rocky Graziano that I was looking for Sully.

Graziano told me that he thought he saw him selling newspapers at a newsstand in Manhattan. Now which one? I decided to go to New York and called my friend Dotty DePaola, explaining that I was coming up to the city on a mission. She had a car and agreed to drive me around in my quest for Sully.

Call it luck, call it karma, call it whatever you want, but what a surprise it was when I spotted Sully in front of the third newsstand hawking newspapers. "Whatta ya read?" He bellowed. "Whatta ya read?"

"Sully!" I shouted.

With cap awry, Sully whirled around and his eyes narrowed trying to make me out. It was my name that brought everything back to him and he stopped hawking papers long enough to say hello.

I explained what we wanted from him and he agreed to come to Miami. I knew it would be good for Billy but, I also thought it could be good for Sully. I made all the arrangements for him to come down and set him and Billy up in a nice place to live.

To let Billy earn some spending money, I put him to work as a busboy at the Top of the Home. I don't know how many jobs Billy had before, but he was the kind of kid that walked to the beat of his own drum. On the first night he worked, I explained to him in detail exactly what his duties were as a busboy and that he was to listen very carefully to what the waiters or the service captain had to say to him—in effect, they were his bosses. A few nights later I found him in his busboy uniform, sitting at a table with some customers. He talked to them like he knew them.

I excused myself to the couple and pulled Billy over to the side and asked, "You know these people?"

"No, but they're very lovely aren't they."

"Lovely? What are you, a screwball? Who gives a shit if they're lovely? You're a busboy for crissake. You're supposed to clean their table, not sit and drink a glass of wine with them."

Another Billy incident involved our salad/dessert lady, Edie. Edie was a wonderful, hardworking woman who'd survived Hitler's death camps. She spoke in a heavy accent and came screaming to me that Billy, the new busboy, had just called her a "kike." She was furious. "Nobody calls me a kike," she hollered. "I survived the death camps not to be insulted here."

I couldn't believe Billy would do such a callous thing so I went and asked him what happened.

"I don't know," he answered in his heavy cockney accent. "I just asked her if I could have a piece of kike (cake)."

Eventually Billy became Cassius Clay's (Ali) sparring partner. Working with Clay was an unbelievable experience for Billy, who by then had become an accomplished boxer. In an interview with Sports Magazine, Angelo Dundee was quoted as saying, "I've got a boxer, Billy Williams, who is so aggressive that after he knocks his opponent down, he stands over him like he wants to kick him."

Well, to anyone that knew Billy this wasn't particularly news and that was one of the problems we had with him. He was one of the dirtiest fighters around, but for some reason he never realized it. He'd hit you low, he'd hit you on a break, he'd hit you on the back of the head, he'd hit you in the balls, and he'd do this all while the fans responded by booing.

It happened right from the start in his preliminary fights. The fans saw he fought dirty, and I believed because of that he started drawing larger crowds. They came in hopes of seeing him get knocked out. When he stepped into the ring holding his little Union Jack flag, the crowds' boos were like a roar. He came back to the corner and said, "Why are they booing me?"

"Because you're a dirty fuckin' fighter." Sully would answer. "That's why."

The odd thing was the fight promoter, Chris Dundee, loved it because Billy started drawing more people than the main events would. Things were looking good for Billy as a heavyweight prospect.

A friend of mine, Bill Alheim of Miami-Dade College, was the most successful basketball coach of any junior college team in America. He put all his ball players through a vigorous weight-training program. He thought Billy Williams would be the perfect prospect for his program. Billy was almost six foot two, but he weighed less than 200 pounds. Alheim thought with proper weight training, Billy could put on twenty to thirty pounds and be faster than he was. Alheim wanted to test Billy at the University of Florida where they had a special machine to determine if and how weight training would be beneficial. I thought this was an exciting opportunity, but Angelo didn't see it that way. He was dead set against it. He didn't think weight training was any good and that bulking up a fighter would actually slow him down.

I made the decision to send Billy to be tested there anyway. While he was on campus during the testing I got a call from the

University asking if I had sent them the right person. I couldn't believe what I was hearing and was sure there was some kind of mix up. The said they weren't the ones that were mixed up. It seems that Billy's arm strength tested below normal and so did his legs. They told me, "We have women here in the program that are stronger than this kid."

"You didn't tell him that did you?"

"Of course not. All our findings will be confidential, but because Mr. Williams was a professional fighter we find this very unusual." They went on to explain that he had a very low percentage of fat in his body, which meant he could easily put on twenty to thirty pounds and his reflexes tested in the top 1.5% in the world.

This was probably why he was such a good boxer. Who cares if you can knock down a wall if the wall ain't there when you swing at it? In reality Billy was the perfect candidate for Alheim's weight training program.

Angelo knew nothing about it, but I made arrangements for Billy to start weight training right after his next fight. Billy was the main event of that fight. It was a ten round heavyweight bout. He had a record of ten wins with no defeats.

The day of the fight, Billy came down with a sudden case of tonsillitis and his throat was killing him. Normally we would have canceled the fight, but the house was packed and Billy wanted to go on. To insure a win I wanted to psyche Billy up. I said to him, "If you win tonight, I'm sending you home to England for a couple of weeks to see your family."

It was like I hit him in the ass with an electric prod. We did all we could do to control him. Sore throat and all, Billy got in the ring and almost killed his opponent in the first round. The poor guy didn't have a chance. As soon as the bell rang, Billy ran out of his corner like a raging maniac and almost beat his opponent to death. Billy was still punching him on the canvas with the crowd booing and the bell clanging, as the referee, Angelo, and Sully tried to pull him off.

Billy's throat got worse. He couldn't even talk so we rushed him to the hospital where they operated on him the next morning.

After the operation, Billy was so anxious to fly home, he wanted to get out of the hospital. He drove everyone, including all the doctors, nuts. Two days later they released him just because he was such a pain in the ass and I made arrangements for him to fly home to London. I brought Billy and Sully to the apartment and helped Billy to bed so he could get a good night's sleep before his trip the next afternoon. I was happy thinking that things were settling down and drove home to get some sleep myself.

No one could have foreseen what happened next. I was awakened out of a dead sleep by the ringing phone and then heard Sully telling me that they were at the hospital emergency room and the cops had Billy.

At the ER, Sully explained that after I'd left, the couple that lived next door had been drinking. They got into an argument and their screaming and hollering woke up Billy. First he banged on the wall, but the screaming continued so he got out of bed, went next door, and pounded on the door. When the guy opened the door, Billy told him to stop screaming. The guy told Billy to go f**k himself so Billy promptly knocked him out. That wasn't all. Billy's throat started hemorrhaging. Sully got him in the car and they headed to the hospital with Billy driving.

On the highway, Billy started bleeding all over and sped out-of-control. A State Trooper pulled them over and saw a bleeding, screaming maniac get out of the car and come at him. He immediately called for backup. In trying to subdue Billy, the trooper got knocked out too. When backup arrived, they handcuffed Billy and took him to the hospital only because of Sully's pleading and explanation of what had happened.

Impossible, I thought as I drove to the ER. When I got to the hospital, I called a Captain I knew with the State Troopers and he straightened out the problem Billy had about hitting the patrolman. A few days later, after Billy recuperated and got out of the hospital, the doctor said he was okay to fly so we put him on the first plane back to London.

Angelo had big plans for Billy, but it all went down the tubes. When Billy was back home he got in much bigger trouble.

Albert Dimes called to tell me Billy's sister's boyfriend hit both her and Billy's mother. So Billy tracked him down, gave him a beating, then ran a car over him three or four times. Somehow the guy lived, went to the police and—no surprise—Billy was arrested and sent to jail.

"Poor Billy," Albert said of him. "What a fellow—couldn't even run the gizza over right."

That was the last time we ever saw Billy, but a couple of years later I did get a phone call from him in prison.

"Hello, Dick how are ya?"

I recognized his voice. "Hey, Billy, when did you get out?"

"I'm not out. I'm still her Majesty's guest."

"You are?"

"Yeah, here speak to the screw." And he puts the prison guard on the phone.

"Hello...how are ya?"

Now I find myself in a conversation with an English prison guard. After a few nice pleasantries I invited him to be my guest if he ever gets to Florida then he puts Billy back on the phone and the first thing he asked me was, "How's Sully?"

"How's Sully? I'll tell you how the f**k he is—he wants to kick your ass for losing him his shot at the heavyweight title with ya. That's how he is."

Sully Emmett went on to become a legend in his own right as the caretaker of the world famous 5th Street Gym in Miami Beach.

One day Sully, as he was simply known now, called me to say, "You remember Humphrey, the guy in Joe Palooka comics? Well, I got one here for real and the son-of-a-bitch can fight. He's a mudturtle that weighs about 400 pounds and you should see him punch. Come on down to the gym tomorrow and watch him spar."

The next day I went down to the gym and watched the Humphrey character work out and commented to Sully, "Boy, this guy is big...I mean really big."

"Yeah," Sully answered, "but look at the way he moves around pretty good."

"Okay," I replied. "I'll get him a four rounder and we'll see what happens."

Within a week I got Humphrey a four rounder. I got the promoter to add him onto Roberto Duran's card and everything was set. If he won I planned a promotional campaign with him looking just like Humphrey Pennyworth, with a shirt where the buttons kept popping off and chickens following him. I had the whole thing planned out...that's if he won as Sully said he would. The arena was packed. When Humphrey stepped into the ring and took his robe off I thought his opponent, who barley qualified as a heavyweight, was going to faint.

The bell sounded and Humphrey came out of his corner like a bull, snorting and waving his arms all over, throwing right hands and jabs. As they circled each other you could see fear written all over his opponent's face whose strategy now became to run and hide. Humphrey chased him all over the ring, throwing a record number of punches but only occasionally landing a glancing blow. Nothing tires a fighter out as much as throwing punches that miss their mark and hit only air...this takes a tremendous amount of energy.

At the closing seconds of the round Humphrey had his opponent cornered in a good position, so he wound up to throw a deadly right hand. If it had landed they would have booked him for murder. But as it happened, he missed. The force of the punch spun Humphrey around like a top and he landed on his back. He was so exhausted that he couldn't get up—no matter how hard he struggled. The referee had no choice but to start counting. Humphrey tried and tried but he couldn't get his fat body to stand up and was counted out. The man knocked himself out. This may be the only fight in the history of boxing where the fighter won by a TKO and never threw a punch. Sully was in the ring when he spotted me seated in the first row and put his hands up and shrugged as if to signify...*whatta ya gonna do*?

Duran won the main event but the next day the front-page sports story in the Miami Herald ran with the picture of Humphrey struggling on the ring floor.

An early days Cassius Clay (far right) outside of the 5th Street Gym, Miami Beach, Florida. (Dick Cami)

Because of my interest in boxing I was often in the 5th Street Gym where I'd see Cassius Clay working out. However, in the era of segregation, he had never been able to come into the Peppermint Lounge. After the 1964 Civil Liberties Act was enacted Clay came in to the Peppermint to see his good friend Dee Dee Sharp who had just had a hit with *Mashed Potatoes* and was headlining at my club. From that time on he came into the Peppermint most every night with his main man Budini Brown and his crew. One of the crewmembers was called "Blackie" and I had a kid working for me called "Whitey." They developed a nightly routine of greeting: "Hello, Blackie...Hiya, Whitey."

I'd seen Clay spar at the gym a few times and was amazed at how fast he could move for a big guy. Seeing him now he looked even bigger to me, well over 6 foot and 200 pounds. I figured him in the Peppermint would be good for business. He was getting a lot of press, all over the sports pages with a whole new way of talking, bragging about how he was going to kill that "big, ugly bear" Sonny Liston.

To know Cassius was to love him. He was a perfect gentleman at all times and in every way, including with the ladies. He was almost shy, a teetotaler whose indulgence was ice cream. He even asked for permission to park his bus outside in the parking lot by the main road. It was a big bus that had a gigantic cut out picture of him in a boxing stance on the side. He knew it would be good exposure and it was good publicity for us too. We all knew he was something special but I was also a student of boxing, and to think that he would beat Sonny Liston was a real stretch. Not only to me but to the betting world as well who gave Liston favorable odds of 8-1.

I shared my concerns with Clay's trainer and my friend Angelo Dundee. "Styles make fights, Dick," Angelo said. "The best thing that can happen to us is that Liston thinks he's the favorite. He's gonna lose...no way can he beat my kid. Liston is just too slow. Clay's reflexes are so fast Liston ain't gonna have a chance to land that ferocious right hand of his. Who cares how hard you can punch if there ain't nothing there to hit?"

I could only give Angelo a look but he was right, though there were whispers that the Black Muslims may have had a hand. When Cassius Clay beat Sonny Liston and became the Heavyweight Champion of the World he changed his name the next day to Muhammad Ali.

Angelo Dundee told me after that there was a meeting with the Black Muslims where they tried to get rid of him. They wanted a black trainer. Ali, with characteristic loyalty, was adamant that he would stand by Angelo no matter what, settling the issue with the simple question in typical Ali speak, "Can you do what he do?" That was that. I remained good friends with Angelo Dundee throughout his life but after the Liston fight I rarely crossed paths with Ali. The last time I saw him was at Angelo Dundee's memorial service.

There was a lifelong bond between World Heavyweight Champion Muhammed Ali and legendary boxing trainer Angelo Dundee as seen when the two reunited in celebration of Dundee's 80th birthday, 2001. (Dick Cami)

Grandson, Rich Cami IV, surprised by Muhammed Ali's signature light fingered handshake to prevent anyone from squeezing his hand, 2001. (Dick Cami)

By the time Cassius Clay established himself as Muhammad Ali, Sully Emmett was firmly entrenched as a fixture at the 5th Street Gym. As the keeper of the door, Sully earned a little money from spectators coming into the gym to watch the fighters spar, charging them four bits to get in. One day a reporter from *Sport Magazine* came to the gym to watch Ali work out. As he came up the steps into the gym, he was confronted by Sully who said, "Four bits."

The reporter, who had never paid for anything before, answered, "Press."

Sully shot back, "Press ya pants, ya mudturtle ya, and come up with the four bits." This broke up the reporter who went into his pocket and gave Sully a fiver.

When Ali trained at the 5th Street Gym, Sully always doubled the entrance fees.

Traditionally, on the last day of his training before a big fight, Ali would spar fifteen rounds, after which he gave a press conference to the gathered throng of reporters. Ali, covered with sweat, looking down from the ring, firing back answers to the reporters' questions was an impressive sight.

Ali, clever as always, decided to inject some humor into the situation. He went to Sully beforehand and told him that when he wanted to end his press conference he'd give Sully a high sign by tugging on his towel. At that time, Sully was to tell all the reporters to get out and call Ali a "mudturtle."

So now the stage was set. Ali had sparred fifteen rounds with Billy Williams and come to the end of the interview session with the reporters. He gave the high sign to Sully who stood up and yelled, "All right all youse guys, get the hell outta the gym... whatta ya think I got all night, come on let's move." Then he turned to Ali and shouted, "And you, ya big mudturtle, get the hell outta the ring now. I wanna go home already."

Ali, who was six foot four, jumped over the ropes and down in front of the barely five foot Sully. Shaking a gloved hand in front of Sully's face, he went into one of his tirades. "You old man. You too old for me to hit in front of all these people but if you follow me into my dressing room, I'll take care of you."

Of course, the press couldn't believe what they saw. Ali walking toward his dressing room with Sully following behind with a big ash on his cigar was a comical sight to behold. Once they were both inside the dressing room, Ali closed the door, picked up a chair, and started banging it up and down on the floor making a commotion while he shouted, "Take that you old man."

Two seconds later the door opened and out walked Sully, still with his cigar clenched between his teeth and the big ash intact. When he dusted off his hands indicating that he'd taken care of Ali, the gym exploded in laughter.

Having known Sully Emmett all those years, from his Freeport days to the 5th Street Gym keeper, I shouldn't have been surprised when he brought fourteen-year-old old Kenny Klingman up to the restaurant for dinner. It became clear as Sully explained the situation that here was one final fighter who had found a place under Sully's wing. I didn't foresee right off just how close that association would become, the depth of the loyalty that would develop on both sides, or the bond that would go way beyond the gym or fight game.

Sully told me that Kenny was traveling from his home, an hour and a half each way, every day after school to work out at the gym. It wasn't just this which impressed Sully, he also saw championship potential. But the kid had a difficult home life, so we came up with a plan. Kenny moved in with Sully and went full time to Miami Beach High School during the week, returning home on the weekends. After graduation Kenny stayed on with Sully. It might have seemed an odd duo—the grizzled and diminutive, 70ish Sully with the over 6 foot, handsome, fresh-faced teenager—but we never thought about it after those first few months.

A few years later when I was up in New York, Kenny won the Florida Super Middleweight Championship. Sylvester Stallone was in the audience, went crazy about him, and asked to manage him. Kenny told him about me and I went to see Stallone at his place in Vegas.

Now we had a new plan. The deal we struck gave Stallone fifty percent. I told him he wouldn't have to put up any money, just promote Kenny as his fighter. This would provide an opportunity for Kenny to climb up the ladder faster in getting bouts to the championship. I moved Kenny out to Los Angeles to train and be closer to Stallone, but it didn't come to anything. Stallone went off with a different trainer who discouraged him from promoting Kenny. At least that's what we think happened. Stallone never really explained the situation, he just became unavailable and unresponsive to our communication attempts.

Ex-boxer, Florida State champion and Bal Harbour, Florida police captain Kenny Klingman with famed boxing trainer Angelo Dundee at Grumpy Dick's Seafood Grill, Plantation, Florida, 2006. (Cindy Aumann)

After dropping $25,000 on the Stallone plan, I brought Kenny back to Miami. Bouts with his name on the bill filled the house for promoter Chris Dundee. Kenny won one fight after another and was ranked eighteenth in the nation when he got an offer to fight number one ranked Mustafa Hamza for $100,000. It was an unheard of opportunity for an incredible sum of money at the time. But there was a major concern. There are fighters that anyone can get in the ring with and even if they lose come out unharmed, and then there are fighters like Mustafa that can cause permanent damage—even if you win.

It was an agonizing decision but I had my own bond with Kenny and felt he wasn't ready and that it was just too risky. Coincidentally, there was probably no time in the history of boxing that the middleweight division had been filled with so many great fighters. Based on all this I took Kenny out of boxing.

Kenny opposed it with all his heart. Even to this day, so many years later, I know he would probably wish he could go back. Still, as I watched his successful career in the Bal Harbour police force, capped by retiring as a captain after twenty-five years I know it was the right thing to do.

A grand jury, casting a wide net in an investigation into the possible misappropriation of Teamster funds captured Sully Emmet. Sully, who was totally innocent of any misdoing, had absolutely no information, and whose only involvement was by association, was subpoenaed to appear before the grand jury in Detroit. There was nothing to do but hire legal counsel to represent him. Two astute lawyers well known to me, Dave Goodhart and Henry Gonzalez, agreed to meet him in Detroit. He had been advised to wear a suit, which to Sully meant his best attire. To him that translated into a brightly colored sport coat, Hawaiian shirt, checkered tie with plaid pants, and bright blue sneakers. Picking him up at the airport, I could imagine Goodhart, who knew Sully better, being amused and Gonzalez aghast. This might have been an indication of the comedy to come.

Gonzalez prepped Sully, instructing him to answer any questions by pleading the Fifth Amendment. They rehearsed his reply over and over to be sure he understood and got it right. During a grand jury investigation, the lawyer cannot accompany his client during testimony. However, the client has the right to go out and consult with his lawyers during the process, which Sully was instructed to do if he had a problem. The prosecuting attorney was advised that Sully would not be answering any questions, having been advised to take the Fifth Amendment.

He hadn't been long behind the grand jury closed doors before, not Sully, but a perplexed, sympathetic prosecutor came rushing out. "I thought that you said your client would be only taking the Fifth?"

"Why? What happened?" Gonzalez asked.

"The first question I asked, he answered and then added, 'I take the Fifth.'"

"Did it go on like that?"

"Yes, he answered every question completely before adding 'I take the Fifth.'"

Gonzalez was allowed to explain to the grand jury that his client was advised to not answer any question only to invoke the Fifth Amendment. After some confusion, the grand jury simply excused Sully.

When I managed fighters, the great Angelo Dundee trained every one of them. One day in the 5th Street Gym he said to me, "Stick around Dick, Rip Valenti from Boston is sending in some hot dog fighter that just got kicked out of the Navy. He's only sixteen years old. His name is Vinnie Curto. I'd like you to take a look at him."

"Sure," I answered.

It wasn't but a few minutes later that I saw this young kid come up the steps into the gym and peer in much like Paul Newman did in the movie *Somebody Up There Likes Me*. I got a kick out of him right away. Angelo wanted to see what he had, so he decided to let him spar three rounds with Jimmy Ellis, who at the time was Muhammad Ali's sparring partner and later went on to become the Heavyweight Champion of the World. Vinnie was only a middleweight but this was a common practice.

Now the strangest thing happened when they started off boxing. Jimmy Ellis started throwing punches right away, but he couldn't lay a glove on Vinnie who bobbed and weaved away from every single one of them. It went on like that for three rounds. The harder Ellis tried to hit Vinnie, the more widely he missed. We all looked at each other and smiled at this surprising spectacle. Not only did Vinnie side-step Ellis's punches he connected with plenty of his own. Ellis was infuriated. We were all amazed.

Afterwards, while Angelo cut the tape off of Vinnie's hands he said, "You know Vinnie, your sparring today really impressed Jimmy Ellis."

To which Vinnie replied, "No kidding…was he in the gym watchin'?"

Our jaws dropped. He'd just given a boxing lesson to Jimmy Ellis and didn't know who he had sparred with. Angelo gave me that, *we got another Lulu on our hands,* look.

Vinnie went on to become a classic high-ranking middleweight, so good that nobody wanted to fight him. I ended up being his financial advisor for a while. In the mid-nineties he told me he wanted to enter the cruiserweight division. I thought he was crazy and told him so, but lo and behold within a few fights he'd won the division title.

Pete Scalzo, a former Featherweight Champion of the World, had retired to Hollywood, Florida. He was a frequent guest at Top of the Home where we became very close. Pete was quite the comedian and had a gimmick where he imitated an old Greek immigrant, speaking in a heavy Greek accent mixed with double talk. He was known as Pete the Greek. He was fantastic. Not only did he look the part, but he had all the mannerisms of an old Greek immigrant. When he met someone he would say, "How are you yourself? Happy to meet me." Everyone laughed.

There were many funny bits that he did with guests at the Top. I always introduced him to someone as their Greek counterpart. One time, the Broward One Hundred, a very prestigious business organization, asked me if I could bring him to a luncheon as a gag speaker. The guest speaker was the Speaker of the House, Tip O'Neill. They wanted Pete to be his counterpart, the speaker of the house of Greece. I brought Pete in and it was all set.

Tip O'Neill got up and gave the most pessimistic speech you could imagine—total gloom and doom. After he was done, there was a small smattering of applause and then Pete was introduced as the Speaker of the House of the Acropolis. He got up and went right to the microphone without hesitation and said. "Don't you worry about nothing, we the Greeks give you all the gas and oil you want."

The audience went crazy with applause. Then he went on to say, "I don't know how the speaker of this country can get by on what they pay him. If it wasn't for my brother who is a bookmaker I don't know what I'd do myself. We both own the business—he robs me, I rob him—we rob each other."

Petey went on and on and the audience loved him. Tip O'Neill objected vigorously, but finally caught on to the set up.

My father-in-law told me he owned a piece of land in the Bronx by Yankee Stadium with the boxer Jake LaMotta. Johnny dissolved the partnership because he feared the potential consequences of Jake's impulsivity and unpredictability. Very few people who knew LaMotta had a good word to say about him. He was not well liked. His wife Vickie, on the other hand, was a lovely person and adored by all, but had the bad fortune of marrying Jake. The legendary Vickie LaMotta had been a friend of Johnny's forever. She and Jake were both from 149th St., Johnny's neighborhood. Johnny introduced me to Jake LaMotta when he came into the Wagon Wheel in 1957 and I've known Vickie since 1959 in Florida.

After she divorced Jake, she married his opposite, Tony Foster, a nightclub singer and emcee who worked the hotel circuit in Miami Beach. I considered them both good friends. Years later, when they signed to do the movie *Raging Bull,* Vickie called me to make a reservation to celebrate the occasion at the Top of the Home. "Jake will be with us," she added. "With his new wife, some stripper."

Talk about disasters. Early in the evening, I went into the lounge and saw Bam, a goodfellow from 149th St. sitting with Christine, Jake and Vicki's daughter. I mentioned that I had set a table aside for her mother and father's party, assuming they would be joining them, but Christine said, "I wouldn't sit with him if he was the last man on earth." Of course, I was surprised.

Then Bam motioned with his eyes. "Give us a table on the other side away from them." Which is what I did.

When Vicki came in with Jake I put them at their table and figured that Vicki knew Christine was in the restaurant. After Bam and Christine finished dinner they came back into the lounge to have a drink with Al Miniaci and me at the bar. Within a short time, Jake also left his table and came to the bar to buy a cigar. He spotted Miniaci, who he knew well, and strolled over to give Al a big Gompa hug. Out of the corner of his eye he noticed a beautiful woman sitting with Miniaci and started eyeing her up and down like a piece of meat, not recognizing that it was his own daughter. She was very attractive and it was probably the most embarrassing moment I've ever encountered. Everyone at the bar knew Christine was his daughter except Jake. An awkward silence hung in the air forever. I figured it was my place to say something.

"Jake." I waved my thumb and said, "This is your daughter Christine!"

He looked like I hit him in the head with a bat. "Yeah," he cried out wide-eyed and bewildered.

Christine's eyes welled up in tears as she leaped off the bar stool and ran into the ladies room. I immediately went to Vicki's table and told her to go to the ladies room. "I think Christine needs you," I added.

Returning to the bar I met Jake going back to his table. He looked very uncomfortable as he came up to me. "Geez... I don't blame the kid. Ya know I ain't seen her in over thirteen years, and besides that, I never ever sent her nuttin'."

I had emotions for Jake that night very few people ever had—I felt sorry for him.

When we opened the Peppermint Lounge in Miami Beach, I saw Rocky Marciano there occasionally but I really got to know him at the Top of the Home where he came in frequently to dine.

What a lot of people don't know about Rocky was that he was bashful. I don't know what you call the phenomena but socially he was shy, I mean incredibly shy. I can't tell you the amount of times after I introduced him to someone they'd ask afterwards, "Dick, was that really Rocky Marciano?"

It was hard for them to believe. First of all, he was no giant, standing at just 5′ 10″ with the demeanor of an introvert. As a result I was always explaining, "Yes, believe me…that was Rocky Marciano."

One thing he wasn't shy about was when he got in the ring. Many people agree that he was one of, if not the best, boxers of all time. The man was an animal. After he trained he went home and trained. When he got in the ring he was a tunneled, dedicated punching machine. He never stopped—never. You can see it all in his films. Although Rocky was very nice and gentle, he did have a big fault. He was tight with a buck, maybe more than tight. To give you the right picture, someone came up with another word "mean"—which is beyond being cheap. God Bless Rocky, and I truly loved him as a friend, but damn… The truth is the truth. If he wasn't so tight he might have been with us much longer. He died way too young in a fatal small plane crash on the eve of his 46th birthday. Anxious to return home after attending a dinner in Chicago he had bummed a flight.

One evening at the Top of the Home, he came in with "Fat" Tony Leone to have dinner. Fat Tony wasn't a wise guy. He was a hustling businessman who at one time played with the Cleveland Browns. He was the nicest guy with a naturally happy personality. They came from Tony's apartment to the restaurant. The maître d' sat them at a window table and I joined them. As the conversation flowed, Rocky extended his foot out from under the table and I couldn't help noticing that he was wearing a beautiful pair of black alligator loafers. There was no doubt that they were custom made. In fact they were so beautiful I was mesmerized looking at them. All of a sudden I hear Tony say, "Hey, Rocky...I got a pair of shoes just like that."

Rocky answered in a flash, "These are yours."

I almost fell off the chair. Here's what happened. When Rocky was in Tony's apartment earlier in the evening he wandered into the bedroom, saw the shoes in the closet and tried them on. They fit so good he left them on.

When Rocky went to the restroom Fat Tony turned to me saying, "What am I gonna do, ask for the shoes back? He's got all that athlete's feet and everything."

There's another story about Marciano I can hardly believe, but it was told to me by Mike Marinelli—the most honest of men.

It was at a time when President Nixon wanted to make a trip down to South America but his advisors weren't quite sure how Americans would be received considering the political scene there at the time. So the State Department put together a small contingent of noted Americans to send down and test the waters. Marinelli and Rocky were among those asked to go.

Rocky showed up at the airport to meet the South American delegation with a few things in a pillowcase. Marinelli couldn't believe Rocky's luggage was a pillowcase. Feeling they had no choice, a few of the fellows chipped in and went to the shops in the Miami airport and bought Marciano luggage and clothing. This was a ploy Marciano had often used, which netted him luggage and clothing at others' expense. Marinelli told me with all of that, it was surprising to see Rocky wearing such an expensive pair of shoes.

Jim Bishop and Hy Gardner were two well-known, syndicated columnists carried in the Miami Herald, and good patrons of Top of the Home. One night, deciding they deserved a night out, they came in with their wives and were joined by their friend and talk show host Sam Gyson. I joined the party at their table.

Bishop's next column reported on the evening:

There is a smidge of magic getting four homogenous guys together. The conversation was on people we liked. All of us knew Rocky Marciano, and we talked about what a lovable dumb bastard he was. He gave his heart...to anyone....

Once, playing golf, I accused him of flattening Joe Louis in the

Garden and turning his back in contempt as the referee counted the Brown Bomber out. Marciano was stunned: "I didn't feel no contempt," he said. "Joe Louis was my boyhood hero. I turned my back so no one could see I was crying."

Completely the opposite of his brother Angelo Dundee, Chris Dundee was another person in the fight business who had a reputation for being frugal. Chris was a big name in boxing and wrestling. He promoted the first famous fight between Sonny Liston and Cassius Clay.

Angelo related this story to me one night over a plate of his favorite pasta. In the early days when he and Chris shared an office in the Miami Beach Convention Center, the phone rang on Chris's desk. When he picked it up it was a long distance operator with a call from a fighter who was scheduled to be on Chris' next fight card.

"Person to person for Chris Dundee, please."

"Yes, operator," said Chris. "Who is it?"

A desperate voice broke in. "Chris it's me, Charlie Walker, I'm stuck in Cincinnati and need five hundred bucks."

There was a moment of silence before Chris answered. "I can't hear you."

Charlie repeated the request and Chris gave him the same answer twice more.

The operator finally cut in saying, "Mr. Dundee, he says he needs five hundred dollars."

To which Chris replied, "You heard him, you send it."

Somebody up there Likes Me starring Paul Newman was the story of how Rocky Graziano became the Middleweight Champion of the World. Long ago when Rocky held the title, he acknowledged the fact that he couldn't have both fame and privacy, and he wasn't about to give up one for the other. Every time he was out having dinner with a friend, his wife would read about it in the newspaper the next day. If he went to a nightclub it would be the same thing—a picture of him was always in the tabloids.

According to the press, his life was filled with sizzling romances and beautiful women. Luckily his wife understood the way the press worked, but that didn't mean he didn't fool around.

Rocky had a gimmick, if there was a beautiful girl he wanted to have sex with, he would approach her and say, "Are you aware that a champion horse gets a million bucks to be a stud?"

Regardless of the answer he would go on to say, "Well, I'm a champion, but in your case I'll make the exception and do it with you for nothing."

Georgie Levine, Rocky's father-in-law, had a record as long as my arm and in many ways was tougher than Rocky. We got to talking and he said, "Don't let that son-of-a-bitch son-in-law of mine fool ya, he's one tough bastard, that Rocky is." Georgie went on. "I remember when he fought Fritzie Zivic, it was a non-title bout, a ten-rounder in The Garden. Rocky split Fritzie's nose in half and almost killed him. After the fight Fritzie asked me, why did Rocky give him such a beating? Does he have it in for me or what?"

Georgie tried to reassure him. "I don't know but I'll find out."

When Georgie asked Rocky he got mad and said, "I ain't got nuttin' against him but what the hell does he think I was doin' in there—playin' around? We're in the fight business for crissake. When I goes inta the ring I goes inta win. Ya get me?"

Fritzie Zivic was the Welterweight Champ of the World when he fought Rocky but after that fight, he never fought again.

Years later when Georgie was in an Atlanta prison, Rocky was on the boxing team that visited the prison. He told Georgie their next stop was to see President Johnson at his ranch in Texas. Georgie saw this as an opportunity for Rocky to ask Johnson to give him a pardon. *What the hell,* Georgie thought it was nothing for the President to do, besides that, he knew President Johnson was a big fight fan. What pissed Georgie off was that Rocky never got back to him.

When the boxing team came back to Atlanta the following year, Rocky wasn't on it but Georgie asked Sugar Ray Robinson if Rocky said anything about the pardon to President Johnson when they were there. Sugar Ray didn't know anything about it. Finally after Georgie got out of prison and they were having a Sunday dinner at home, Georgie asked Rocky, "What happened with you and Johnson?"

Rocky hemmed and hawed and before he could answer, Georgie, who had a fork in his hand, thrust it deep into the top of Rocky's shoulder. He then picked up the carving knife and yelled at Rocky with one hand waving him on. "Come on you lyin' son-of-a-bitch I'm ready for ya."

Georgie always did get a little emotional when he expressed himself. This put a damper on the rest of the family dinner, to say the least.

I remember when I promoted a wonderful charity function for the Boys' Town of Italy. It was an American charity for orphans in Italy. I asked Rocky Graziano to be the Master of Ceremonies.

"No problem," he agreed.

Also on the dais was Johnny Desmond, the fabulous singer, Harold Gibbons, the number two man in the Teamsters under Jimmy Hoffa, Lou Fugazy who once owned the Diners Club and Hal David, the songwriting partner of Burt Bacharach.

It was a hundred-dollar-a-plate affair and the room was filled to capacity. After a three-course dinner, Rocky was the first one to get up and speak. He looked good in a tuxedo, but it didn't disguise all his rough edges. As he walked to the microphone he muttered to himself, "What the hell is the name of this charity again?"

"Ladies and Gentlemen, it's a pleasure to see you all here because this is one of my favorite charities, yes sir, the…uhh... the errr..." Rocky stuttered trying to remember the name of the charity.

Straining to remember he saw Dick Byno and leaned away from the microphone and asked him, "What the hell's the name of this charity again?"

Byno stood next to a battery of TV reporters with their cameras. He covered his mouth and in a loud whisper said, "The Boys' Town of Italy."

"Oh, yeah," Rocky smiled. "The Boy Clowns of Italy."

The place broke up. Then someone said, "That Rocky... what a character. Always joking."

A family celebration with Cindy Byno, Dick Cami, Rocky Graziano and Dick's son Rich, 1976. (Dick Cami)

Just being with Graziano was an experience. After we had lunch one day, Rocky asked me where I was going. "I'm going down to the Battery," I replied, "to get some restaurant equipment."

"I'll go with ya," Rocky said. "That's my old neighborhood."

As we walked the streets, people from all over shouted greetings to him...store owners, pedestrians, and construction workers hanging off rafters shouted things like, "Hey Rocky—keep punchin' champ."

I couldn't believe how popular Rocky was and told him he should run for mayor. "You'll win in a landslide," I said.

From there we went around the corner into Little Italy where everything changed. We came across a storefront that was a card room for The Boys, and to my surprise, sitting outside on an orange crate was Don Cheech, a good friend of Johnny Futto's who knew me well. He gave me a big hello, greeting me with enthusiasm. Then Don Cheech looked at Rocky and said, "Whatta ya gonna do—play or what?"

"No...No Don Cheech." Rocky faltered. "I'm just with Dick, looking for a store."

"All right then," Don Cheech said. "Go where yas gotta go." And threw his hand down.

Everything is relative, I guess.

Rocky Graziano putting in a golfing foursome including Teamster Vice President Harold Gibbons leaning on golf club. (Dick Cami)

Chapter 17

Jimmy Hoffa & The Teamsters

In my experience just about everyone not only knows about Jimmy Hoffa but has an opinion. The most frequent question I am asked is, "What happened to him?" regarding his still unexplained disappearance. I do have a theory about that, but first, let me share a few stories about Hoffa and my relationship with him. Jimmy Hoffa started out as a labor organizer in the 1930s and was elected president of the International Brotherhood of Teamsters in 1957, a position he held until beginning his prison sentence ten years later. Even before being elected Teamster boss, he had been under U.S. government investigation—most notably by the McClellan Committee. He was generally considered a personal target of Bobby Kennedy in his capacity on that committee and later in his role as U.S. Attorney General. Hoffa evaded numerous early charges, until being found guilty of the misuse of pension funds in 1964. He appealed his conviction and it was during the three years as the appeal played out that I first met him.

Hoffa had an apartment in Bal Harbour, Florida where he wintered with his wife, Josephine. My close pal Bill Johnson and his wife came in the first time with the Hoffas, and during the course of the evening I joined them at their table. Hoffa was short and stocky. My first impression was that he was honest, direct and to the point, a straight shooter, and more comfortable attending to business than socializing. He became a good and frequent customer. As you might expect he was a meat and potatoes man, and as you might not expect—a teetotaler. Nothing I saw ever changed my first impression. Although he had some rough edges, I found him to have strong and unwavering loyalties. First to the union, secondly to Josephine, and third to his family. With a strong work ethic and amazing memory he was well aware of the goings on at every "local," both nationally and internationally, and knew over 1500 union delegates by their first name. He might be the most misunderstood man in America, which I think was due largely to the determination and doggedness of the Kennedys, who ironically did not have some of Hoffa's better qualities.

Top of the Home guests NYC cop Dick Byno with Teamster President Jimmy Hoffa, 1972. (Dick Cami)

On the evening before Hoffa was to go to prison, he and his wife dined at the Top with Bill and Jennifer Johnson. Josephine asked Johnson if they were going anywhere after dinner. When Johnson said they were going over to the Diplomat Hotel to see a show with comic Frank Gorshin, Josephine asked if they could go too and clearly really wanted to. Johnson looked over at Hoffa whose eyes narrowed to slits before he reluctantly nodded yes.

The couples took separate cars to the Diplomat. Johnson got there first and waited outside for Hoffa. When Jimmy arrived and Johnson approached Hoffa said, "I have better things to do with my time than go to nightclubs. I'm holding you personally responsible for forcing me to come here this evening." Johnson without so much as a blink accepted the responsibility knowing very well that Hoffa was only doing it for Josephine and under the circumstances.

The Diplomat personnel were very familiar with Johnson. He grabbed the maître'd and told him in no uncertain terms no one should announce that Jimmy Hoffa was in the audience, or in any way draw attention to him. "We wanna keep it all low key." With that, the maître'd led them through the kitchen to an obscure ringside table. This pleased Hoffa who just stared at Johnson in appreciation. Everything went smoothly and Hoffa and his wife stayed at their table until the room emptied while Johnson went outside to get Hoffa's car so it would be waiting for him when they came out.

Before he went to prison, Hoffa designated Frank Fitzsimmons to be in charge of the Teamsters. A decision I believe was based more on emotion than reason, and would prove to be not only a mistake but eventually lead to Hoffa's fate. Fitzsimmons was content to be a figurehead more interested in his daily round of golf than any day-to-day union business. He couldn't be a waiter in my restaurant—that's how incompetent he was. Under Fitzsimmons' blind eye and inaction, locals throughout the country began to develop independently and go in all directions, far from their cohesive functioning under Jimmy Hoffa. There had long been rumors of mob ties—remember the Kennedys' mission against organized crime and the unions—but now the situation was perfect for major Mafia takeovers.

The right man for the job of Teamster boss during Hoffa's time in prison was the heir apparent, longtime International vice-president, and number two man under Hoffa, Harold Gibbons.

Gibbons was everything Hoffa wasn't. He was a tall, distinguished looking college grad, suave, intelligent, and sociable with no rough edges. He was also a Don Juan who women flocked to and who never did anything to discourage them. He was a frequent Top of the Home guest, often coming in with Bill Johnson and always with a woman on his arm. Like Hoffa, he was diligent and hardworking, putting in legendary hours and steadfastly dedicated to the worker and the Union mission. But, by the time Hoffa went to prison, the two weren't talking.

The riff happened at the time of President John Kennedy's assassination. Gibbons ran St. Louis, and like the rest of the country, lowered the flag over his Union hall to half-mast in honor of Kennedy. Hoffa was furious when he found out and called Gibbons saying, "Are you nuts? This bastard is trying to kill us and you lower your flag on a guy like that..."

Gibbons firmly replied, "Jimmy...today the President of the United States was murdered. The flag will stay at half-mast on my Union hall." That was the last time they ever spoke and even though Hoffa no doubt knew Gibbons should have been his replacement, he gave the nod to Fitzsimmons.

During the time Jimmy Hoffa was in prison Josephine continued to frequent the Top, most of the time alone. I would always try to sit with her. I could tell that she was not just lonely, but that she was only living for the day when Jimmy would get out. He was her love and her life.

Harold Gibbons also continued to come in for dinner and I got to know him quite well. His story was one of a larger than life character, from his birth as the youngest of twenty-three children to his eventual involvement in politics, and to what I guess today would be called social justice. I am not sure how the topic came about, but one time he told me a story of himself as a young boy, cold and hungry on the streets, when he was invited into a woman's home and given a warm meal. The punchline of that story was that during the course of the meal he realized that the woman was a sister he had never met!

His commitment to the members of the Teamsters went well

beyond any job, and I came to admire him as truly remarkable. He believed in something I have seen on the internet called "total person unionism." From my interaction with Gibbons, I would describe it as a belief that unions should provide a total life support system for their members and families. It would include not just good wages and a pension, but fully address any medical, housing, education, or other major life needs—a total community. I do know that in his area he did just that, developing and providing housing at a reasonable cost, constructing a hospital, and addressing concerns with desegregation and the provision of quality education. He held an annual benefit concert in St. Louis, raising a million dollars a year to support those projects. Harold Gibbons and Frank Sinatra were mutual admirers and great friends. It was Frank who played a major role in the benefit concerts, not only performing, but providing an entertainer list of who's who, including the Rat Pack and countless others. Johnny Carson emceed at least once, performing gratis.

During the years I attended the concerts, I had some interesting experiences. Once, while flying out of Miami to the St. Louis benefit, I found myself seated next to Tommy Whalen on the plane. Whalen was a well-known mob link between the Capone mob in Chicago and St. Louis. He was well known to me, as he and his wife "Champagne" Eleanor Holm, the Olympic swimming champion, were frequent guests at Top of the Home. As a couple they couldn't be missed. Frequently arguing like characters on the old radio show the Bickersons, they were both good looking, interesting conversationalists and as I frequently witnessed on our dance floor, marvelous dancers.

This particular time Whalen was alone, and knowing that so many men in the underworld like to occasionally push fate, I wondered if the trip for him to St. Louis might involve some illegal matter. We acknowledged each other as we boarded our flight and coincidentally were seated next to each other in first class. Tommy had the window. Our conversation was normal for us and the flight uneventful and on time. Well, that is until we were about to descend and Tommy reached under his seat for his small, leather travel case. As the plane wheels came to a halt he opened the case and took out a snub nose .38 caliber pistol, opened the cylinder, and checked it out. Satisfied it was loaded, he clipped it into his coat pocket. When he noticed that I was looking he said, "I still have a lot of enemies here in St. Louis."

You have no idea the apprehension that gave me as we descended the plane steps together and proceeded to walk into the terminal. I don't know if it was my imagination, but it seemed like the whole time we were in St. Louis he wanted to be by my side.

The living room of Harold Gibbon's penthouse apartment was furnished with huge sofas and chairs covered in bright fabrics. The picture window that faced the city's skyline was quite a distance from Harold's bedroom where he lounged with this evening's beauty. At 2 a.m. the beauty's boyfriend stood, held the St. Louis telephone book in his hand, and threatened to rip it in half.

Earlier that evening at the Jefferson hotel's fine dining restaurant, I was part of Harold Gibbon's party waiting to be seated when I decided to go to the bar and have a drink. I was standing next to this girl, a ravishing beauty and her boyfriend when I overheard her say, "Oh, my God—that's Harold Gibbons over there." I turned and noticed how excited she was.

"Yes," her boyfriend replied in a low voice. "You've got no chance of meeting him, he's a big shot."

"Oh, you're probably right," she said.

I broke in with a flat voice. "You want to meet him?"

She turned and smiled. "That would be something." She answered with a convincing wail in her voice.

"Listen," I said. "I'm in his party and after diner we're going to go his apartment, if you'd like to join us there I'll give you his address."

She held her breath then let out a screech, "Oh, my God...yes!"

This had happened many times to me when I was in Gibbon's company. I'd seen women actually melt down when they were asked to go out by him. As I've said he was an all-American lady's man without equal. When I joined Gibbons at the table, he wanted to know who that pretty girl I talked to was. I told him the story and that she and her boyfriend would join us later at his place. He seemed pleased with the news.

At Gibbon's apartment, everybody in any way connected to him seemed to be there. The place swarmed with beautiful women, but for whatever reason, Gibbons seemed to be intrigued with the beauty I'd met at the bar. Somehow he maneuvered her away from the crowd and headed to his bedroom, leaving me with the boyfriend who in time became infuriated at her absence. In total frustration he picked up the thick telephone book and sneered. "I wonder where my girlfriend could be?" He proceeded to rip the book in half.

I seemed to be the only one that saw this as a threat. I made my way to Gibbon's bedroom where he and the girl were on his bed engaged in a lovemaking position. I frantically called out, "Harold! Her boyfriend is looking for her and let me tell you he's pissed."

"Really?" Gibbons calmly replied. "Let him know she'll be right out."

Shortly thereafter, the girl appeared in the living room where her boyfriend approached her. Not to betray the situation she waved her hand and spoke in a bright voice, "Mr. Gibbons was just showing me the rest of his apartment, it's so beautiful."

The boyfriend, harassed and unhappy, quickly grabbed her by the arm. "Come on, we're getting out of here."

"Why?" she replied. "The party's just getting started."

"Not for us." He glanced at his watch. "It's all over."

He got their coats—no negotiation—on the way out the door she gave me a wink.

Frank Sinatra was a complex man, and often when asked to tell a story about him I have asked, "Which Frank?" Many stories involve his "bad boy" persona usually seen when he had been drinking, but Gibbons told me an entirely different story. Sinatra was in St. Louis for one of the benefit concerts. At breakfast one morning, Sinatra read in the local newspaper about a house break-in gone wrong. A young black girl who was babysitting for the family at the time had been cut with a broken bottle and suffered serious eye injuries. Gibbons said that morning he got a call from Sinatra telling him what he had just read. Sinatra asked Gibbons to see what could be done to help the girl and pledged to give $10,000 to start for any medical expenses. He wanted to help, no matter what it would take, to restore her eyesight fully and fix any injuries to her face. Sinatra also gave instructions that his involvement remain anonymous.

Jimmy Hoffa had served about five years of his fifteen-year sentence when I was sitting with Harold Gibbons in my restaurant and Johnny Meyer joined our table. Meyer was a mover and shaker who for years worked for Howard Hughes and had now moved on to be with Aristotle Onassis.

"Onassis in Miami?" I asked.

"Yeah, he's on his yacht, *Christina,* docked in Miami. We're flying over to Greece tomorrow."

"It's quite the coincidence," Gibbons said. "Because I was just going to ask Dick how to get in touch with you about going over to Greece to see Tom Pappas. I've got a million dollars to contribute to Nixon's campaign fund, of course, that's if he agrees to pardon Jimmy Hoffa." Despite the intense animosity between the two men, Gibbons now talked about facilitating Hoffa's early release from prison.

Meyer invited Gibbons to fly over to Greece with himself and Onassis but Gibbons declined, saying he had to attend a board meeting the next day. The men exchanged phone numbers and Gibbons agreed to call when he got to Greece.

Tom Pappas was better known as "Esso" Pappas because he was the distributor for ESSO gas in Greece and that part of the world. He was also a prominent republican and Nixon supporter. I've seen a variety of explanations for the pardon of Hoffa and this is just what I heard. I don't know any details of what happened between Gibbons and Pappas. I do know that after Gibbons flew to Greece Jimmy Hoffa was pardoned by Nixon, receiving an early parole.

Interestingly enough, whatever influence Gibbons had at that time with Nixon wasn't lifelong. When Harold Gibbons became increasingly political and outspoken against the war in Vietnam, he ended up number one on Nixon's enemies list.

The pardon from Nixon and early release from prison carried a stipulation that not only prohibited Jimmy Hoffa from reclaiming his title as president of the Teamsters, but also prevented any involvement in union business until 1980, which would have been the date of his release had he served his full prison term. However, Jimmy Hoffa was a prime candidate for radio and TV interviews and appearances. Although hard to know exactly his intentions, he couldn't have thought it would hurt to stay in the public view.

He accepted a televised debate with William F. Buckley on the subject of prison reform to be held at the University of Michigan. I made sure I tuned in to see it. As I watched the debate, I couldn't get over how well Hoffa did. This was Buckley, the famous debater—people feared him—and here was Jimmy Hoffa getting all his major points across, big time. It was the first time I ever saw Buckley with such a flat, lackluster attitude. *What's going on?* I wondered. By the end of the show, there was no question Hoffa had won. I was so impressed with Hoffa's knowledge of the subject I thought he should go into the field of prison reform rather than go back into the Teamsters—ever.

The very next night, Hoffa came to the Top of the Home for dinner with Josephine, just the two of them. As soon as he saw me, he smiled and motioned for me to come over to his table.

"Hi, Jimmy," I said. "I saw you on the Buckley show last night. Man, you did great."

"Really, I'm glad you saw it. Sit down." He pointed to an empty chair opposite him. "I wanna tell you about this bum."

As I sat down, his eyes narrowed and he spoke slowly. "I heard that this Buckley was no good. He tells ya one thing that he's gonna talk about then when he gets ya in front of the camera—wham—he figures he can catch ya off guard and switches the subject. So I decided to study him. I went to the library and did some research on him. One of the things I found out, he went to the same school in England that Chamberlain went to. Chamberlain, the English Prime Minister that Hitler made a fool of."

"As you know," Hoffa said going on, "the debate was supposed to be about prison reform. So I started laying out some good points that I thought were important, like prisoners should be allowed to take a shower once a day."

"Then when Buckley held up his hand and said with that grandiose attitude of his, 'Uh... uh...uh...I went to school in England and we were only allowed to take a shower once a week.' I knew I had him."

"That's when I put in my zinger, 'That musta been a pretty stupid school. Was that the school Chamberlain went to?'"

"Did ya see Buckley's jaw drop when laughter came from the audience?"

Hoffa smiled. "He just stood there on the platform for the rest of the hour and it was like I'd cold cocked him. After that he wasn't much into accepting any more challenges. I still had a lot more to say when Buckley ended the debate but I decided to just stand up and wave. When I said 'Thank you' and the audience broke out in applause, I knew I'd destroyed Buckley."

"There's no doubt about that." I couldn't help but smile too.

"How's the roast beef tonight?" Hoffa asked.

"The best like always, Jimmy," I replied.

"You know when I was away, I can't tell you how many times I dreamt about your roast beef."

"Thanks, Jimmy" was all I could muster up to say. Walking away, I thought this was a prime example of what I'd heard Hoffa say so many times—Study your enemy and know your subject.

Against everyone's advice not to pursue regaining control of the Teamsters Union or re-seek the presidency, and despite his parole restriction, Jimmy Hoffa wasn't about to go away quietly. He just couldn't accept that he'd had his run. His name still had power and he was popular with the rank and file, which in the end proved fatal. Seen as a real threat to the new status quo he had to be stopped. After his five year absence, local control and independence, and widespread mob influence was not about to be relinquished.

The answer to the question, "What happened to Hoffa?" may never be exactly answered. But the story as I know it came from Joe Franco, one of Hoffa's bodyguards and so called ambassadors of violence. In my restaurant one night, Franco casually remarked, "I should write a book about the 'Old Man.'" Franco was from Detroit and because I'd never heard Hoffa referred to as the 'Old Man,' I thought he was talking about some Detroit wise guy. Only when Franco mentions Hoffa's name did I sit up and take notice.

At the time, I knew a literary agent who I contacted about the possibility of a book. He contacted noted crime writer Richard Hammer who suggested that Franco put his story on tape. Working with Franco and his tapes, Hammer wrote *Hoffa's Man*, where you can read the long version of this story.

The short version is that under a totally bizarre circumstance, Franco claimed to be the last person to see Jimmy Hoffa alive in the parking lot of Detroit's Red Fox Restaurant. The restaurant was in the same shopping mall where Franco's girlfriend worked in a beauty parlor. Franco suspected her of cheating and was in his car keeping her under surveillance when he saw Jimmy Hoffa drive into the parking lot. Embarrassed, Franco slumped down in his car because he didn't want to be spotted by Hoffa who he knew would think spying was a weaselly thing to do. Hoffa waited for a while before getting out of his car to make a phone call. Josephine Hoffa reported that she received a call from Jimmy saying that whoever he was meeting hadn't showed and he was only going to give them a few more minutes before leaving. One of Hoffa's absolutes was never be on time—always be early. So it is probable he was there before the appointed meeting time and after waiting what he thought was a sufficient length of time was getting impatient and ready to leave.

However before he left, Franco reported seeing a car drive up with three men, one black, all in suits. One man approached Hoffa and showed him something that Franco took to be some kind of badge and Hoffa got in their car. When they drove off, Franco followed them for a distance until they turned down a small dirt road that led to an airport. At the point of the turn Franco knew he couldn't continue to follow without being spotted so he just drove on. So ends the trail...

What happened to Jimmy Hoffa seems pretty clear. Exactly how, by who, or where he ended up are questions unlikely to ever be answered. Most suspicions and speculation centered on mob suspects, but Hoffa had made equally powerful enemies of union leaders and the government. Alone or any combination of those groups could have played a part in Hoffa's disappearance.

It may be anticlimactic, but I couldn't tell Hoffa and Teamster stories without including a few about Barney Baker. He was another member of the group dubbed Hoffa's ambassadors of violence and not without reason. A big guy, 6'4" and over 400 pounds, he used his size to develop a reputation for a unique organizing style. He once collected an overdue debt by hanging a man by his ankles out a window twenty or so stories up. Another time, after finding out who the company boss was, he walked into his office, picked up his desk and tossed it down a flight of stairs. Then announced, "I'm here to organize yas."

Long before he had anything to do with the Teamsters, he may have been the best-known Irishman to come out of Hell's Kitchen even though he was half Jewish. Early on he had plenty of reputation, and endless stories preceded him.

In the mid 1930's when Hitler came to power he put together the Jugend Bund Deutscher, which was shortened to HJ. They were a group of Aryan super boys between the ages of fourteen to eighteen that formed a corps of potential adult leaders. The HJ was an important stepping-stone to future membership in the SS. Hitler maintained training academies for the HJ, designed to nurture future Nazi Party leaders. Only the most radical and devoted HJ members could attend. Hitler couldn't forget Germany's dismal record in the 1936 World Olympics games so he called for a youth boxing match between his HJ group and an American team. The bouts took place in 1937 in Nuremberg, where members from all over Germany converged for the annual Nazi Party rally.

Barney Baker was the heavyweight on the American team. Because of his heritage, he wore a Star of David on one leg of his boxing trunks and a shamrock on the other leg. Each winner of a division was awarded a prize of a German product. Barney easily won the heavyweight division and for his prize selected shoes, fifty pairs. He picked out a wide range of styles and colors and completed the arrangements to have them shipped to America. When Barney got back home he discovered the boxes contained all left shoes—one hundred of them! Later when Barney worked on the docks, any shipment from Germany that landed in his area got "special" treatment—his compliments.

The movie *On the Waterfront* was based on the Longshoreman's local that included Baker. Barney was the model for Marlon Brando's movie character ex-boxer Terry Malloy and the famous line, "I coulda been a contender!"

Leaving the docks, Barney became the bodyguard of Farmer Sullivan, the boss of Hell's Kitchen Pre-Westies. The Italians wanted to make a meet with the Farmer and set a location over in Jersey. At the meet a car pulled up and four gunmen opened fire, killing Farmer Sullivan in a blaze of bullets but only wounded Barney. It wasn't their fault, the .32 caliber bullets that entered Barney's body found their mark, but just never got past the thick layer of hardened lard lining the outside of his stomach.

Shortly thereafter, a second car of Italians came by to verify the results and saw Barney, a bloody mess, staggering down the road. One of the Italians who knew him asked, "What happened, Barney?"

"Farmer just met his maker," Barney replied.

They put Barney in the back seat between two gunmen and as the car sped off toward New York City, Barney pondered his fate. He knew if they went through Staten Island, he wouldn't live, they would finish him off and dump him in the swamps. If they went straight through to the Holland Tunnel, he knew he would survive the ordeal. "Barney, which way you wanna go back to New York?" One of the gunmen asked.

"I don't care," he replied figuring he was dead anyway. "Take me any way youse want...it don't matter to me."

A few minutes later, Barney saw a sign out the window reading, "Holland Tunnel" with an arrow pointing straight ahead. The decision had been made to let Barney live.

Time was short. "Cockeyed" Johnny Dunn had to get Barney Baker over to Ma Cassidy's house before she went to work at Madison Square Garden. Barney, on the lam, was wanted for questioning about the murder of a union official at the Zodiac bar over on Tenth Avenue. Ma, in what would be just another day to her, was to put Barney up until some witnesses could be reached and neutralized. Dunn and Baker made their way through a series of side streets and alleys then over a back fence until they arrived at the convenient rear entrance of Ma's apartment.

Within a few days there was a knock on the door and when she opened it, there stood two New York City detectives. "Hello, Ma," Detective Broderick said.

"And what would you be wantin' here?" she said giving him a stern look.

"We've been told you've got Barney Baker here with you?"

"Now what would a Jew be doin' in a good Irish home like this?" Her steely eyes stared him down as she stood fast and barred the door.

The two detectives just turned and walked away. Barney and his ferocious appetite stayed on for two more weeks, practically eating her out of house and home. She provided all the food and necessities Barney needed without a word of complaint, until all the arrangements were complete and "Cockeyed" Johnny Dunn came back to pick him up. As they left, Ma Cassidy shouted out after him in her fine Irish brogue. "The next time ya be bringin' him to stay here, ya better be bringin' a cow with ya."

Food was never far from Barney's mind. In fact, in his prime he was a world-class eater, besting Fat Butch in an eating contest at the Dunes Hotel in Las Vegas by downing twenty whole chickens. He shared with me his secret of having small chickens cooked just right so he could just suck the meat off the bone. Nonetheless, I've never related this story when it hasn't been met with eye rolls to the ceiling and the listener repeating, "Twenty chickens?"

Years later, when Barney Baker was one of Jimmy Hoffa's personal bodyguards, I heard this story about him. Baker was with Hoffa at the Drake Hotel in Chicago during a series of contract negotiations. Hoffa was getting impatient and became adamant about completing the negotiations. He announced to all his officers and stewards they would be locked in the hotel room until the contracts were finalized.

Hoffa slammed his fist on the table saying, "We're gonna stay here for as long as it takes. No matter what, nobody's leaving this room. So go and make all your calls and arrangements now because I don't wanna hear any excuses. We may be locked in here for a week. Once we start nobody leaves this room, and that's final. Everyone here understand that?" You could practically see the smoke coming out of his ears.

Somehow that translated to Barney that he'd better stock up on food. After all, if nobody's leaving the room for a week, they'd need it. So while everyone made their respective arrangements, Barney got room service on the phone.

Everyone returned and the meeting resumed with Hoffa going over the points to be negotiated. All of the sudden the doors of the suite swung open and in came a long line of food carts, one after another, being rolled in by room service waiters. Hoffa looked amazed and confused. "What the hell is this?"

Barney piped up. "I figured if we're gonna be locked in here for a long time, we'd better have some food on hand."

Everyone in the room stifled a laugh as an infuriated Hoffa shouted through clenched teeth, "Get those god-damn carts outta the room now—and, I mean right now."

At the time of this story, Barney worked out of Allen Dorfman's Teamsters Insurance office in Chicago. He decided to join, for a few dollars by mail, the House of Joy, a religious organization somewhere in California, which entitled him to all the perks of a minister. Now he went around telling everyone that he was the Reverend Baker. For a couple of bucks he got a collar plus a manual of instructions for religious rites.

Dorfman had recently moved his offices to a new location. Nobody there knew the old Barney Baker, just the new Reverend Baker. Barney and Dorfman were having lunch across the street from their offices when a waitress rushed up to Barney and asked him if he could assist with someone who was dying in the lobby. Certainly this was the last thing Barney ever expected to be asked but he answered in his best minister's voice, "Yes, my dear, you go ahead and I'll be there shortly."

Barney went to his car to get the book of instructions on how to perform the last rites. Armed with the book, he made his way back to the lobby where he saw a lot of people standing around the fallen guest laid out on the floor. "Stand back," Barney yelled. "Stand way, way back and give this man some room to breathe. I will attend to him."

Barney didn't want anyone to hear that he didn't know what he was doing. He leaned down, got in close on one knee, and with his book close in hand put his head next to the victim and poked his shoulder while he whispered his version of the last rites. "Hey... how ya doin'. You all right or what?"

As Barney spoke to the victim, his eyes began twitching and he started regaining consciousness, coming out of a diabetic coma. Barney immediately stood up and started shouting, "Hallelujah, it's not this man's time to meet his maker!" Fortunately by that time, the paramedics were there and able to take over.

For all the stories I heard and the wacky and wild things I witnessed, Barney Baker was hard not to like. You may actually know something of him yourself as he came to prominence nationally at the time of President Kennedy's assassination when Jack Ruby repeatedly called the Teamster offices asking for his help.

A LOOK BACK

Part 2

The Boys

Chapter 18

Mikey the Hat

Preface

I knew a "Mikey the Hat," a combination part-time bartender from a joint down the road from Top of the Home and daring cat burglar. We got friendly when he became a regular at my restaurant. He always worked in disguise and thought of himself as something of a Robin Hood. With nerves of steel and a heart of just enough gold, he admitted to only robbing insured jewelry so only the insurance companies – who he'd say were the real thieves – got hurt. He once told me that he returned a ring after he found out that it was a mother's memento from her deceased daughter.

His Story

I'm home in bed with my wife Jeanette. Usually Thursdays are my I'm outta town night, but my girlfriend, Billi, is in Hollywood Memorial recovering from plastic surgery. She's havin' a breast reduction. An exotic dancer at the Ha Ha Club, a titty bar, she's twenty-three with a perky attitude and built like a brick shit-house except for her tits. First she had them enlarged, then she had them lifted because they started saggin' from all the wild dancing she does. Now finally she's decided to make them smaller. She's like a yo-yo goin' back and forth to the hospital with the tits.

So here we are in the morning when our little girl, Christine, comes and jumps in bed with us. The little things girls do. Geez, she's the love of my life...my little blue-eyed redhead is. Everyone in our family is dark, they're dark skinned and dark eyed—everything's like a shade of light tan. Where did my little girl come from? This happens sometimes to Sicilians. There's always that light skinned, blue eyed, redhead way back in our genes. "Morning, Daddy!" she says brightly, "Remember we're going to the beach today."

"I remember baby," I answer. I often forget dates, but never with my family. Jeanette raises her head and stares at me. "I'm going to make a nice picnic basket." She gets up and goes into the kitchen and I yell out after her. "Don't forget the peppers and eggs!"

Jeanette, my petite brunette wife, is the nicest thing on God's earth and the best wife any man can have. I make no claim at being the perfect husband, but I do strive to fulfill everyone's needs, not just mine. We have a nice house in a nice neighborhood and two nice cars. Jeanette has all the clothes and jewelry she ever needs and my baby Christine wants for nothing. I have the good luck of love and know it. I earn way over a million bucks a year, much more than we need to live on comfortably.

I'm fortunate enough to be able to take care of Jeanette's mother back in New York. She's a widow without anything, who worked all her life like a dog with nothing to show for it. She raised her family alone working in a retail store for some cheap bum who paid her in cash. So, in the end she has no Social Security, no insurance, no nothing—all she has is me. But, I don't mind, in fact I'm happy to do it, she's a wonderful woman. I put my younger brother in the construction business, he's a smart little guy that Sonny is. I gave him a couple of hundred thousand and so far he's turned it into a couple, maybe three million. What we don't spend I stash away for a rainy day. In my business, this is a must.

It's also a must that I have to be in shape. I'm slender and wiry and not big, but I have strength in my shoulders, upper-arms, and back. I work at it. I jog, I swim, and I have sex—lots of sex. I'm medium height, medium weight, and medium looks without any distinguishing features. I'm very common looking and have a face that can be easily forgotten. I'm always overlooked too. I mention this because it's another important factor. Maybe my stealthy movement is responsible for that. "Oh, Mikey!" Jeanette's always pleadin' with me. "Will you please clear your throat or something so I know you're around?"

She tells me that I'm just like a little kid. I laugh at her. I was born in the Bronx to parents who emigrated from Palermo in the sixties to open a pizza parlor. My father died in the middle of a double pepperoni to go, and my saintly mother, God rest her soul, left us a year later. My brother, Sonny, and I finished our childhood in foster homes—an experience so ridiculous that I hate even to think about it. I'm a dedicated family man who loves his wife and child deeply, but I do sleep around. I love women and believe there are different kinds of love. All right...all right...I know all you women out there are sayin' that's bullshit and don't buy into that philosophy, but that's the way it is with me. My life is a series of complications and a fella who does what I do needs some kind of release.

To me, I don't do anything wrong. Of course, the New York City Police Department, the Manhattan District Attorney's Office, the FBI, and especially Lt. Ring Sloane of the Broward County's Sheriff's Office in Fort Lauderdale all think differently. I figure in a few years I can retire—although I love what I do.

I'm Charlie the Plumber, I'm Jack the Gardner, I'm Joey the used car salesman and I'm—the good Lord be willin'—Mikey the Hat. My real name is Michael Candillucci, but they nicknamed me "The Hat" because I'm always in disguise when I do a caper.

My Mentor

Ft. Lauderdale, a few miles away, is where whites with money move to escape Miami and all those Latinos, Marioletto's, and fuckin' Haitians. That's why I got out of Miami. Lauderdale, now there's a great place for a thief to work amongst the people. I'm fortunate enough to have the personality to attract the ladies and the quiet nature to scope out where the good shit is at. I'm successful because I have a formula. Not that it's an original formula and I make no claim to being like Cary Grant the cat burglar in *To Catch A Thief*, but I do strive to be the best I can. All of my jobs are tightly orchestrated. I only take valuables that are insured so nobody gets hurt except for the real thieves, the insurance companies—the rat bastards that they are. In the army I trained with explosives, and I fine-tuned that skill into an art form. I can put just enough plastique on a safe to blow it open and not make a loud sound. I went to school to become a locksmith. My fingers are so nimble they can quickly feel the way to most any combination. I can duplicate any key from a Medlock, to the most complicated one for a safety deposit box.

The first thing I do when I plan a caper is to know everything about the people I'm going to rob. Who are they? Do they have the goods? When do they come and go from where they live? The second thing is to plan out everything in detail as to how I'll actually pull it off. I go through it step by step: when to go in and when to come out, alternative plans of escape, and finally, how to get rid of the goods. Very seldom do I sell it personally. Here's where you have to be very careful otherwise things can fall apart—fast. Burglars sometimes aren't as smart as you think they are.

When I was in the can, Lewisburg to be exact, I met the saint of all cat burglars, Joe Diamonds. He's a loner from the word go and a walking illustration of how to do it. He taught me everything I know: how to look on cops and security guards as the enemy, and if there's dogs involved, forget it. "Figure you're an ISIS terrorist and they're Special Forces," he says.

He shows me how important traffic patterns and the weather can be. The best time to rob someone is at night or when it's rainy—forget about bright, sunny days. Another good time is when there's a big party or wedding going on. They can be away, or even at their house during this time, while they're so busy socializing with their guests they never realize what else is going on.

This may be a totally upside down way of looking at the world and society, but it's how I first got started. It seems like the standard forms of behavior don't apply to me. In school they teach you to be honest and not cheat, but what happens when you get out? You find out that everyone cheats, lies, and steals, including a lot of cops and politicians, so it's good to understand their mentality. Joe also taught me to have tunnel vision and to concentrate on the business at hand—nothing else is important. He raised a finger at me and said, "Remember...nightclubbin' ain't important and forget about broads. That's all bullshit and doesn't count."

Joe influenced me tremendously to be constantly alert and relentless, although he lost me a little with the broad comment, but the man's a wizard. He taught me how to judge a jewelry store in seconds: pretty much disregard the little shops and those that have a lot of doors going in and out. The first thing you do when you go in is to act like you have a lot of money and ask to look at something expensive like a big diamond ring or large necklace. This will tell you how many people are employed and give you a chance to see where their vault is. Window displays will give you an idea of the range of jewelry they have. Size don't always mean a thing. Sometimes the best stores are the smaller ones that are beautifully designed with custom built furniture and handmade rugs, where a well-dressed clerk appears with a tray of expensive goods for you to examine. If you don't like what's on the tray, send them back for something else.

Joe Diamonds made a point of forgetting about all shops with security guards, whether they're dressed in a uniform or not. Silent alarm systems usually have a trick button in plain view to fool you into thinking that's what they're going press when they're in trouble, but the truth of the matter is the clerk will hit a hidden silent alarm button, which most times is outta sight on the floor by his foot. The silent alarms in display cases have to be deactivated before a salesperson can open them. And sometimes, if you're lucky, they forget to activate them again when they move to another counter.

The Man to See

In downtown Ft. Lauderdale, there's a restaurant called Sal's Charter Grill. Sal's not a big shot wise guy, but he is from the streets of New York and can settle an argument with an overhand right if he has to. Oddly enough the food in his restaurant is very good. He has an active lounge that gets going around twelve o'clock at night. Every booster, con guy, and fence that's anybody is there mingling with the regular customers and other patrons. Even Lt. Ring Sloane occasions the place. Sal knows everyone and everything besides all the old time entertainers—Frank and Dean, too! A big picture of Frank Sinatra hangs in the entrance signed by Frank. "To my Pal Sal, keep punchin'."

Sal is a word mangling storyteller and in New York he knows every human south of 52nd Street. If he goes north of there he gets dizzy. "The air's too clean up that way," he says.

He had persistent problems with the NYPD and decided to move south to Ft. Lauderdale. Within a short time, he established himself and could get you a line on anything or anyone in South Florida. Sal is one of my contacts. I am on a mission. I walk into his joint and see him behind the bar taking a liquor inventory. Without losing the bottle count he says in a heavy Nu Yawk accent. "Hiya, Mikey. How ya doin'?"

"Good but I need something."

"Yeah...what?"

"I'm lookin' to get a piece with a silencer. Can you help me out?"

Sal raises an eyebrow and slaps the bartop. "Son-of-a-bitch...I can't believe you asked me that. A guy was just in here lookin' to dump one."

"Where's he now?"

"I'll have to reach out for him. Gimme a couple a days."

"Sure...wadda ya think he wants for it?"

"About a G-note." Sal looks at me. "Mikey, let me ask you somethin'. I gotta guy, Bob Welch, who's lookin' for a cornflower blue sapphire. You ever hear of dem?"

"Of course, but they ain't easy to come by. Even when you have one, you can't be so sure that's what it is because they're so hard to identify, all colored stones are, but those are all but impossible. You almost have to be a gemologist."

Sal looks around and says, "He knows where one is."

"So?"

"So," he leans in and says in a mock whisper, "maybe I can introduce you to him and make a score."

"Maybe, but in the meantime see what you can do for me about the piece."

"Absolutely."

A Jeweler

Things got so bad with the fences that Joe Diamonds decided a long time ago to become a jeweler himself and break down his own swag. He convinced me to do the same and set me up with the jeweler that taught him. When I got out of Lewisburg, I went to work for Benny Hirsh for about six months. Benny has a small office in the Seybold Building in downtown Miami where he sells some bigger pieces discriminately, but his real shtick is watches and jewelry repair. Most of the important jewelers in Miami send their repair work to him—antique watches and especially Rolexes because he's an authorized Rolex dealer. He taught me how to break down jewelry, identify precious stones and reset them along with how to melt down gold and remake new settings.

I asked Joe Diamonds once, "When you go in to make a score, with all the phony synthetic stones around how do you tell the difference between them and the real diamonds?"

"Ooooh." He ran a hand over his mouth. "You gotta be so careful today."

And, of course, I was. Who the hell wants to rob a phony diamond? He taught me how to identify synthetic stones and real pearls. Diamonds if they look perfect through the loop they're probably phonies and pearls you rub across your teeth. If they're gritty, they're real. If they slide, throw them back, they're phony.

When Benny Hirsh finished with me I was a full-fledged jeweler. This is important. Now I could break down any piece of jewelry and never have to worry about it being identified.

Trouble

Early Sunday morning, I'm in the apartment I keep for cleaning up my swag jewelry when the phone rings. I pick it up and hear, "Mikey?"

"Yeah...who's this?"

"It's Laura," she says. "Mikey you've got to come over right away."

I hardly recognize her voice it's trembling so much. "Come where?"

"To my house." I look at my watch. It's ten-thirty in the morning.

"Meet me at the Rascal House at eleven," I say, "and we'll have breakfast."

"On motel row?"

"Yeah...the Rascal House."

"Okay, Mikey...I need your help—"

"All right, all right," I interrupt. "Don't worry about it. We'll talk about it there."

I thought things were going good for Laura, now what the hell is this all of a sudden? Laura is a hooker, but she doesn't have a slut's mentality. She told me she was giving it all up because she met the right guy. I walk through a light drizzle from the parking lot to the entrance of the Rascal House where she's standing under the canopy waiting for me. A gust of wind whips her skirt around revealing long, shapely legs. Laura is well built, the sort of build you see on a model, not an ounce of flab with an incredible face and long blond hair. She sees me and runs her hand through her hair, shifting her weight from one foot to the other. We go inside and sit at a table in the back. She's wearing rose scented perfume and a dress that clings in all the right places—beautiful.

A round-bellied waitress with bright orange hair waddles over and looks at Laura. "What's on ya plate today, honey?"

"I'm not eating...I can't...just a cup of coffee, please." Laura sighs and turns to me.

"Gimme a couple over easy with hash browns, toast dry and coffee, black."

Laura is visibly shaken and speaks in a low tone, like someone's close by listening. She has a tendency to be too verbal and looks like she needs a shot to calm her down, but it's too early for that.

"Mikey." She starts right in. "You have no idea of what hell I'm going through. I'm so upset, there seems to be no justice in this life. Just when everything is going right for me...this happens."

She grabs my hand and I can see she's struggling with something bad. I've known her for a long time. We have this chemistry between us. She starts to ramble on and it's obvious the situation must be serious.

"Look." I squeeze her hand back, interrupting her babble. "Take it easy, slow down. Why don't you tell me what your problem is and let me see if I can help you? And for crissake, don't leave anything out. If you want my help I gotta know the whole story from the beginning. Now go ahead...tell me everything."

As she begins, her body trembles. "I met Kevin socially... not through work. Oh, Mikey he's been so wonderful to me. We hit it off right away. In a matter of weeks he asked me to marry him. He's well off too, very well off. He started a small computer company with something about a chip and the stock market. I don't know about chips but...anyway now he's worth millions. One of my old tricks, you may have seen him around, Rodney? He's a private investigator, about fifty, six feet tall with thick black hair and heavy eyebrows. He specializes in brainwashing and mental destruction. In my case it's both, plus bribery."

"A rat bastard might be a good way to describe him." My face twists in disgust.

"Yes, that's right." Laura nods confidently. "He's a vermin in every sense of the word. Since I've been with Kevin, I've stopped working, but Rodney won't leave me alone. I plead with him but he won't listen. Somehow, he found out about Kevin and now he wants twenty-five thousand dollars to keep quiet or he's going to tell Kevin everything about me."

I'm transfixed at what she's saying, these things aren't done in my world. I start to fume, this is just plain wrong. "Son-of-a-bitch." I pound my fist on the table. "Where do these assholes come from? Laura, listen to me. You're a sitting duck for a guy like Rodney. Does this Kevin really love you and all that other happy horseshit?"

"Yes...oh yes."

"Well, then just tell him the truth...he's probably gonna find out anyway." That is if he didn't already know. Only a handful of women could pull off a dress like the one she's got on.

"Oh, I can't do that Mikey," Laura said, breathless. "I'm too afraid and I'll die if I lose him. He comes from a very moral family. His father is the pastor of a big church in Manhattan. It'll be too much for him to bear if they find out. Oh, Mikey, I don't know what to do." Her perfectly shaped chest quivers in her V-neck dress.

"Take it easy...take it easy." My hands bob up and down trying to comfort her, but she starts sobbing and a tear rolls down her cheek. I look around uncomfortably as the orange-haired waitress approaches the table with our order. I have a sickly smile on my face when she slams the eggs over to me and looks at Laura.

"You sure you don't want anything, honey?"

"No." Laura says trying to compose herself.

The waitress shoots me a dirty look. "Don't let 'em get to ya, honey. These guys are all alike." She throws a look at me and turns away.

I remain silent. "You see?" I wave a hand at the retreating waitress. "I'm always getting a bum rap. You got a number for this Rodney asshole person?"

The elation surging through Laura is visible. "Oh, Mikey, I knew you'd help me."

She scarcely knows what to say and finally throws her arms around me with a bear hug and hangs on. The voice of the waitress drifts over from the service stand as she speaks to another server. "Boy, we're such suckers. I should put a little poison in that guy's coffee and save her a lot of trouble right now. She seems like such a sweet kid."

The Rat

Riding home, I mull over the problem and make a decision. Some guys say one thing then do something else—not me. I stop at a payphone and dial a number. It rings. "Yeah," a rough voice answers.

"Smiley?"

"You got the wrong number buddy."

"Lissena me asshole...I got the right number."

"Who is this?"

I lean into the booth, forcing my voice into a low, mock whisper. "Right now let's just say I'm someone that's very close to you."

"I don't know what you're talking about."

"Lissena me...the party's over my friend. We're talking about Laura."

"Laura? Who Laura...the hooker? What do I know about her?"

"Way too much."

It's quiet a moment, and I hear the noise of a TV in the background. "She's a whore...that's what I know. What's your concern anyway?"

"My concern is that you owe me."

"I owe you? Who the hell are you, a cop?" His rough voice is edged with sarcasm.

"Lissena me, it don't matter who I am...you still owe me."

"What the hell are you talkin' about?"

Can't this guy get it through his thick skull? I lay it on heavy. "I'm talking about you bothering Laura. Now you're gonna pay me to protect her."

"Oh...yeah...right. You got some case."

"Five thousand."

"Five thousand?" Rodney's voice goes up. "Five thousand what?"

I begin speaking in a language that Rodney understands and he quickly realizes that the best thing to do is go along like he's going to make the payment. I figure that if he has any balls he's gonna insist on meeting me in person—then try to kill me.

"Why should I pay you?"

"Let's say that it's a form of insurance."

"Insurance for what?"

"Insurance that I don't nail your kneecaps to your front door.

I'm your ultimate nightmare, asshole. Trust me, I'll squash you like a bug."

There's a silence. "It'll take me a week to get that kind of money," he says in a low voice.

"I'll call you in three days. Oh, incidentally, Rodney, lissena me...if by some strange coincidence Laura's fiancé finds out that she's a hooker, forget about everything because there ain't enough money in the world to help you out then. You'll be toast."

"Yeah...yeah...yeah."

"Good...I'm glad we understand each other, because if you don't, it'll be too late. You're gonna wake up one morning and find yourself dead."

The Cornflower Blue

Sal corners me in his place Saturday night. "You remember Bob Welch, the cornflower blue guy? I told him what you said about the gemolo... something...gist or whatever."

"A what?" I smile.

"I don't remember what ya fuckin' called 'em. Ya know the guys that look at the stones...what the hell did ya call 'em?"

"A gemologist."

"Yeah, yeah that's right...a gemologist." A broad smile comes to Sal's face. "Anyway...he wants to meet ya."

"What do you know about him?"

"He's been coming around here for a couple of years and as far as I know he's all right. He knows where one of those stones is sittin' in a safe. Easy pickin's he says."

"All right I'll meet him."

I'm in disguise for the meeting that Sal sets up with Bob Welch. That's not only a change of name, but also a change of appearance just in case we accidentally meet later he won't be able to recognize me. This didn't just happen overnight. I worked at it a long time. The change of hair color is a wig. I use makeup and a completely different wardrobe. I even change the way I walk and the way I talk. It's like I'm an actor playing a role. I found a lingerie shop in Surfside that specialized in underwear fetishes.

"Good morning," I mumble to the salesperson. "Do you have anything that can make my wife's...you know." I point to my ass. "Look bigger...uh...here?"

"Yes, sir." She gives me a polite smile. "We call them fanny pads."

I buy a load. Elsewhere I purchase shoes with three-inch heels. That brings me up to six feet. It takes a few minutes to adjust when I first walk in them, but then I'm fine. In Wig World I buy every wig imaginable: wavy, long hair, kinky, and in a variety of all colors. I throw them away after every job. For makeup, I usually go to JC Penney where the prices are right. I watch to see how the saleswoman applies false eyelashes, paints on green eyeshadow, and places black beauty marks on her customers. I always buy loose fitting jackets and pants in medium blah colors, nothing that stands out. Sunglasses are effective, and contacts in different colors are a good way to throw someone off.

I arrive at the meeting early. My appearance is so deceptive even Sal doesn't recognize me. I walk up to him and say in my normal voice, "Whatsa matter, paly—don't you say hello to an old friend?

Sal's eyes narrow as he recognizes my voice. "Mikey...is that you?" He glares with a knowing smile at me.

"Yeah, it's me."

"Holy shit, Mikey? I'll be damned!" Sal's clenched fists drop to his hips. "I don't believe it. I never woulda made you out if you didn't talk to me. Welch ain't here yet?"

"You sure this guy is...solid?"

"I hope so." Sal shrugs. "I've known him a long time but you know I don't trust any of these wasps, so be careful."

"I understand."

I'm at the table in the rear drinking mango daiquiris when Sal brings Welch over and starts to introduce me but I put up my hand and stop him.

"We don't need any names, if that's OK with you?" I look at Welch. "We're all Sal's friends."

He nods in agreement then starts to tell me about the mark's apartment, all trivia: where this is, where that is. I cut him off.

"Lissena me. I only give a shit about important stuff like when the mark leaves his apartment. Do you have a key to enter the apartment? Is there a security system? If you can get the code that would be a big plus and, of course, where the safe is. Can you find out this information?"

Welch looks at me. "I can do better than that. I can tell you when he'll be out of the apartment and for how long...and where the safe is hidden that the stone is in."

"You can?" I keep my manner reserved.

"Yeah, but that's all I can do," Welch says. "You'll have to gain access into his apartment and break into the safe yourself. I only want the cornflower blue. You can keep the rest and believe me there'll be plenty. Can you do that?"

"Yeah...and you only want the cornflower blue?"

"He screwed me out of it. He's a no good lying cheat, that doctor is."

"What kind of doctor is he?" Sal asks.

"Who knows? I never asked him." His hands go out with a blank expression on his face.

The Caper

When I do a caper, I never come and go from my house dressed in disguise. I use an apartment for this purpose where it's very secluded. I always swipe a nondescript small car, easily available at airport parking lots. I'll wait for a party that's departing with a lot of luggage, indicating they'll be gone for a while. I'll always tag the title of that auto to my disguise with a name and phony ID, just in case I'm forced to use it. I have all the duplicate forms, IDs and papers, even a Polaroid and lamination press set up so I can put my picture on IDs to make it all look realistic. I make up a background scenario for my disguises. For example, for Sal's friend's caper I'm Benjamin Flowers, born in a farming community near Charlotte, North Carolina, named Cumbleton. I graduated Boone College, just recently moved to Ft. Lauderdale, and until something comes in from one of the ad agencies I've applied to, I'm looking for a waiter's job because my funds are low.

Getting out of a disguise is a lot faster than getting into one. I take my time and do a good job and presto here I am, Benjamin Flowers, the nice guy from North Carolina and you know what—I love it. I can handle both identities easily and do everything that has to be done.

I take it slow driving up to Hillsboro Beach, a little community north of Pompano, to the doctor's apartment building. He lives in a high-rise complex he owns right on the ocean. I arrive early and park across the street in a parking lot on the intracoastal. With my binoculars, I can see clearly into every car that comes out of the underground parking garage. Welch gave me the name and a picture of the doctor. He's such a goofy looking bastard, there's no mistaking him. So here I am for twenty minutes slouched in a cheap rental car, when I spot an old Cadillac pulling out. My first reaction is that it can't be the doctor's car. He wouldn't be driving a bucket of bolts that old, but just for sure I look anyway and in the middle of my binoculars I see a freckled faced, red-headed goof, grinnin' like a hyena—it's the doctor. I gotta laugh. Sal's friend told me he would be driving an older car, but this is old. I mean old. Well, I'm thinkin' he must be an eccentric.

The condo apartment is what real estate people call "prime property." Among other things, his apartment is the penthouse of this magnificent building that's right on the ocean—one of a kind to say the least—the whole top floor. I cross the street and enter the underground parking garage and get into the elevator. I press the penthouse button, but nothing happens. I press the button of the floor beneath it and the elevator engages. I leave the elevator, go to the fire exit and walk up one flight, pick the lock, and enter the hall of the penthouse level. A window in the rear is slightly open, this tells me the alarm isn't set. I quickly lift the window and climb in. Slowly I make my way to where the safe is. I can't help but take in the magnificent apartment. It has a gigantic sunken living room with a huge flagstone fireplace against the wall. I see a spotless custom kitchen off to the side stuffed with fancy equipment, plus more rooms than I can count. I continue toward the doctor's bedroom in the back. The silence is broken by the sound of footsteps. "Who are you?" bursts into the air.

"Holy shit." A chill shoots up and down my spine and I feel my skin prickle.

She stands there dreamily and the gaze from her half-opened eyelids covers me from head to toe. It's a moment or two before I can speak, but I quickly regain my composure. She's gorgeous and has the body of a showgirl. "I'm a friend of Doctor Jordan," she says.

She notices I'm wearing latex gloves. "Oh...what happened to your hands?" Her speech is slow like she's in a fog. There's another moment of silence and her eyes continue to stare into mine.

"Allergies, I have allergies," I say. "That's what the doctor is treating me for."

"Oh...is that what he does?"

I reluctantly return her smile. She isn't tall, but looks tall. Her makeup is flawless and her beautiful blue eyes are bloodshot. "I just met him. I didn't know."

I can see she's a party girl. "He's letting me and my girlfriend stay here for a couple of days." She wobbles a little. "You wanna do a line with me?" Her sad eyes glance toward the bedside table.

A bowl of coke rests on the table, half empty. "Yeah...sure." I look around wildly. "I'll be right back. The doctor wants me to do something for him in his bedroom. I'm gonna close the door now, okay?"

"Okay." She slurs the word into a melancholy little song.

This has gotta be quick. I crack open the safe and for sure Sal's friend was right. There it is...the cornflower blue sapphire, a small but perfect gem. In the light, the star jumps right out at you and there's more than enough jewelry in the safe to make me happy. Within minutes I'm back in my car. I turn the key in the ignition and the engine roars to life. I put it in gear and drive off casual as you please with a smile on my face. "Wanna do a line with me?" I say to myself.

Bad Break

The next day I stop by the Charter Grill and give the cornflower blue to Sal. Two days later, the world gets flipped upside-down. I'm in the kitchen fixing a cup of coffee, when there's banging on the door. I'm not expecting anyone. Like an idiot, I open up to find two cops staring at me.

A grin spreads from ear to ear across Lt. Ring Sloane's face. "Well, well...if it ain't Mikey the Hat." His voice is metallic. "For years I've been waiting for this. You've always been one step ahead of us but now, my friend, things look different. Now it looks like we're one step ahead of you. You are under arrest on charges of burglary, unlawful entry and distributing stolen merchandise." He turns and shakes his head. "Read him his rights, Gallagher."

I feel like wilting when I'm handcuffed and taken into custody. It isn't until late afternoon that I'm arraigned and the judge sets the bond at five hundred thousand dollars. I'm out in two hours. The next morning I'm in my lawyer Dave Goodhart's office, and he immediately goes for the phone and stabs a button. "Hold all my calls, Stephanie... until I tell you."

"How did they come to me, Dave?" I glare at him.

Goodhart ponders for a time. "It seems when Dr. Jordan was robbed he told the cops that a guy named Bob Welch set him up and that he would have his cornflower blue sapphire in his possession."

"Fer crissake." I have to contain my anger.

Goodhart continues nonchalantly, "Then they went to Welch's home with a search warrant and found the cornflower blue sapphire ring. Lt. Sloane gets him quivering in his pants and he rolls over. He's willing to testify that he told you where the doctor's jewelry was and all he wanted in return was the sapphire ring. They got him to identify you from a mug shot. Think about it, Mikey...unless you can prove you were in Boo Boo Africa or somewhere like that, it'll be better for us to plea bargain now for a lighter sentence."

"He's full of it. He could never identify me."

"I spoke to Sloane who said the guy who did this is a real pro. There were no signs of forcible entry, no fingerprints, and he claims the bimbo they have as a witness was too stoned to give them any details about a man who apparently was in the apartment at the time—a perfect crime if there ever was one," Goodhart continues. "If it wasn't for the doctor telling him about

Welch's passion for the cornflower blue, the case never would have been cracked. They also have Sal, the owner of the Charter Grill, as a target of the investigation but he's denying everything, of course. He knows nothing about a ring, but rather claims that Welch wanted to borrow some money from him and he refused so that's probably why Welch is making the claim—said he got rude about it too and almost had to call the cops because he was afraid Welch might get violent and beat him up."

I have to laugh at Sal. Calling the cops...that's a good one. My moods are swinging. One minute I feel good and figure there's no way I can get nailed, the next I'm cursin' and crackin' my knuckles over goin' to trial and losin'. Goodhart tells me there's no way I can beat this rap—even if I didn't do it, they'll frame me.

"Let me see if I got you straight." My eyes focus on Goodhart. "The cornflower blue sapphire ring puts me on the spot. All they have is Welch's testimony—the testimony of someone given immunity. Because of Sloane's persistent questioning, Welch finally confesses that Sal, from the Charter Grill, provided him with the thief that broke into the doctor's apartment and in return he's given the sapphire ring for the lead. From the description of the thief's height and demeanor, Sloane determines that the thief is none other than me, so Sloane provides a mug shot to Welch who identifies it as me. How else can he do that? He never saw my real face. I was always in disguise when I met him. What a crock of shit."

"It'll be Welch's word against yours and who cares?" Goodhart frowns.

Something in the air has changed my luck. There isn't much I can do to reach Welch, but there is one thing I can do and that's what I do best—go in and nab the stone. Without that evidence, they have no case. All I have to do is break into the property room of the Broward County Sheriff's office and steal my file and the evidence. Not a particularly big deal I think, but it's hard to concentrate on a plan because of the way my mind keeps drifting back to Laura and the way she looked that morning at the Rascal House. I know it sounds weird but I promised Laura to keep this snake off of her back. I can't let that scumbag Rodney ruin Laura's life. If the truth gets out it'll be all over for her. It's a terrible situation and her fear is easy to understand. In fact, it's getting to me—sort of an angry misery that keeps naggin' at me. The difficulty is trying to remember what comes first, her heartaches or my own hard luck story? It's like a mission, but I know that before I can help her I have to help myself. It'll take me a couple of days to figure out how I'm going to proceed with the plan to break into the sheriff's office.

Finally Sal connects me with Eugene, an embittered former sergeant, who was with the Broward County Sheriff's Office. He had been a dedicated policeman for the Sheriff's Department for seventeen years, then one day he was set up as the fall guy in a sex scandal and given an ultimatum: resign or be indicted. The man is pissed, and for some good money he gives everything up to me. Detailed descriptions of where the file and property rooms are, plus employee shifts and recommended times to go in. He reconstructs a floor plan and tells me how to access the building. Geez, I can't ask for more than that.

"The best time to go in," he says, "is about 4 a.m. Nobody's around then except for security, and they're usually sleeping or watching TV."

I make the decision to go in as soon as possible, disguised as a maintenance man. The Broward Sheriff's Office is located in downtown Ft. Lauderdale behind City Hall. It's one of several buildings right outside of the business district. On bicycle I get close, about three blocks away, then go the rest of the way on foot, nice and slow. I pause on the corner, glance around and see no one. I look up at the lightning zigzagging around some angry clouds. Jesus! This is all I need now, for it to start raining. Then, just like that, another flash of lightning comes out of the sky and thunder starts rumbling. About two seconds later, I feel a few scattered raindrops—shit. I should have known, this ain't my night. Soon I'll be in the parking lot of the sheriff's office.

It's a big building with louvered shutters and it's dark in the rear. By the time I run through the rain to the locked rear doorway, I'm soaking wet. To gain entry I use a wire and go up the back stairs—it's pitch dark. Eugene was right though, somehow the department never kept a bulb in the stairwell. My flashlight guides me past three floors of offices to the fourth floor landing, to a door that leads to where I'm going.

Alone in the detectives' offices, I start searching through the files. It isn't long before I find mine along with a four-foot rap sheet including ten aliases, seven social security numbers, and five different birth dates. I've been up on every charge imaginable but murder. I come across a memo Lt. Ring Sloane has written to the FBI about me. I shift uncomfortably as I read it. It states that a high-ranking member of an organized crime family, who's in protective custody, has told him that I was a made member of the Gambino crime family. That dirty rat bastard, Sloane. I'm thinking after all the trouble I went through to not connect myself to the mob, this bastard lies to the Feds and puts me right in the middle pretty good, the lyin' prick that he is.

I'm so engrossed in reading the memo I almost didn't hear the elevator bell ring when the door opens. I recover quickly. Who the hell can this be now? It's three-thirty in the morning for crissake. I hear footsteps coming down the hall and slide behind a file cabinet. I still have a good view from inside the room through a glass window. My mouth is dryer than anyone can imagine. To my astonishment, it's the maintenance man. He wasn't due in for over another hour. The son-of-a-bitch is actually coming in early. He must be a thief himself. I'm thinkin' *why is he here now?*

He has a tool box and starts repairing the floor buffer right outside the office. I can't take a chance he'll see me so I force myself to be patient and soundlessly lean in to watch him finish. After he leaves I move into the property room. The simple lock affords me quick entry. I shine my flashlight around the glassed-in room, which has half opened blinds. I wait a second to compose myself then begin to search for the cornflower blue sapphire. I examine the evidence boxes carefully. It's slow and tedious work. The rows of boxes seem endless. Ten minutes later I'm still looking when I hear a noise. At past four in the morning, a man who does my kind of work has a very high level of energy. I press myself up against the wall, behind a file cabinet, and to my surprise I see a uniformed police sergeant coming into the room holding boxes.

He goes to the opposite wall and puts the boxes on a table.

What the hell is going on here? Now I take another look across the room and I'm dumbfounded. Holy shit—it's Lt. Ring Sloane coming through the door. A dim light outlines him and the box he's carrying. I take a quick breath and hold it. My heart hits the floor. This is becoming a ridiculous nightmare. My brain is spinning.

"I could get my ass reamed for this, Sloane," the Sergeant says.

"Yeah...well don't worry about it," Sloane answers. "I saved your ass plenty of times."

"Which file did you want?"

"Bob Welch's"

"Okay, here it is."

The sergeant hands the evidence box over to Sloane. He goes through it and takes out the cornflower blue sapphire ring. Then he starts switchin' it out with another stone. What a break this is for me. I'll bring this out at the trial and the case will be dismissed. Without the real gem sapphire there is no case. Sloane doesn't know it, but he's doing me a favor. I'm jumping for joy inside. Sloane takes out a penknife and slowly begins to loosen the prongs that hold the stone. He begins to work the blade in deeper against the setting, trying to be careful to do as little damage as possible. As soon as he replaces the stone he gives it back to the sergeant who leaves. I hear another noise and my heart beats faster. *Who the hell is it now?* It's gettin' to be like Grand Central Station in here. It strikes my funny bone and I start grinnin' a little. Two apples come walkin' into the property room and Sloane's face turns serious.

"Lt. Sloane?"

"Yeah."

"I'm Gerry Lancaster, DEA and this is...well, you might better know him as Digger. He works undercover for us, so you can speak freely. Our mutual friend said you wanted to see me."

Sloane doesn't answer and takes a step back. He wipes the sweat off his upper lip with his fingers.

"You okay?" Lancaster says.

Sloane nods. "Let's get to it. I want some little prick off the streets."

"Okay, who is it?" Lancaster replies. "Anyone we know?"

"Mikey Candillucci, he's known as Mikey the Hat. Something else, Bob Welch, the one we've got testifying against him at trial... he's one of your informers right?"

"Right."

"We ain't gonna have a problem with him backing out are we?"

"No chance of that." A slow smile spreads over Lancaster's face.

These rotten bastards, I thought. They must have stool pigeons behind every lamppost.

Sloane goes on. "I need some horse to plant in Mikey's car. We need to send him away for good. That's why I asked you here. Can you get me the right kind of heroin—uncut, the real China white—enough to show that he's a dealer. Can you do that?"

"Sure we can." Lancaster's eyes sparkle. "But understand, we have to make the bust."

"Absolutely. We'll coordinate that."

At last the truth dawns on me. What vultures they are. They shake hands and leave. These guys are so secretive that half the time their bosses don't even know what's going on, and the other half, they don't care. All they care about are arrests. It's at this moment I first think about killing Sloane. If I had a pistol then I would have killed the both of them. I wish I'd done it—finding these guys shot dead in the sheriff's office in the morning would have been something. Besides that, it's what they deserve.

They leave and Sloane has my file with him. I know I'm gonna have nightmares over this. Nobody's ever gonna believe me. I wish I had a tape recorder. I'm still stuffed behind a file cabinet, laying low. It is so quiet I can hear the sweat running down my back.

When it's clear, I make my way back out into the parking lot, but stop short. What's that? Another noise? I think I see a dark figure, might be a cleaning man? I'm not sure and in a second it's gone. I decide to wait, but maybe I shouldn't, maybe this is a mistake. I hold my breath for a long time. Nothing...it's nothing.

Shit...I'm getting paranoid. I gotta get a grip on myself. We got a Murphy's Law goin' on here. I start to get a bad feeling, there's just too many things happening. It's got me worryin' that I'm gonna run into someone on the way out. Everything is becoming more than it actually is. Bad things come in bunches, especially at times like this—in the middle of the night—in the dark. I'm thinkin' about how I should have done things differently and now, of all things, I start thinking about this fuckin' Rodney and how he's really starting to bug me. In the dark he becomes a bigger rat than ever to me.

A muffled sound rustles nearby, giving me a sinking feeling. I know exactly what it is. I realize the odds of getting out of the parking lot are against me and the only thing that can help me now is a miracle. My head comes up and I feel a hot flash. I blink, rub my forehead then look up at a cop. *What did I get myself into?*

"Put your hands up," a cop shouts. "Police."

"Aw shit!" Everything is different. I'm in the middle of a nightmare and I feel the blood throbbing in my head, my mind shouts for me to make a run for it. I might make it, but who knows—I'm dead meat.

"Fuck it." I shudder and raise my hands over my head. He handcuffs me and takes me into custody. Jesus. I'm so major depressed there are no words I could use to describe the way I feel.

Unfinished Business

I'm arraigned for trespassing. It's a miracle Goodhart got me out on bail again, he found a loophole—they didn't read me my rights. I've got four weeks before my trial date and for sure I'll be convicted. Four weeks to get my life in order and set up Jeanette and my beautiful baby, Christine. Clear the calendar. So what is my calendar? I ain't gonna be goin' to jail if I can help it I'll tell ya. Jail is a hellhole and not for me. I was there before. I know once I'm in the can, this time, they'll be working to keep me in. As a last resort, I'll take my chances on the lam.

Laura has no idea of my situation. She asks me to come to her apartment. After leading me into the living room, she sits next to me on the sofa, her large soulful eyes looking up at me for help. She looks like an angel, so young and helpless. My arms come up and go around her. I want to protect her from this asshole that's hounding her.

"Any news about Rodney yet?" she asks, the strain of anxiety evident on her face.

"Yeah." My voice is low.

"You contacted him?" She kneels down beside me, and trembling, grabs my hand. "What did he say? Oh, please Mikey, tell me."

Any bad news would be devastating to her already fragile state, so I just tell her that I made a date for a meeting next week. In the meantime, I assure her he won't talk. I kiss her forehead and she stops trembling. In Laura I see a saddened woman before me. I want her to be stronger, but somehow I realize more fully now how deeply this situation touches her. I know if she loses her fiancé, her life will be over. Silently she's begging me to do the impossible. I can't deny that I'm determined to see this out, no matter what it takes. I'm living in a strange, unreal world between a happy carefree family man and the secret life of a burglar, which I believe can go on forever. I remind myself that nothing ever does and consider the situation. I know that Laura is counting on me. She trusts me and the little comfort she gets now is from believing I'm looking out for her. It's funny...because I'm the one in the Bermuda Triangle and am thinking I need someone to help me out.

Doing It Right

"Hello...this is your friend again," I say blunt into the phone. "Talk to me."

Rodney is instantly defensive. "I'm ready to drop this off...just tell me where."

"Lissena me...no drop offs buddy." I'm adamant about this. "You gotta deliver the package in person. You and I are gonna have a heart-to-heart."

"Tell me where and when."

"You know where Markham Park is?"

"I think so...off 595?"

"Yeah...I'll meet you there tomorrow at 3:30 in the afternoon. Wait at one of the picnic tables in parking lot number five. I know what you look like...I'll find you. Lissena me, if you decide to get cute or try anything, believe me you won't live out the week. I know where you live."

There's nothing more to say. I know Rodney still has the receiver up to his ear and I want him to hear the click when I hang up. I want him to stew over what I said.

At Sal's Charter Grill

I estimate Sal's age to be about sixty-five. Years ago he had a handsome face. His teeth are still all his, although a little yellow now, and his smile is still knowing and a little secretive. When I ask him how he is, he says that his nose is getting' bigger, his earlobes are growin' larger, and his balls are droopin' about two inches lower than they were a few years ago. I've heard his stories more than a few times. "The silencer?" I ask.

"I got it for ya." Sal's voice lights up. "And it comes with a pistol too."

"Ooh, that's good."

"Follow me."

Sal jumps up, spry for his age, and I follow him to his office in the back. He pulls up a chair for me to sit on. Behind his small desk he opens a drawer, pulls out a box, and places it on the desk. He opens the lid and two pistols with silencers and bullets to match gleam in the light of his desk lamp. They are Berettas, nine millimeter parabellums with magazines that hold eight. What beauties—just what I was looking for.

"You're the man, Sal. What do I owe you?"

"Nuttin...take 'em. Consider it my gift to you."

"Thanks, but I can't do that."

"Mikey...after all I put you through with that piece a shit Welch I feel responsible. Go ahead and take 'em."

"Are these pieces hot?"

"Stone cold...untraceable."

"I'll take them both." I reach into my pocket and pull out a wad of bills and peel off twenty C notes and plunk them down on the desk.

"Mikey...don't do this." Sal sounds a little disappointed.

"I have to."

"Why?"

"Because Sal, when I want something from you I want you to know that it's for the money. You get me? No freebies—no any other or I'll pay ya laters. With me it'll always be for the money up front...you'll never get screwed."

"Okay...I get ya." Sal leans in. "Ya know somethin' Mikey?" His voice drops down to a whisper. "You're beautiful."

The Meet

The next day, I put on coveralls like the park caretakers wear. I raise my head and hold it upright as I put contacts in—a special pair that resemble cat's eyes. I glance into the mirror and I'm riveted. I look awesome. The bizarre look on my face would unnerve anyone. This Rodney is gonna shit. I lower my eyes and feel a twitch in my nose.

This is one of my best disguises yet. I'm pleased. I place the pistol with the silencer in a shoulder bag and adjust the strap. I have to hold the pistol in the bag, ready to use, yet it has to look normal. Sheltered by the trees in the park, I can watch anyone who walks on the trail up to this spot. I also have a good view from this height in the parking lot. I make sure I'm here early and enjoy the advantage of being first. It's a nice part of the park, very quiet. I close my eyes and listen. It's so restful, so peaceful, it's nice to relax and daydream for a change. A few cars roll slowly into the parking lot. I glance at my watch. It's a few minutes before three o'clock. I'm convinced that everything is proceeding smoothly and that Rodney will be on his way here, I'll be five thousand richer and Laura's situation will be taken care of. But, it isn't to be. I wait and wait, but Rodney never shows.

First Things First

The minute I walk in the house, the phone rings. It's Goodhart. He isn't going into details, but the picture is clear enough. If I'm not willing to help myself, what can he do? The next morning I'm in his office.

"You couldn't leave well enough alone could you?" Goodhart's eyes narrow. "You had to go in there and take a shot. What's the matter with you?"

"That's the million dollar question," I answer.

"I know." Goodhart smirks. "It always is with you. So where does this leave us now? What kind of life is this going to be for your family?"

I'm silent. Anything I might answer would sound too brainless. I'm ready to take my medicine. Goodhart expects an outburst of anger or some kind of display of despair, but I won't give him the satisfaction. I simply shrug my shoulders, fold my hands on my lap, and stare at him.

"I'm sorry," he says. "Look, you have no choice but to plead guilty, and now is the time before the case begins. Let me do it... say yes. If you don't let me go in and negotiate with them you'll be going to prison for a long, long time—longer than you have to." He hounds me, almost shouting.

"All right...keep ya shirt on, will ya?"

Goodhart's anxiety is visible. "You're a psycho...you know that?" He stands up from behind his desk. "Mikey, besides being your lawyer, I'm your friend, you son-of-a-bitch. I love you, but I'm telling you the judge is not going to be swayed by sentiments of any kind if we go to trial. But now, and I mean right now, there's a chance I'll get you a lower sentence."

"I see." I hesitate, reluctant to agree. "What kind of a deal can you get for me?"

It takes all morning and a ton of coffee to figure it out, but Goodhart's argument finally convinces me that I have no chance of winning in court. Fuck it. I decide to plead guilty for a lesser sentence.

"The State always wins in these kinds of cases. The defendant? Only about two percent of the time," he says. "It's just the fact of the matter."

The Sentence

In Florida State Criminal Court at sentencing Friday the 13th, I stand up before the judge, hesitate briefly then plead guilty.

The judge acknowledges me then starts to speak. "Michael Candillucci, being accepted a plea of guilty, this court sentences you to a maximum sentence of seven years in a Florida State Penitentiary. You will hereby be remanded and taken into custody to begin serving your sentence. Do you have anything to say?"

"Yes, I do your honor." I smile my way into an explanation. "It's my tenth wedding anniversary this Sunday. Your Honor, may I please be allowed to stay out on bond to celebrate it with my wife and family? I won't see my little girl for a lot of years, Your Honor. They're the only thing I've got left. I'd like to be with them this Sunday for the last time, then turn myself in on Monday. If you can find it in your heart, it's only an extra day. Please, your Honor."

The prosecutor shoots out of his chair. "We vigorously object, Your Honor."

The judge looks over his spectacles at him then asks, "Was the witness hostile toward the prosecution or the State Attorney's office at any time?"

"No, Your Honor."

"Did he agree to plead guilty and save the State the cost of a trial?"

"Yes, he did, Your Honor."

"Then I'm going to overrule your objection and allow the defendant to turn himself in on the 16th of the month, this Monday."

"Yes...Your Honor." The prosecutor nods wistfully.

"You've got balls, Mikey," Goodhart murmurs softly shaking his head. "I'll give ya that."

On The Lam

Ever since my arrest, my nerves have been strung out. I lay awake every night asking myself am I sure I've covered all my bases. Then I start thinking how did I get myself in this position? Everything was going so good for me, what happened? I was riding high—a great home life, a great wife and kid, and great girlfriend. Plenty a scores, plenty a broads, then it all starts to fall apart. I couldn't help but think that it all began with helping Laura out with something that had no personal gain in it for me whatsoever. My world started crumbling because I was just doin' a favor. It's as simple as that. It's all like a bad dream.

My decision to become a lamister is final. I move around my bedroom slowly, lookin' for the right size suitcase which I find almost immediately. I open the drawers to choose some clothes to take and my attention falls on some photographs. I hold the pictures of Jeanette and our little baby, memorizing them, before placing them back down. It doesn't take me long to collect a few things to wear: two pair of pants, one suit, and half a dozen shirts to match. I grab several pair of shoes—all comfortable ones.

It's difficult to decide what jewelry to take. A watch, a couple of rings. All these are more sentimental than actually valuable, although the watch is a Tudor. Then my underwear and shaving things. After I lock the suitcase, I take it and put it in the garage in a storage cabinet. Only Sonny knows where it is. Sunday night on the way to the Charter Grill for our anniversary party I whisper to Jeanette. "When I get out, we'll make a new life."

She turns her head and looks at me. I smile and her eyes twinkle. "Yes, Mikey. A new life...will I be part of it?"

You could've knocked me over with a feather."What are you talking about?" Something's wrong with Jeanette. I finally pump it out of her.

"You're going to leave me, aren't you Mikey? You found someone else." Jeanette says on the verge of tears.

Like I need this now. I want to throw up. This is a low blow. I can't imagine what in the world she's talking about. I can't even believe she'd think I'd leave her.

"You think I'm nuts?" I reply. "You're all I got left, you and the baby. I need you to stick by me now on this. You're my million-dollar baby for crissake...why you talking like this? What happened? I wanna know."

"Last night, I answered your cell phone when you were in the shower. I thought maybe it would be an important call, but it was a girl...she was crying asking for you. She said she had to reach you. She knew I was your wife but it was important and that you and her are doing some business together and without you her life will be nothing. She won't be able to go on. Do you love her, Mikey?"

My head shakes back and forth. Holy shit, it's nothing but heartaches for me. I see a roadside flower cart and stop the car and jump out. I carefully look at all the flowers then raise a pot to my nose and slowly inhale the aroma of a rose. I buy it and get back in the car, smile, and give it to Jeanette.

"If you take care of this rose plant like you did me, it'll last forever or until I see you again, which will be sooner than you think."

The car fills up with the aroma of the rose. It's intoxicating and she places the plant between us. I know she likes the gesture.

"Jeanette, don't ever think I'd fall out of love with you for some other woman. The girl that called you is a hooker and it's true what she said, but all I'm doing for her is a favor—no romance whatsoever. I swear to you on our baby Christine's eyes. Honey, believe me that's all that it is—a favor. You believe me don't you?"

Jeanette's smile is slow and timid. "I should believe you, shouldn't I?"

"Damn right."

She leans over and gives me a big soft kiss on the cheek, but I know she doesn't believe me. I look in the rear view mirror and notice that a van is following us. They're feds. We arrive at the restaurant and I make sure everyone sees me throwing the keys to the parking attendant then slowly walk inside.

Sal gives me a big hug. "Here's the man himself." He escorts us to our table. Up to now, except for the trial, it all seems a game and I'm always winning. The narrow escape from New York, my early release from prison, all my capers, my risky selling of jewelry has always gone well and there's plenty of money in offshore accounts. Now for just doing a favor for an old friend, a hooker no less, my wife thinks I'm cheating on her. Geez.

Sonny Boy, my brother and all his millions in New Jersey, obtained the finest appeal lawyers for me but still, the writing is on the wall. There's no question about it. If I stay here I'm going to spend a lot of time in jail.

"How this ever could have happened to you, I'll never know." Sonny Boy shakes his head. "I'm so pissed the way the guy fingered you. I get the blues just thinking about it."

"Sonny, it's a little late for that now. I did a stupid thing and it backfired, and the bottom line is I can only blame myself." I grin. "But wait till we hit 'em with the surprise, I'd love to be there to see the expression on their faces."

"You're abso-fuckin'-lutely right," Sonny says. "I'll be there and let you know—the cocksuckers."

All this seems to be for nothing. Poor Laura, she'll get messed up anyway that's for sure. The cops are unfair. Lt. Sloane is unfair and life itself ain't exactly a bowl of cherries. I sip my whiskey and thoughtfully look at Sonny over the rim of the glass. Time is running out. I know I can't tell Jeanette that I've decided to run. They woulda' burned me for sure if they got me in the slammer. I took my chances with the law and this is the way it has to play out. I motion my head and Sonny moves to the back of the restaurant by Sal's office...I am not about to make any sudden moves. I know there's a team of cops having dinner in the restaurant watching my every move even though Sal put them at a table that's hard for them to see me.

"Jeanette," I say. "I don't want you to stay at home. I think it's good for you to go out and get a job. I'm not trying to talk you into anything, it's your decision to make. You don't have to if you don't want to, but it's all right with me." I'm doing small talk here, biding time.

"I'll do whatever you want me to, Mikey." Her eyes fill with tears as the impact of the situation finally hits her.

"Gimme a kiss, baby." I start feeling depressed myself. "I love ya more than life."

She turns and gently kisses my lips, a short kiss but a sweet one. "I love you, Mikey," she says. "I love you so much."

My eyes are drawn to the back again. The minute hand is counting down the time. I squeeze her hand and get up. "I'll be right back," I head toward Sonny. "Well, maybe not right back I mutter to myself, but back for sure."

Vengeance Is Mine

I look at Sonny. "It's time to rock and roll. I'll wait to hear from you. I want you to do me a favor, as soon as they see I'm gone they'll grab the house, all the bank accounts and the safety deposit box too...right?"

"Of course."

"Don't go anywhere near the safety deposit box."

"Why?"

"Because I want them to find the two envelopes I left in there for my friend Lt. Ring Sloane."

"You did what?" Sonny cringes.

"Yeah. You heard me right, and a note written out to you."

"A note to me? What does it say?"

"It goes like this:

Dear Sonny,

I'd rather just disappear than grow old and gray in prison. Here are two envelopes with twenty thousand in each. Make sure Lt. Ring Sloane of the Broward County Sheriff's Office gets one and tell him the other one is for his DEA buddies Gerry Lancaster and Digger. This is their payoff for not framing me in a drug rap.

"Jesus H Christ." Sonny grins from ear to ear. "That's a lot of money, but it's worth it, you're brilliant."

"Who knows whether it's enough, but it'll certainly fuck him up with his department and the Feds. The prick really deserves to get whacked."

I slip into my disguise, then out the back door into a waiting car in the alley and turn the key. I pull out through the rear alley and work my way in and out of traffic toward I-95 heading south.

I'm alone, wearing my new wig. It's a wavy, blue-black color and looks good on me. Sonny had picked up my suitcase and put it in the trunk. I'll pick up more stuff along the way. The wigs and the ID kit are the most important things I need, that and my makeup kit. Continuing south, I keep to the speed limit, frustrated watching the speeding cars fly by. In a few minutes I'll turn off of I-95 and head east.

All of a sudden it hits me like a thunderbolt and I make an unexpected left turn onto Biscayne Boulevard, heading north toward Aventura. I remind myself there is only one course of action left. This Rodney dude is a first class rat and all I want is to finish what I started out to do, which is to stop him from ruining Laura's life. Although it seems pointless now, I couldn't help myself. I know where Rodney's apartment is and pull into his parking lot. I get out of the car with the insane idea of killing him. I retrieve my silencer from my shoulder bag in the trunk and walk to the rear of his building. Getting in is easy—the lock is old fashioned. I make my way in, scurry up two flights of stairs, and slink into the hallway. I never act this impulsively, and I'm amazed by it. I draw several deep breaths and hope my prey is home. I stand motionless before Rodney's door, silencer steady in my hand as I pound on the door in three sharp raps.

"Who is it?" A voice rings out.

I can tell it's Rodney's. My face breaks out in a sly grin. You can almost keep time by the beat of my heart.

"Maintenance, sir."

"Who?"

"Maintenance man, sir, I'm here to change your air conditioning filter."

A voice comes up from behind the door saying. "Now? You must be kidding? It's too late, come back tomorrow."

"It'll just take a minute, sir."

Rodney mumbles something inaudible and opens the door. Without a moment's hesitation I shove the door open and press the silencer against Rodney's shocked face and he blurts, "What the fuck is this?"

"Here's what it is, asshole." With that, I swipe the pistol across

Rodney's face and send him to the floor then kneel down beside him and squeeze off a round that shatters his knee. Rodney clutches his leg and wails.

"That's for Laura."

I then press the silencer against Rodney's other knee and squeeze off another round, "That one's for me. I'm letting you live because I wanna see you suffer but if I hear one more word outta your mouth about Laura I'll be back to finish you off for good no matter where you are. You got that, asshole?"

I leave Rodney on the floor in a bloody heap and make my way back to the car, quickly disappear into the darkness, and proceed to the intracoastal and onto the Castaway's dock. Waiting there for me there is a chartered boat that Sonny arranged to get me out of the States and to an island in the Bahamas. Just a routine night fishing charter—that's all it appears to be. The only consolation I have, is that I took a clumsy crime and turned it into a work of art.

The night is warm and the wind comes up from the south. The charter boat slowly chugs its way out through Haulover Inlet. I open the door of the cabin and shuffle outside to the aft deck and sit in the fighting chair. I lift one leg, then the other foot onto the footrest and sit immobilized with a double whiskey in my hand—then it hits me.

"Holy shit...I forgot to kiss the baby goodbye." My face turns sullen. "Damn..."

The corners of my mouth turn down and a faint look of depression crosses my face. I gaze out over the water. Somehow the Miami Beach skyline looks different at night. I'm there a long time after the lights of the skyline that shimmer across the Gulf Stream have vanished, thinking about Jeanette and the baby. I can't believe it—I'm lonely already.

My cell phone rings. I see who it is and answer.

"Oh Mikey, this is Collette. A terrible thing has just happened to me. Can you come over to my place right away? Please?"

"I'm sorry, honey," I reply. "I'm out of town." And I throw the cell phone overboard.

Chapter 19

Sibbey Mamone and Santo Trafficante

It all began when Sibbey Mamone had to go on the lam and Johnny Futto took over the Gangplank, his New York City club, and reopened it as the Peppermint Lounge. Sibbey retained a piece of the profits. In later years, Sibbey and I became close and he shared a story with me of what happened to him when he was a kid.

It was the 30s, the iconic Cotton Club was swinging, and Sibbey's brother was the dentist up at Sing-Sing. Once a month their mother made up an Italian care package for Sibbey to take to his brother, Dr. Mamone. Before one of Sibbey's Sing-Sing visits, Dr. Mamone called to ask him to pick up the wives of inmates Owney Madden and Farmer Sullivan, and bring them along so they could visit their husbands. Sibbey did this for over a year until Owney Madden, the owner of the Cotton Club, and Farmer Sullivan were pardoned.

A few months later, young Sibbey and a couple of his boys got the idea to promote a dance downtown in Little Italy. It was their first entrepreneurial undertaking. They rented a hall, set the date, and someone recommended they should print up a program to sell ads to make a little extra money. Then it came to Sibbey, why not go up to the Cotton Club, the hottest club of the day in New York City, and ask Owney Madden to take out an ad. After all,

Sibbey reasoned, he had driven his wife up to Sing-Sing all those times and never asked for anything, not even help out with the gas money. The boys dressed in their best suits and ties went up to Harlem. When they got to the Cotton Club, a long line wound down and around the block. Sibbey, unperturbed, went right up to the front of the line where a big, burly doorman took a look at him.

"Don't even think about it kid." The man's voice rumbled like an attack dog on alert. "We got a full house tonight. Go home, ya mudder wants ya."

A thousand possibilities ran through Sibbey's mind but he simply answered, "I'd like to see Owney Madden, please."

"Who are you?" The doorman looked a little confused.

"Tell him that Dr. Mamone's brother, Sibbey, is here?" Sibbey's voice, which was sincere and filled with emotion, moved the doorman. Without any further ado, he whispered into a bouncer's ear who in turn went into the club.

"Wait over there on the side." The doorman shooed young Sibbey and his two friends away from the door. "And don't yas be botherin' anyone."

Feeling they were in over their heads, one of his friends said, "Come on Sibbey, I think we'd better go."

Sibbey just shook his head. "No way." And stood there waiting, steadfast.

In a matter of minutes, the bouncer came out and motioned for the boys to follow him into the club. He led them right into the main showroom past everyone, up to the front of the stage where two waiters squeezed in a ringside table for three.

"Holy shit," Sibbey said in a surprised tone. "Madden thinks we wanna see the show."

They had never been in a nightclub before and were nervous thinking about how they were going to pay for the drinks and tip the waiter. They weren't prepared for this. Shortly thereafter the waiter came sauntering over to the table, tipped off that it was a VIP party, "A very good evening gentleman…what'll it be?" He asked.

Sibbey, resisting a meltdown, replied with a weak smile,

"Three Seven and Sevens...please."

"How we gonna pay for dese?" Sibbey's buddy leaned in with a look of panic on his face. "I don't even like Seven and Seven," he added.

"Who cares," Sibbey said concealing his own panic. "That's all I knew what to order."

Shortly after the drinks arrived so did Owney Madden with a big smile on his face. Sitting down with them he finally thanked Sibbey for what he had done for him.

"You're my guests here tonight," Owney said. "So don't even think about going into ya pockets, the drinks, tip...everything's covered."

When Owney was about to leave he got up and asked if there was anything else he could do for them. Sibbey took the chance to explain he was selling ads in a program for a dance they were promoting.

"How much? Owney asked.

Sibbey cleared his throat and started to give the prices of the various size ads. "We've got four different size ads for different prices and...."

"No…no." Owney stopped him. "I mean how much for the whole thing. I'll take everything. Don't worry about it, kid. Just figure it out and let me know how much it is."

Sibbey was too dumbfounded to speak.

"And incidentally, what are yas doin' for music?" Owney said.

"Oh…we've got a band." Sibbey's tongue was now going faster than his mind.

"Well, tell them to take a break between eight and ten," Owney commanded. "Because I'm sendin' Cab Calloway down to ya, my band here from the Cotton Club. And make sure ya advertise that they're comin' so the people'll know."

This set off a surge of adrenaline. When the boys left the Cotton Club, they half ran, half jumped, half flew, feeling so high like their feet weren't even touching ground.

An enormous moon filled the sky the night of the event, with lines forming around the block. The place was so packed it seemed like thousands. Seven-thirty and Sibbey swallowed hard, stepping outside to watch the moon disappear into a bank of dark clouds and wondered whether Cab Calloway would show. Fear stabbed at him thinking what would happen if Owney forgot his promise. *What would we do,* he thought, *refund the money? We'll have a riot on our hands.* Then, as if by magic, precisely at a quarter to eight, two trucks pulled up with Cab Calloway and his Orchestra.

They set up and played for two hours, just like Owney said they would. The air was electric—nobody flew higher that night than Sibbey and his boys. Oh, what a night.

No way to know what would or would not have happened had John F. Kennedy lost the election. I do know that many believed it was the mob, especially those connected in Chicago, that had been instrumental in putting Kennedy over the top. Patriarch Joe Kennedy had rumored connections to the mob for years. Scatsy had even told me years before the presidential election that Frank Costello had once done business with Joe Kennedy who had not kept to their agreement. Costello wouldn't go for it and it was *pay what you owe me or end up in the bay time.* The contract went to Johnny Futto to select someone to do the job. It was resolved when mob people from Chicago intervened on Joe Kennedy's behalf. It wasn't much of a stretch to think that the father had intervened this time on his son Jack's behalf.

Johnny and I were at the Tampa home of high-ranking Mafioso, Santo Trafficante, having a sandwich when the conversation turned to the Kennedys. Santo didn't mince curse words or names when talking about the Kennedys. A mild looking and sounding man, I'd never seen him so worked up or so bitterly angry. It was clear he felt that the Kennedy sons Jack and Bob had crossed lines with their involvement with women in and out of the White House, and their manner of pursuit of both the union and the Mafia. "And the worst part," Johnny concluded, "was that we helped put them in—and they know it."

"Not for nothing, Dick, how do we make the best of what's left?" Scatsy was grim and worried, feeling the full effect of his brother Johnny Futto's murder and thinking maybe we might be next.

"Let's keep the facts straight," I said. "We know Johnny was no rat." I consoled him. Scatsy forced a smile and it was like I became his new brother. Our fears of being killed eventually subsided and the stigma from the suspicion of Johnny being a rat was lifted.

When Johnny was alive he would tell the boys, "Stay away from the Top, I don't want you guys stinkin' up the joint." Now that Johnny Futto was gone, there were plenty of reasons for the wiseguys to stay away. Me, Scatsy, and the Top of the Home became a hot, off-limits ticket. Mafiosos always had an inside track as to what was happening in the law arena. It finally became obvious to them that I refused to talk to the cops about Johnny being murdered. I remember Johnny telling me, "If anything happens to me, you play a dead hand...and stay away from finding out who did it."

It was several months later when Santo Trafficante showed up—he was the first. I'll never forget that night. Julie, our maître d', called down to my office and told me someone was up there looking for me.

"Who is it?"

He was silent for a moment then said, "I think you'd better come up."

I made my way up to the restaurant from my office, which was one floor below, then walking through the kitchen to the dining room. There sitting in a heavy silence was Santo Trafficante. All of a sudden he looked up at me and smiled. It had been five months since I'd seen him, and now that he was here I was dumbfounded. And to think he was smiling. I never saw him smile—never. My mind had been poisoned against him, thinking possibly he had something to do with Johnny being murdered, or at least approved it. Every scenario passed through my mind. All that vanished instantly when he stood and gave me the traditional goomba kiss. Santo's tall frame dwarfed the table. "I was looking at this beautiful view you've got here...pretty impressive. Sit down and have a drink with me." Santo sat down and rested his hands on the table. His tone became serious. "I'm glad to be here. It's been a long time—too long."

I felt as if the whole world lifted. Why I was so amazed to see him is hard to explain. It meant everything in Johnny's world. At the time, I didn't know the real story behind Johnny's death, but I knew it couldn't be because he did anything dishonorable. In fact, in time I found out it was just the opposite: it was because he did the honorable thing.

A little later in the service bar, Scatsy was behind the stick when he looked over as I approached. "Santo just came in," I said. "And, asked how you're doing."

In the middle of making a drink his hands froze, like he'd been kicked in the stomach. "You fuckin' kiddin' me?" His eyes went back to the martini he was pouring out. His face turned red. He barked at the nearby waiter. "Whatta are ya waitin' for, a bus? Or are ya gonna put an olive in the martini and take it to the table?" His eyes filled with love as he looked back at me, "We'll be all right, Dick. Don't ya worry about nuttin."

"You bet your ass we will, Scatsy," I replied. We were back.

Not too long after that night, Meyer Lansky came in, then his daughter with her husband, Vince Lombardo, who became regulars. Then other mob figures started showing up: Jimmy Blue Eyes, Sam the Plumber with his whole Jersey crew, Jackie DiNorscio, Jerry the Jew, Anthony Accetturo, and then from Chicago Jackie Cerone, Gussie Alex and Gus Zappas, Boys from Boston and New York, and so many more who initially had stayed away from The Top. They now came and brought their hugs and kisses.

In a way Johnny, in death, was vindicated. I believed it was a sign of respect for him. It became clear how many of the wise guys loved him. One night, for some reason, there was an unusual number of wise guys in for dinner. It was strictly social and I put them over on the south side at two big tables. A guest came up to me that night and said, "You know, Dick, if a bomb goes off in here right now, the crime rate in America will go down by 50%." He was probably right. I met more mob guys at the Top of the Home after Johnny was gone than I ever did with him at the Peppermint.

I first met Donald Tucker when he was Speaker of the House of Florida. Whenever he was in South Florida, he frequented the Top of the Home, and we became good friends. One night he was in with his wife to be, Joan, sitting way up front at a window table when Santo Trafficante came in with his lawyer Henry Gonzalez. It was the first time I met Gonzalez. At that time, the FBI was hounding Trafficante on the conspiracy theory suspicion of his involvement in the assassination of President Kennedy.

As I sat Trafficante and Gonzalez, Santo noticed Tucker and asked if I knew him. I was taken aback a little because I was afraid he would want to be introduced or want some kind of a favor. I hesitated, cautious, but the next thing I knew Tucker was at my elbow and patting me on the back saying, "We're having a great meal here tonight, Dick!"

I saw this as the moment to make introductions. "Donald", I said, "I'd like you to meet Henry Gonzalez, a very dear friend of mine." And pointing to Santo Trafficante I said, "And this is my Uncle Sam." Santo nodded. We talked for a few more minutes before Tucker went on his way.

As I sat down with Santo and Henry I took in the wide, rare smile on Santo's face.

Chapter 20

Byno, Trigger Mike, Betty Jarwood, Tony Goebbels, and Matty the Horse

Before any of the following happened, let me give a little background of interest on my longtime friend from Freeport, Dick Byno. As a kid of fifteen, he was full grown and looked much older than he was. With a passion to join the Marines, he forged papers allowing him to get in just at the end of WWII. He cut a handsome figure and was assigned to the Marine Corps Honor Guard.

Maybe the most famous marine of all time is the highly decorated John Basilone. He was awarded the Congressional Medal of Honor during WWII for valor in the South Pacific before being returned stateside to help the war effort. Not happy to be removed from battle, he wasn't content until, at his insistence, he was sent to rejoin his outfit on the front lines. He was subsequently killed in action and awarded the Navy Cross. Byno's first assignment was Basilone's funeral in New Jersey.

At the service, there was some immediate connection between Byno and Basilone's mother. Her eyes shot to him like an arrow and held his gaze. Perhaps she saw something that reminded her of her son, John. In the middle of the ceremony with tears in her eyes, she got up, walked over to Byno, gave him a hug and her son's Marine ring. A startled Byno stared straight ahead, stoic.

Eventually the ring went to Byno's son when he became a Marine Corps colonel.

After the war Dick Byno became a Nassau County cop. In those days police officers weren't paid much so Byno supplemented his income with a floor care business. It was around '63 when Byno called me to ask if my father-in-law, Johnny Futto, could recommend him to do the floors for Carlo Gambino and Terry Zappi, who had just built homes out in Massapequa, Long Island. Gambino was number one in the Mob then. Johnny did the favor and called me back to tell Byno that it was OK for him to go to Gambino's house where he'd be expected. For some reason I neglected to tell Johnny that Byno was now a cop.

Byno went to Gambino's house in his civvies and knocked on the door. One of Gambino's boys answered and in a gruff voice asked what he wanted.

"Mr. Gambino here?" Byno answered. "I'm here to wax the floors."

When Byno entered the house he noticed that the floors were marble. Byno had never even seen a marble floor before but when Gambino came he explained how these floors would need special care on a weekly basis. Gambino said okay and Byno brought in his equipment and started polishing. Four weeks later, Byno hadn't billed Gambino yet and realized that he needed some cash to pay bills so he went to Gambino's house to collect his back pay. Now he was in a police uniform, something he hadn't thought about when he walked right up and knocked on the door. Another one of Gambino's boys answered and was caught off guard when he saw a cop in uniform.

Byno said, "I'm here to see Mr. Gambino, please."

"What for?" The wiseguy raised a suspicious eyebrow.

"I'm here to get my money."

The wiseguy couldn't believe his ears. He craned his head and had Byno repeat himself. Then he left to get Gambino. Gambino approached, and by the serious look on his face, Byno realized he didn't make him out and probably thought that he was just some strange cop trying to shake him down. He knew instinctively it would be best to identify himself right away.

"It's me, Mr. Gambino, Byno," he said lifting his cap, "I was wondering if I could get paid for the floors. I'm a little short this month."

Gambino stepped back in amazement. "That's a you," and gave him a broad smile of relief. Then he turned and called down the hallway. "Momma...come over here and look at who's a copa."

From then on. Byno and Gambino became close friends. The FBI took note of this and wanted Byno to wear a wire, but he refused.

"I just do the floors for him, I don't want to get involved," he told the FBI.

Soon after that he was reassigned to the police force's Marine division. This did little because Gambino's house was on the water with a dock, so Byno saw more of him than he had before being transferred.

It was a beautiful Sunday out on the Great Bay of Long Island, and even though Byno and his partner were on boat patrol duty, they'd had more than a couple of beers. Towards the end of the day Byno realized that they hadn't given out any citations yet. At that moment Vincent Squillante's yacht went speeding by. The patrol boat, with Byno at the helm, took off after it in hot pursuit with no idea at the time that Squillante was the mob's garbage king, or in Gambino's Family.

Byno stopped the yacht, but somehow when he asked for ID he accidentally tripped his boat into forward. It shot ahead, ramming a big hole in the side of Squillante's yacht. Squillante screamed down from the fore deck at Byno.

"What the... Why you bastard...look what you did to my boat!"

Unfazed, Byno wrote out a ticket for speeding and not having his boat under control. When Squillante read the charge on the ticket he went ballistic. "I'll kill you...you son-of-a-bitch if it's the last thing I ever do." He went on and on. As Byno drove away, he looked back and saw Squillante on deck waving his arms, jumping up and down, and screaming at the top of his lungs.

"Boy," Byno said to his partner. "That guy gets easily excited."

Later Byno found out who Squillante was and called me for advice because he knew he was in trouble. By this time, my father-in-law, Johnny Futto knew Gambino liked Byno so he told me to tell Byno to go to Gambino himself knowing he'd help him out. Johnny also advised that Byno should apologize to Squillante. After all, he was the one that was out of order.

Vic Centrella asked me if I could help him get the front door parking concession at the Fountainebleau Hotel in Miami Beach. Of course, the first thing I did was go to my father-in-law who made an appointment for me to see their contact, "Trigger" Mike Coppola. The appointment was made for noon on the following day at the La Gorce Country Club. I took Victor along with me in case there were any questions. As soon as we entered the clubhouse, I spotted Trigger Mike. He put up his hand discreetly, signaling me to wait. It was obvious the FBI was watching him, so I told Victor, "Let's sit here."

A few minutes later Trigger Mike gets up and as he walks by me, signals with a slight gesture for me to follow him. I nonchalantly get up and tell Victor that I'll be right back. I walk at a slow pace behind Trigger Mike and follow him into the men's room where he goes right up into a urinal—I do the same in the urinal next to him.

Now while we're there, he kept looking forward and asks me in a low voice what I want. I tell him about the Fountainebleau parking concession and he says, "OK...I'll get back to you." He then zips up and leaves. I do the same and go back to where Victor is sitting.

"Come on, let's go."

"Let's go?" His mouth hangs open in surprise. "What happened with Trigger Mike?"

"I just saw him," I said.

"You what?"

"Come on, I'll tell you outside."

Bottom line: Trigger Mike got back to Johnny and told him 'no luck' with the parking concession.

Betty Jarwood was a most amazing person. A lady that personified the word class, and one of the most gracious, polite, and interesting women I'd ever met. I know that's saying a lot, but when you've met as many women as I have you're allowed to draw some conclusions. I can honestly say that every time she came to the Top of the Home she had another interesting story to tell. I met her in her early seventies, but even then she was attractive and one of the best-dressed ladies anywhere. Each time she came to the Top she wore another custom-made outfit—never ostentatious or gaudy, simply elegant.

One time, Favo the Spic, one of Meyer Lansky's boys, saw me talking to Betty and filled me in on her background. She was a Ziegfield girl who married Louie "Lepke" Buchalter, one of the most notorious mobsters of all time. He became the administrative head of "Murder, Incorporated," a group formed to carry out murders for the Mafia. In March of 1940, he was sentenced to a term of thirty years to life for racketeering and sent to Leavenworth Penitentiary. Not much later he was double-crossed and sentenced to death after Abe "Kid Twist" Reles cooperated with prosecutors in convicting him of murder.

After a short stint as a widow, Betty married Arthur Jarwood, a New York nightclub owner. Their marriage wasn't exactly storybook so they decided to separate. This was when she moved to Florida and frequented the Top of the Home. After she came to the Top a few times, I sat with her and we were both amazed by each other's knowledge of wise guys. She couldn't get over that a young guy like me knew so many underworld characters. Frankly, I was also surprised too, meeting a lady who knew so much about the life.

I had just seen the movie *Funny Girl* and I asked Betty if she knew Fanny Brice. "Oh, yes," she replied with a quick laugh. "We did two crossings together."

Another time when I stayed at a suite in the Pierre Hotel in New York, I was amazed how large and luxurious the rooms were. When I got back home I asked her, "Did you ever stay at the Pierre?"

"Oh, yes, Dick." Her face brightened. "I lived there for eight years."

When Lepke got the chair, she moved to Palm Springs and became friendly with a lot of Hollywood screen characters—William Holden, the actor, for one. When I mentioned that I was going to Africa and would be in Kenya, she told me that Holden owned a beautiful vacation spot there called the Mt. Kenya Safari Club. I gave her the dates I would be there and she gladly called Holden to make reservations for me.

The Big Game and Safari Club was way up by the equator near Ethiopia. On our way we stopped at a large outdoor market. Bill Johnson, who I traveled with, walked around with our guide while I stayed by the car. Within a few minutes this beggar came hobbling towards me who looked like he had been in a fire, that's how horribly disfigured he was. I gave him my pocketful of loose change. He was so thankful that he grabbed my hands and held on, shaking them vigorously for a long time before he released them.

When Bill got back I pointed out the poor beggar to him and he asked, "Wow...what happened to that guy?"

"Probably got caught in a fire," I said.

The guide quickly corrected me. "No, he's a leper."

There's nothing that could quite describe the feeling I had then at that moment—even after the guide said, "but he's not contagious."

How does he know? I wondered.

It was a Saturday night and the Top was jamming, I saw a hand from a table in the distance waving me over. It was Tony "Geobbels" Ricci. Tony was in his eighties, six foot four, curt and right to the point. Tony was one of the first guys to go on the lam from Brooklyn to Chicago. And the one who told Al Capone, "Come to Chicago, it's good here."

As I approached, he pointed to his plate. "This is the best fuckin' duck I ever ate since I was with Al in Chicago."

I was confused for a moment. "Al?"

"Al Capone. What's a matter with you?"

"Of course," I answered, thinking I should have known better. If you're from Chicago and mention "Al," it's Capone.

I loved Matty "the Horse" Ianniello. I knew him since the beginning with Johnny Futto. You can say what you want about wise guys. But, I can tell you this from first-hand experience, you'll never find a more right guy than Matty the Horse.

All your high-falutin and double-dealing politicians, philandering religious leaders, and back-stabbing, high priced CEO's, can take a lesson on ethics from Matty. His life was quite a ride from the beginning in Little Italy to South Pacific war hero, alleged drug dealer, multiple restaurant/nightclub owner, and convicted crime boss. To put it plain, he was the "go to" guy in New York City. Most of his life was spent straightening out guys that screwed up. He's gone now, but he left a few pretty good stories behind.

One day, "Fat" Tony Salerno went to Matty the Horse and told him to make a list of guys who should be considered to become made men.

"We gotta bring some guys up," Fat Tony said.

A few days later Matty had the list ready and gave it to Fat Tony.

Upon reading it, Tony asked, "Who's these guys? Who's this Richard Andalucci?"

"That's Dicky Rags," Matty the Horse said.

"Who's Johnny Bramante?"

"That's Jellybeans."

Fat Tony shouted back at him, throwing the list at his face. "Why don't ya give me their real names fer crissake? I don't even know who these other fuckin' guys are."

Chapter 21

Burt Halpern, Judge Helfant, and Sally Burns

Burt Halpern was not a train wreck waiting to happen, he was one that kept happening over and over. He was a New Yorker who went at things in his own way, sometimes that way was innocent and sometimes it wasn't. He was an inch, perhaps two, over six feet and powerfully built, with wide shoulders. His head would leaned forward with a fixed stare that made you feel you were in the ring, facing an opponent. It was exactly four months after his startling escape from a Mexican prison that he was drawn into perhaps the most perplexing criminal situation he had ever been in. It was so mystifying and inexplicable to the authorities that it went to the top of their unsolved crimes. Every avenue led to a dead end.

It all started one summer evening when Burt met Mona, a beautiful ex-model. He saw the exhaustion in her face, perhaps she had too much to drink. She turned to him and said out of the clear blue, "I'm not pure you know."

Burt remained silent.

"A friend of my father's came to me one night." Mona kept her eyes fixed on the table in front of her, relating the story. "He wanted everything and I gave it to him...I was only fourteen. I don't know why I'm telling you this."

Touched by her confession, he reached out and held her hand.

"That was a long time ago. You should forget it."

What Mona wanted was something meaningful. She had a lifetime of loneliness and longing, but she felt that could all change. Burt went on to discover she had just inherited the estate of one Henry Blount, a California real estate mogul who had numerous assets, totaling millions. The ironic part; Blount had been over eighty when she'd just turned twenty-four. They had only been married for four months. No one was more surprised about the inheritance than Mona.

Burt had just made a big score himself gambling in Vegas, so to celebrate the two of them, strangers who felt a need for each other, decided to lease a private yacht out of Miami and take a pleasure cruise through the islands of the Caribbean. The only other person on board was Captain Geraldo. Burt preferred it that way and stocked the boat with all sorts of provisions, planning to do the cooking on board himself. Burt set the ground rules early as to what the trip was about. He was only interested in the present and didn't want get into the past or the future. He'd been there before and knew once Mona got to know him she'd probably be like all the others and want to know where he was born, what his lousy childhood was like, how his parents were occupied, and all that kind of crap. He had no interest in going there. After Burt laid it all out, Mona seemed pleased. They sailed out of Miami into the Gulf Stream and four days later came to the Turks and Caicos Islands. The scuba diving there was matchless and they had the best fresh conch in the world. Until you've eaten a conch fritter from the Turks and Caicos you haven't lived.

Sailing on from there, they took their time with sunny skies on calm seas until they got to Trinidad where Burt decided it was time to leave the boat and check into a hotel. Mona welcomed the change. By this time, Burt was more pleased than surprised that they had bonded. After a few days on Trinidad someone mentioned how beautiful Tobago was, so off they went to the small island close by. They were having a lovely day doing the tourist thing when the hammer dropped. By mistake, Burt used one of his stolen credit cards and they were both arrested and held in the local jail. The police chief of Tobago noted that the credit card was tied into an international drug smuggling ring that was wanted by Interpol. He took pride in the arrest.

Burt and Mona spent the night in the same cell, curled up on a single bunk. The jail was a dump and after a few minutes in the cell they could smell camphor in the cracks of the walls. Burt couldn't believe this was happening to them.

The police chief had an eye for Mona. He dragged her out of the cell for questioning in his office, where he had the jailer hold her down while he caressed her breasts and put his hand in between her legs. She never mentioned this to Burt because she knew he had enough problems, but the incident prompted her to bribe the police chief to let them go. When the Police Chief heard Mona's proposal he grinned happily. Mona was brought back to the cell where she told Burt about the bribe. He was amazed and made arrangements to have ten thousand wired into the local bank to pay the dirty police captain off.

Everything went according to plan, except for one unforgivable mistake. After the police chief took Mona to the bank, he not only took her money he took her too, raping her in an ugly fashion in the back of his van. When she was brought back to the police station, she and Burt were released. As they made their way to the yacht, Burt became suspicious of Mona's apprehension and barely audible voice. She broke down and confessed she had been raped.

It was like a bomb went off in Burt's brain. Blood surged, popping the veins in his neck while Mona quietly sobbed. He told Mona to continue to the boat where he'd join her soon. She pleaded with him not to go back but her pleas fell on deaf ears. Finally, she left for the boat. Burt headed back to the jail where he slipped in unnoticed, subdued the jailer by taking his weapon away and demanded to know where the police chief was. After the jailer told him the chief lived next door, Burt slammed his pistol into the back of his head, knocking him unconscious. He tied and gagged him, dragging his body into a cell and dumping it there.

Upon entering his house, he encountered the chief right away. He held back nothing, giving him a severe beating. "Think about that the next time you wanna rape somebody, you bastard." Burt glanced at his watch, grabbed the money sitting out on the desk then made his way to his yacht. The whole episode took no more than ten minutes.

You would think that would be the end of the story, but after they got underway heading for Puerto Rico, Captain Geraldo overheard them talking about what had happened and figured he could capitalize on it. He told Burt that he'd keep quiet for an additional five thousand dollars. Burt didn't hesitate a second. He planted his right foot and threw a perfect right hand into the Captain's jaw. Then he grabbed him by the throat, dragged him over to the rail and tossed him overboard.

When the yacht was well outside of Puerto Rico they came upon a small fishing vessel. Burt went alongside and was moved when he saw how concerned the fisherman was about the direction they were going. "You are heading to nowhere, Señor... out to the open sea. Please follow me I am going back to Puerto Rico."

Burt invited the shabbily dressed fisherman on board and said to him, "Your boat looks like it's in bad shape."

"Si, Señor. I save for the day I can have a boat such as this to fish with but I'm afraid it is just a dream."

Burt said on the spot, "I'm going to make you a deal and give you this boat."

The fisherman was stunned. "You really mean it, Señor?"

"Yeah, I do," Burt said. "You'll have to paint it over and change the name so no one will know where it came from. If you can live with that, this boat is yours. All we want is to arrive quietly into Puerto Rico."

The astounded fisherman could only nod. Burt didn't wait around Puerto Rico and went right to the airport with Mona. Standing in the center of a crowd, his concerns were enormous. He felt all eyes around were silently staring at him. It was Mona's fate that concerned him. There was a problem with tickets for the flight. The flight was overbooked and everyone was concerned. Would they get on board? The rain outside hammered down on the airplanes and there was a tropical depression approaching.

When Burt got to the counter, the agent looked up, shocked to find the hundred dollar bill Burt placed in his hand. He hesitated for a second then asked for their names. When Burt replied, the agent said, "Oh yes, Mr. Halpern, of course. There are two first-class tickets in your name. The flight is full," the agent said, "so we'll be taking off right away before the storm gets here."

Burt and Mona rushed out of the terminal and to the ramp. "Good riddance," Burt said under his breath as they boarded the flight to Miami.

A few nights later they came into the Peppermint Lounge, both looking happy. "You must have had a good time in the Caribbean," I said. "I hope you didn't get in any trouble?"

"Naw." Burt shrugged, an air of nonchalance in his tone. "Just a nice quiet cruise."

"Actually quite boring." Mona smiled.

If you've ever seen *The Godfather* or watched *The Sopranos* you might think you know what life is like in organized crime. Whether you know them as La Cosa Nostra, The Mafia, or simply The Mob and bought into the Hollywood interpretation of these gangsters, you couldn't be more wrong. In the middle of the last century while FBI Director, J. Edgar Hoover, was denying that organized crime existed, the Boys were forming powerful syndicates in the country's major cities. Some of these bosses were cowardly backstabbing petty thugs who would sell out their mothers to protect their own skin.

It came as a shock to discover that Nicky Scarfo killed Judge Helfant in Red Morgan's restaurant in Atlantic City. The judge and his wife had been faithful customers of mine in Florida at the Top of the Home. To me, you couldn't meet a nicer guy. I often wondered why Scarfo killed him. You'd think he must have had a good reason, but then again I remembered there were a lot of guys in that life who never needed any reason for what they did.

It was a strange time in Atlantic City with the city just on the verge of getting casino gambling. Everyone was jockeying for position and deals were being cut way before the gambling arrived, so in effect, nothing would surprise anyone. The whole thing stunk. I believed it was over a bribe, taken, refused, or not followed through on.

Judge Helfant was a wealthy lawyer before he became a judge. He owned a motel, a restaurant and a few other businesses. A person who takes a bribe is seldom killed, but the person who doesn't follow through on the agreement is almost certainly destined for some ugly fate. So went the rumors.

Nicky Scarfo survived many years before he was finally convicted of Helfant's murder. His other crimes and murders are too brutal to mention.

So many celebrities came to Miami's Peppermint Lounge that we hired an in-house photographer and provided a small dark room where he could develop his pictures. Although he was very good at what he did, like anything else, occasionally there was a slip-up.

There was no reason for what happened — no reason on earth — except for one Sally Burns. Sally Burns, an alias for Salvatore Granello, was a made member of the Genovese crime family and the biggest crook in town. If you read stories about the mob in Cuba or the Kennedy assassination, you'll see Sally Burns' name pop up. This *Time Magazine* article is a good example.

Mafia Spies in Cuba, Recharging
The CIA Spies, Spies Everywhere.

It is well known that when the CIA had dirty work to do in Cuba, it turned to an organization that had long tentacles around that country: the Mafia. In 1961 the CIA, according to reliable sources, put out a contract to Mafia Leaders Sam Giancana and John Roselli for the assassination of Fidel Castro (TIME, March 17). In a separate and equally futile action, TIME has learned, the CIA enlisted other Mafia figures to do some spying in Cuba in preparation for the 1961 Bay of Pigs invasion. The Mafiosi were Russell Bufalino, now the mob boss in Scranton, Pa., and James Plumeri and Salvatore ("Sally Burns") Granello, of New York City. Before Castro overthrew Dictator Fulgencio Batista in 1959, the three men controlled a racetrack and a huge gambling casino near Havana.

Sally was a three hundred pound, barrel-chested man, who could pick up a chair by one of its legs and easily hold it high over his head. That may not be an unusual feat for some, but when Sally did it someone would be sitting in the chair. So we always gave him and his wild behavior a lot of leeway. Even the night he picked up a customer sitting next to him and threw him two tables over because he was talking too loudly—we let it slide.

One night, Sally came into the Peppermint with a very attractive girl and he wanted their picture taken. Of course, our house photographer obliged him, and a short time later came running to me, trembling.

"Why are you shaking?" I asked.

"A customer threatened to beat me up because the picture I took didn't come out right. I offered to take another one but he pushed me to the floor, cursing."

"Our bouncers usually handle incidents like this," I said.

"I went to them and they told me to see you."

"Point this customer out to me."

When he did I blurted out, "That's Sally Burns. You're lucky you only got pushed."

Later in the evening, singer and actor Johnny Desmond came in. Sally called me over and asked if I knew him. I said I did.

"Can you introduce me and have your guy take a picture of us?" Sally asked.

"Of course I will, Sally."

I made my way over to our photog. "Come with me. I'm going to introduce Sally Burns to Johnny Desmond, and Sally wants you to take their picture."

He started shaking again but I said, "Don't worry about it. Just take the picture."

So there was Sally, posing with a big smile with his arm around Johnny Desmond. When our boy raised his camera, Sally hissed at him through his smile. "This one had better come out right. Get me?"

We all knew what that meant. Thank God the picture was perfect and our photographer avoided what could have been a near death experience.

Sally Burns and Johnny Futto were close. Burns' biggest ambition was to earn a legitimate buck but like with so many other wise guys, this wouldn't be easy. He figured the quickest way to accomplish his goal was to attach himself to a respected businessman—someone that feared him, of course.

Burns shuffled through a pile of papers then slammed the desk with his fist in frustration. "I don't know shit about real estate, but what I do know is that I'll break that Sol's fuckin' legs if he doesn't go in and take that escrow money"

"How big's the score?" Johnny asked.

"About 350 large."

"What does he want to do?"

"He wants to stay with it and build the building. He says it'll be a bigger score than what we're makin'—and it's legit."

Johnny shrugged. "Maybe it's worth it"

"Yeah..." Burns said, drumming his fingers in thought, "but who wants to take a chance with that? I'd rather bust 'em out and take the escrow money now."

The project was supposed to be a legitimate apartment building on the ocean in Miami Beach. Sol explained how it was a better way of selling apartments, rather than co-ops. He wasn't a pioneer in bringing about major changes in land development, but somehow he was the first to develop the concept of Condominiums in Miami Beach.

The Marlborough House was a beautiful building right on the ocean. The units sold like hotcakes and produced roughly 350 thousand dollars in deposits that were put in an escrow account. This was a lot of money back then and Burns wanted it. Sol pleaded, trying to convince Sally there would be more money if they finished the project with the added bonus of it being legitimate. It all fell on deaf ears. Sol had no choice but to abscond with the funds, leaving the greatest real estate concept of the time to be developed by others.

My friend, Vic Centrella, had the parking concession at the Peppermint Lounge in Miami Beach. Unbeknownst to us, he'd paid Sally Burns five thousand dollars for the front door concession at the Marlborough House. He mentioned this to Johnny one day in a casual conversation. Of course Johnny knew there would never be a front door concession.

Early, on a bright Miami morning a few days later, two overgrown torpedoes pounded on the front door of Vic's house. His wife, Dolores, woke him up and he went to the door with sleep still in his eyes. He woke right up, jumping back when he saw the goons, not knowing what to expect.

"Vic Centrella?" one of them asked.

Vic looked around, cautious. "I don't know whether I am or not."

"Well, think about it fast. Are ya or ain't ya?" The question came in a gruff voice.

"Yeah...I am, I guess," he stammered in reply.

"Here's something for ya from Sally."

They handed him an envelope and left as abrupt as they'd arrived.

Vic opened it and found five thousand dollars. He didn't know what to think or who to thank and it wasn't until later when the scam hit the papers that he realized what Johnny had done for him.

Chapter 22

Robbed, Lou Black and Clarence Darrow, and The Unholy Alliance

About three weeks after the Peppermint closed for the season, we were robbed. Someone broke in and stole everything out of the liquor room and from our giant freezer where we kept a hundred beautiful, pre-cut prime 16 oz. steaks.

Scatsy was livid. "Look at these dirty bastards, they stole everything. Who could have done this?"

"It had to be an inside job," Johnny said.

About a week later, I stood in front of the Peppermint when Tony, our cook, drove up and asked if I'm interested in buying some liquor.

I had my suspicions right off the bat, but I said, "Sure, let me see a list of what you've got."

The next day, Tony came back with the list. I could see right off that it was our own whiskey he was trying to sell back to us. We agreed on a price, but I told him that I didn't want it coming to the Peppermint so he should give me a call the next day and I would let him know where to deliver it. Johnny called Sid Rosenthal and we used his warehouse in Hialeah. When Tony called, I gave him the address and said I would meet him there with the cash.

Johnny and I waited across the street from the warehouse.

When we saw Tony deliver the liquor, we called over and told Tony after dropping it off to meet us at Junior's on Biscayne and 79th Street to get paid. In a little while here comes Tony, all smiles, walking towards us at the entrance of Junior's.

He asked for the money, never expecting my reply.

"Listen, you piece of shit, do you think I'm going to buy back my own whiskey?"

His face turned ashen and he started to shake and stammer. "They'll kill me."

"Good. Let them call me."

Tony turned and started running. That was the last I ever saw of him.

Two years later at a party, I was introduced to Eddie Cook. I knew him right away as the infamous jewel thief. His name was always in the papers. Years later they even made a movie of his life called *Thief* with James Caan.

"Hello," I said extending my hand, "I'm Dick Cami."

"Yeah, I know. You're the guy who stole my whiskey."

The whole scenario flashed before my eyes. "That was you? How the hell did you pull that off?"

"I had a cop playing chickie for me."

"Makes sense. Now I get it. How's Tony?"

"When that son of a bitch told me what happened I grabbed my pistol and threw a couple of shots at him as he was diving into the canal. Who knows what happened?"

"And the steaks?"

"Ohhhh, they were delicious." He smirked.

We both had a good laugh.

The TV screen filled with a rush of reporters practically squashing Candace Mossler, desperate to get her to take their questions about her sensational murder trial, when Lou Black said, "Look at dem reporters mutalatin' up trouble. She'd better remember that nothing she never said will ever do her any harm. They never get the story right anyway."

Percy Foreman, a flamboyant criminal attorney, appeared on the screen and a surprised look came over Lou's face. "Hey!" he said pointing. "He looks just like Clarence Darrow."

By some chance, I was reading Darrow's biography at the time, *Attorney for the Damned*. I was surprised at Lou's comment and asked, "You saw Darrow?"

"Whatta ya mean saw him?" Lou turned to me. "Whatsa matta which you. Don't you remember?"

"Remember what?"

I had no idea what he was talking about but Lou had this thing. If he liked you, he automatically treated you like family and believed that you knew everything that had ever happened to him, even before you met. It was the most amazing thing. He was old enough to be my grandfather at the time—maybe eighty.

"He defended me," Lou said. "Didn't he?"

"Clarence Darrow defended you?" I repeated. "Are you serious?"

"Of course, I am," Lou said looking me right in the eye. "Don't you remember the story?"

"You're kidding me?" I said.

"Why should I kid you?"

"Geez...I'll be damned. Tell me what happened?"

One thing I knew for sure, Lou Black was no liar. He brought a wooden chair from the corner and set it down then went back and got another one. "These ain't very comfortable," he said. "But sit here while I tell ya the story."

"They'll do just fine," I said. "Go ahead, I'm listening."

Lou lowered himself into the chair and started to talk in a low voice. "Ya never know when something good is gonna happen to ya—or bad. It was in the late twenties in the winter and I was bookin' numbers out of an office up in Harlem. It was snowin' something terrible and the wind was blowin' like hell when them three coloreds came into the office and started giving me shit, like who the hell they thought they were. I knew it was a move to take over the location, but I wasn't havin' any of it. Now an argument got going and we tumbled outside into the street. It was in the middle of the day and there must have been about a thousand people walking by...who knows? These guys had bad intentions and I knew it. They were packin' so when we hit the street I took out my gat and started blastin' away. They already had their pistols out and were throwing shots back at me. So there we were, standing close by and blasting away at each other. When it was over, I don't know what happened with the bullets, but it finally boiled down to that I never got hit and all three of dem guys were dead in the street. Don't ask me how, I don't even know myself. Just lucky I guess."

"Wow...lucky isn't the word," I said, mesmerized by the story.

"Now when the cops came..." Lou sat back in his chair. "... they took me and booked me inta da Tombs. I was there for three months and there was no way I was pleading out. No way. There were days when I thought I wouldn't make it. I already spent half my life in the can so fuck them, I was going to trial for Murder One—that's where ya either walk or get the chair."

"Geez...Lou," I said. "That's some situation."

"It was Charlie Lucky," came Lou's sharp response, "that came up with the idea of askin' Clarence Darrow to defend me. Now this Darrow guy was high-class and didn't wanna ruin his reputation wid no two bit wise guy like me so he said he'd do it but not as the attorney on record. Charlie Lucky had to get another mouthpiece for that.

"When we went to trial, Darrow wanted us to get all the witnesses we could. Can you imagine? I thought he was off his rocker because like I told ya there must a been a thousand of them coloreds there on the street and what were they gonna say happened? But Darrow knew what he was doing because when he got them up on the stand and started questioning them, they were all givin' different answers to the same questions. Like they were full of shit. Even when Darrow got the truth out of them, he did it in such a way that made them sound like they were bullshittin'." Lou gave a broad smile. "One guy, one of the main witnesses, was lookin' out his window watchin' from one floor up over me. He said that he saw the whole thing and that those guys never drew no guns, the lying cocksucker that he was.

"Do you blink?" Darrow asked him.

"Yeah." The guy shrugs at him.

"Well, possibly when you blinked that day," Darrow says.

"One of the deceased pulled out a pistol?"

"I didn't do no blinkin' that day...your Honor," the witness said.

"Then Darrow brought out the weather report and proved to the court that if the witness was hanging out of the window like he said he was that day, the snow and wind would have been going right into his face because of the direction of the storm. The witness didn't know what to say. Silence filled the air when the witness clammed up. It went on like that with other witnesses and the jury found me innocent and I walked. I got Charlie Lucky to thank for that. And wait a fuckin' minute, here's the kicker... that Darrow was good and he knew it—he wouldn't take any money. He loved the idea that Charlie Lucky owed him a big one, and that's the way it was. Lucky sent him over to the Red Devil Restaurant where he picked up Darrow's check for dinner."

Unbelievable...

My Uncle Scatsy always referred to his brother Johnny as the "ole man." Ten o'clock in the morning and Scatsy's working his way through the paper as usual. He always started from the back in the sports section and read his way forward to the front.

Scatsy continued reading the paper and didn't acknowledge me when I entered the Peppermint Lounge. Then he abruptly stopped, slammed his clenched fist onto the desk, and cried out, "Look at this shit, Dick, here's a priest holdin' up the crown jewels...can you believe this bullshit? They're still talking about this heist. For crissake it happened more than six years ago. Ma Dawn, the ole man had us help get 'em back."

"Help who? Get what?" I asked.

Scatsy paid no attention to me and continued scanning the article that had a picture of a Monsignor holding up two jeweled crown pieces over his head.

"Holy shit," he said. "Don't make me laugh. They wanna make a ceremony for the anniversary of the miracle of the return of the jewels...boy, that's a hot one."

Scatsy finished the article then threw down the newspaper. "It always amazes me how shit like this, that's so far from the truth, gets reported by the press. And, on the front page no less." He looked at me. "Miracle my ass." He straightened out the fingers of his right hand and vigorously shook them up and down in front of his crotch. "Here's your miracle…right here."

Years prior to this article, thieves broke into St. Rosalia's Church in Brooklyn in the middle of the night and robbed the display of its jeweled crowns. No fingerprints or evidence were left. The police held the usual ongoing investigation, but turned up nothing. The event of a church being robbed wouldn't have been that significant except for one thing. This was Joe Profaci's church. He was one of the reigning bosses of the original five Mafia families in New York City and a deeply religious man who had given untold thousands of dollars to St. Rosalia's, making it the pride of Brooklyn.

I picked up the newspaper and started reading the article. "You and the ole man got this back for the church? You're kidding right?"

"No! We helped Profaci get it back, all the Boys did. I remember going around myself looking and asking everyone if they knew anything about a booster with a green car who'd ripped off a church in Brooklyn. A church janitor remembered seein' a green car parked in the area the night of the robbery, but it was the only clue."

I wanted to know more. "So, what happened?"

Scatsy's eyes settled on mine and he went on to relate the rest of the story to me. "So after they robbed the jewels from the church, the Monsignor goes and tells his congregation to pray for their safe return. Now the church is packed everyday with people praying like he asks. Remember this is Joe Profaci's church. A religious nut, right?"

"Really? You're talkin' about THE Joe Profaci?" I smile. "You keep saying that out loud and people in this town are going to believe you."

"Yeah, why, what's wrong with that?"

"You're telling me that Profaci's a religious nut? I can hardly believe that."

"And he's a great family man too." Scatsy shrugs in an

indifferent way. "And don't ever talk about broads around him. He don't go for hookers or any a that bullshit either."

"Oh, gee I'm glad you told me." I rolled my eyes toward the ceiling. "Like I'm gonna be talkin' to him tomorrow...so, what happened then?"

"Profaci flips out when he hears they robbed his church. He went bananas and called for a major meeting with all the other bosses then asked them to help him find out who swiped the crowned jewels...and get them back."

"And, then?"

Scatsy's face turned somber. "I don't remember everything, but I do remember it was back around '52, sometime in the summer, maybe."

His mind drifted back to recall the events as they unfolded. The silence is broken moments later as the memories flooded back to him. "The boosters cut the wire to the burglar alarm and kicked away the bar to get to the altar, then they reached in and grabbed the crowns. It was actually a clumsy job. Still, they didn't discover the jewels were missing till the next day. The cops had nothing to go on. The usual punks and boosters were brought in for questioning, but ya know, once again, without stool pigeons there was no evidence, so where they gonna go? The case went out the window."

"Wow, then you got involved?"

"Yeah. This became a big thing with the Boys. Every thief had a lot of explaining to do."

This was Joe Profaci's church and he felt like he had an obligation to get the Sacred Crown Jewels back. Profaci was takin' it personal. Ya know, he went to church almost every day at that Saint Rosalia's and forget about how much money he put into the joint? He practically built the whole church by himself, so when this happened, of course, the Monsignor called him first—it became some kinda unholy partnership."

"Man, Profaci must have been pissed."

"You got that right," Scatsy said. "He sounded the battle cry, putting every thief and fence in the city on notice. Every booster knew those jewels were going be returned or else. It was round up time in New York City. Once Joe Profaci gave the orders, all the families responded. There was a wide dragnet. Characters suspected of knowing anything were dug up out of their holes. Profaci pledged he'd get to anyone who had anything to do with the heist. It was dog eat dog time. Thieves realized they might be marked simply for being suspected of knowing something. It was clear they intended to punish anyone who didn't cooperate—loyal or not, in or out of jail. Terror struck hard. Fear was the mob's strongest ally and Profaci used it."

Scatsy continued his trip back in time. "Johnny told me, Chinky, Fat the Butch, Joe Zingara, Georgie Hooks, and the rest of his boys spread the word around the streets that they were looking for the jewelry that was heisted from a church in Brooklyn named Saint Rosalia. It's Joe Profaci's church and they took something of his. This gets a big green light. They want that swag back otherwise a lotta heads are gonna roll...I believed them on that. Johnny never saw Profaci so pissed. We turned the city upside down. Some even got into the act by mistake. A young punk makes a remark he shouldn't have and Noodles carves him up on the spot. During the early days of the round up, any number of lowlifes were held until it was clear they weren't involved with the theft. One canary broke the mystery. He'd heard of a boasting young Puerto Rican who drove a green car."

Scatsy's voice trailed off for a minute then grew in intensity. "To Johnny it became like a crusade. He tells me to get the word out to the kid, to tell the booster to give the jewels back and we'll forget about everything. But the canary was scared shitless. He was so afraid he was gonna get whacked himself that he takes off to the other end of the city to Yonkers somewhere and hides out. He must have gotten word to the booster, because several days later the crowned jewels were returned to the church, by mail of all things...can you believe that?"

"Boy, that's something."

"You're not kidding." Scatsy was all smiles. "The Monsignor gets this package and the jeweled crowns are inside. He's so excited he gets up and runs into the church holdin' them up over his head and starts shoutin' all over the joint. 'It's a miracle...a miracle has taken place! The crown jewels have been returned to the church! It's a miracle! A true miracle! People start fainting in the aisles and suddenly applause breaks out right there in the church. The newspapers write it up like it's some kind of miracle and everybody's happy."

Scatsy sat back and put his feet up on the desk, clasping his hands behind his head. "It's all bullshit. Not only that, but a stone is missing. That was a no-no and not the deal. The booster knew he made a mistake but it was too late. Profaci tracked him down, recovered the stone and whacked him, sending a message out that bad things happen to people who mess with him."

Scatsy noticed the curious smile on my face. "I don't doubt you," I said, "but it just seems so funny to me that a guy like Profaci, one of the most feared mob bosses anywhere, is so religious. I wouldn't expect something like that of him...don't you find that strange?"

"I don't know." Scatsy paused, then gave a reassuring nod. "People only hear one side of the story. Maybe he's like one of them battlin' angels they got...ya get me?"

"Yeah, maybe." I took in what he said for a moment. "If he is, they certainly got the right guy...he knows how to fight fire with more than fire."

"Make no mistake about it," Scatsy said. "Joe Profaci is a very religious man."

"A battling angel." I couldn't help but laugh. "Boy, that's a good one."

Chapter 23

Favo Allan

Preface

Crime and the follies of human misfortune have had a profound influence on mankind throughout history. This story, which spans approximately five years before and five years following World War II, is a hard boiled, stranger than fiction true story about a lower east side street kid who, through a quirky set of circumstances, embarks on a wild and incredible journey through the criminal world with waves of brutality, resulting in a set of uncanny and unintended consequences.

Seated in my restaurant were Chris Dundee, the famous fight promoter, Jake Lansky, brother of crime boss Meyer Lansky, and Ernie Fliegel, a bon vivant fight manager and the inspiration for Al Capp's cartoon character, "Evil Eye Fleegle." I joined their table early in the evening. The mood hummed, jubilant and relaxed. It was one of those rare evenings where the conversation flowed easily with remembered stories of old friends and good times.

"You ever hear of Favo Allan?" Ernie Fliegel asked me.

"No." I shook my head, thinking they were talking about a fighter. "What's his weight class?"

Jake Lansky laughed. "He wasn't a fighter. He was one of the Boys. The problem the police had with Favo was not knowing what he did...it was catching him at it. His is an unbelievable story."

Just then, Jimmy Blue Eyes stopped by our table. "I'd like to have a piece of what you guys are cutting up," he quipped.

Everyone laughed. "Dick never heard of Favo Allan," Chris Dundee said.

"I'm not surprised," Jimmy replied. "His MO was to fly under the radar, and that was all a long time ago. You should tell him the story."

Favo Allan is the story of a deeply flawed and complicated character, bordering on superhuman. Some of the names have been changed, but the incredible saga of events is, to the best of my memory, what was told to me that night.

The Beginning

Living in the gutters of New York, Favo's bizarre behavior served to keep others in the neighborhood at a distance. Some weren't sure whether he was half man, half animal, or just plain wacky. Some tried pinning the name Bugsy on him. He wasted no time in putting a stop to that by issuing severe beatings to those responsible. Once the word got around that Favo would have no part of the nickname, it got reassigned to Benny Siegel, another crazy from the neighborhood.

"Your friend, Fat the Butch just spit in Favo's eye."

"Yeah?" Bugsy Siegel said. "I'd like to shake his hand."

"Ya can't, he's got a lily in it. Favo left him on the floor full of holes."

Bugsy Siegel, an evil kid from another gang, was a close pal of Fat the Butch. So when Favo killed Fat the Butch, as far as Bugsy was concerned, that made them archenemies. Bugsy sent word out they should meet and settle the score between them. Favo agreed, and now sitting opposite each other, the blood in Favo's temples pounded, echoing the storm that raged outside.

"Cullyuns?" he said. "Ya know what they are don't ya? Balls...I don't want ya goin' to ya maker without knowin' what I'm talking about."

Bugsy twisted his face into an expression of stark cruelty. "Since when did anyone give a shit about what you said?" He eyed the gun that laid on the table between them. "What did ya do...swipe it?"

"None of your fuckin' business." Favo spat the words with an angry sneer.

The gun on the table was a .38 special—a policeman's gun. Lying next to it were two .38 caliber bullets. Favo, handsome and well proportioned, looked unconcerned, showing no emotion. Benny was equally good looking and had more than enough size to him. Neither had any intentions of backing down from the agreement they'd made to settle the beef. All in the clubroom were there to be sure of that.

"Who goes first?" Bugsy said in a sharp voice. "Or ya want me to choke it outta ya?"

"That'll be the fuckin' day. We'll toss for it." Favo grabbed a coin. "You call it."

"Tails," Bugsy said.

The coin came down heads. "That's me," Favo said. "I go first."

Favo broke open the gun and took one of the bullets from the table and slid it into the empty chamber then spun the cylinder. "This gun holds six bullets so our chances are one in six...pretty good odds, eh?"

"You got any relatives?" Bugsy said, more than a hint of sarcasm in his voice.

An icy flare came to Favo's eyes. "None of your fuckin' business what I got," he said jutting out his chin.

"Well, stop ya yappin' then," Bugsy said in the same tone, "and get on with it."

Favo's jaw tightened in anger as he put the barrel of the .38 up to his forehead and pulled the trigger. It clicked on an empty chamber. Without any emotion whatsoever, Favo slid the gun across the table at Bugsy. "Now it's your turn asshole," he said.

When Bugsy grabbed it he didn't look so cocky. He opened the chamber and checked to see if the bullet was there. "Let's up the odds," Bugsy said and put the other bullet in a chamber and spun it around again. He slowly raised the pistol and placed it to his temple, but instead of pulling the trigger he yelled out, "Bang!" Then howled with laughter.

As lightning flashed outside, Bugsy stood up and pointed the pistol at Favo's face and started to pull the trigger. Silence settled over the room except for the clicks of the pistol's hammer coming down on empty chambers. It seemed like an eternity but only a split second passed before Favo leaped out of his chair and delivered a devastating right to Bugsy's jaw, that sent him tumbling backwards to the floor unconscious. The gun flew out of his hand, spinning to rest on the floor at Sonny Boy's feet.

Sonny Boy picked it up and tossed it to Favo. Members from both sides hung for a moment in suspended anticipation then began to brawl without abandon. As glass and wooden furniture exploded everywhere around them, the gun went off, leading to screams out on the street. Before long wailing police sirens sounded in the distance. Someone yelled, "Beat it, the cops!"

Seconds later, two policemen rushed in with whistles blowing and took down Favo, clubbing him viciously with their nightsticks. Favo started punching away but as the crowd scattered, another policemen came in and quickly helped to subdue him. It was a scary moment. Favo was arrested for assaulting an officer and disturbing the peace.

Circuit Court Judge Joel Green agreed to hold an evidentiary hearing regarding recantations made by two witnesses against Favo Allan, who said they saw him shoot the gun. If Judge Green found no forensic evidence linking Favo to the shooting, the case would collapse but fingerprints identified on the gun at the crime scene were Favo's.

"I never shot the gun, Your Honor," said Favo. "But, I was there, we were all in a big fight...I only picked it up."

Not one shred of other physical evidence linked Favo Allan to the weapon that had been stolen off the body of a dead police officer two years prior. The accusation against Favo proved how far the prosecution would go to get a conviction. After the fight started, a witness noted a shot went off and the police quickly responded to the scene. Despite Favo's fingerprints on the gun there was no gunpowder residue on his hands to prove that he'd pulled the trigger.

While in detention during the interrogation, a detective

threatened Favo. He stared down the detective. "I don't know what you're talking about. All I know is I didn't shoot nobody."

When it came time for the trial, Favo took the stand and testified in his own defense that he had no involvement in stealing the gun in question. He remained calm throughout and answered each question clearly and respectfully. Rather than risk having his decision overturned by a higher court, Judge Green amended his decision and Favo agreed to plead guilty and do six months on a charge of disorderly conduct.

The reality of rotting away in jail got to him. Favo couldn't imagine how these luckless men lived on the damp, cold floors day-after-day, staring out into the bleak future as the years of their sentences piled up on top of one another like the stones of the prison walls—fate had slipped him a Mickey. He was in the wrong place at the wrong time, but then again he would only be there for six months, and as fate would have it, Kid Twist was his cellmate.

Kid Twist was a member of Murder Incorporated and part of the new breed of tough Jew mobsters running with Charlie "Lucky" Luciano's mob. Favo had heard rumours that he was even tougher than Meyer Lansky. It could be good to know a gangster like Kid Twist, but Favo could care less and wasn't kowtowing to anyone.

Despite his decision to stay out of the messy alliances that always seemed to spring up in jail, Favo found himself sucked in by an old unsettled score between Kid Twist and fellow prisoner, Larry Rosenberg.

Years before, Kid Twist had killed Larry Rosenberg's brother in a territorial dispute. Rosenberg harbored hatred and vowed revenge. Now together in prison, Rosenberg put his plan to kill Kid Twist into action. Favo saw Rosenberg approaching Kid Twist from the back with a knife ready in hand. Like an explosion, Favo leaped over the table, brought him down and picked up the knife that skidded out of Rosenberg's hand, plunging it deep into his gut again and again until the other prisoners pulled him off, but not before one of the guards saw this and claimed that Favo was the killer.

Favo spent several weeks in solitary because he wouldn't talk—sticking to his story that he didn't see anything. Kid Twist got Favo a new lawyer, and in time, he walked out of jail a free man with the respect of Kid Twist. He had made his mark as a man, but didn't expect much to come of it.

On His Way

For the last week, the raw and miserable weather had been the worst he'd seen in a decade—way worse than even the winter of '24. The snow had been falling all morning and no matter how hard Favo banged on the radiator, no heat. He left his apartment on the lower east side and walked down Third Avenue, pausing to look through the snow coming down across Delancey Street. The silhouette of the Williamsburg Bridge rose in the distance, arching over the East River to Brooklyn where he was born. His mind floated back—*I'm a long fuckin' way from there now,* he thought.

He entered Coffee Central, where they all knew him, and hung his coat up on the rack by the counter. Ellie, the gum-chewing waitress, set a cup of hot coffee down at his elbow. He was thinking about Cuba, where all this snow would be nothing but soft rain coming down through palm trees on a beautiful sandy beach. He'd be in a soft bed with a long-haired Latina beauty curled at his side, in a place with open windows letting in gentle, warm breezes to the sounds of the tropics. Yes, that's where he'd be, if the deal were right. After a life of petty crime and gangland violence here was his chance. He finished his coffee, threw down some change, and stood up, then slipped his coat back on and stepped outside.

The sound of tires crunching snow approached the curb. Headlights flashed as a new Dodge stopped in front of him. The driver motioned to open the door. "You Favo Allan?"

"Yeah."

"Good, get in."

Favo climbed in and the Dodge pulled away.

"Nice to meet ya, I'm Meyer Lansky. Kid Twist told me about

you. He said you're a 'shtarke' and that's good enough for me."

"Yeah, well he told me about you too." Favo nodded smugly. "But, before we get started, I wanna make one thing clear. I don't work for nobody."

"That's right." Lansky raised an eyebrow. "We're gonna be partners and like all good partners, we're gonna provide a service for each other."

Favo looked at the glint of determination in Lansky's eyes and remained silent. Kid Twist had told him about Meyer's cunning business ability. Ordinarily Favo wouldn't give two shits for guys like Lansky, especially not for his friend, the rat bastard, Bugsy Siegel who he hated. But for some reason when Lansky contacted him, he agreed to meet him.

Prohibition had been repealed. But with its repeal, bootlegging didn't simply fade away. Because they didn't pay alcohol taxes, bootleggers put out a much more reasonably priced product than the legal distilleries. The Cuban government supplied Lansky with all the sugar he needed to set up direct distribution to still operators and he became known as the Molaska King.

Lansky went directly to the subject of the meeting and asked Favo to make a run with a freighter load of sugar from Cuba, through the Panama Canal, up the Mexican coast, and to a still operator in San Diego. He took out an envelope from his coat pocket and handed it to Favo. When Favo opened it and saw money inside, his heart gave a little skip. "What's this for?"

"Expenses...for you," Lansky replied, stopped for a red light. "Go down to Miami Beach and check into the Bel Aire Hotel. Have some fun for yourself, then ask for Jimmy Blue Eyes. He'll be expecting you...he'll tell you how to get to Havana and who you have to see. Jimmy's our man down there."

"Let's say I go for this deal," Favo said with a trace of cockiness in his voice. "How do we divvy up the money? I don't wanna get screwed, having someone comin' in later sayin' something else."

The light changed and the Dodge inched forward. "Like I said, if we're partners, we're partners." Lansky's words hung in the air. "We're gonna get fifty percent plus costs up front, so that'll be ours. When you deliver the goods in San Diego...you keep what they give ya there. It should be over a hundred G's."

Lansky put him at ease. Favo looked at him, not with just a glance but with a long hard stare and decided he liked what he saw. "Okay, I'm in."

"Good." Lansky assured him with a confident glance. "Remember, this is just a start. I want to expand to the West coast. Kid Twist said you've got what it takes, and now that I've met you, I agree."

Lansky pulled over to the curb. Favo got out but then bent back down to stare inside. "What?" Lansky asked.

Favo arched his eyebrows. "We got a deal, right?"

Lansky nodded with finality. "Right...we got a deal."

Favo waved, acknowledging the final approval and slammed the door shut.

The Trip

The freighter, packed to capacity with Cuban sugar, made its way out of Havana harbor and headed west towards the Panama Canal. Favo leaned against the railing on deck and just watched the stars. As a little kid he'd always felt they held a special destiny for him. Someday, those stars would summon him. The bad things seemed all behind him now. Although, it was a funny thing how he kept thinking about Bugsy Siegel. Of course, he didn't want to see him any more than he imagined Bugsy wanted to see him.

But standing under those stars, Favo vowed that one day he would settle that score. He went up to the bridge and stood next to Captain Dega. It had been a run of the mill trip until they got to the Pacific side of the Mexican coast, where the freighter suddenly developed engine trouble and headed for an unscheduled stop in Mazatlan.

"I don't like that ping I hear in the engine," Captain Dega said. "We're going in to Mazatlan. Luckily I know someone there who will make the repairs quickly so we can be on our way again."

When the freighter docked, Favo wanted to indulge himself and have a little fun, so he asked Captain Dega if he knew any hot Mexican rumba dances in town.

The Captain blinked as though caught in a lie. He shook his head, rejecting the idea. "There won't be any time for señoritas."

"No time? You're kidding...right?" said Favo, looking at him in surprise. "There's always time."

Ramon, another officer on the bridge interrupted with a muffled remark in Spanish. It caught Favo's attention as an insult. "Watch your fuckin' tone." Favo pointed a finger at him. "Nobody's talking to you."

Captain Dega covered the tension with a hasty apology. "It's a joke. Please Señor Favo he only makes a joke. When we dock, I know a place where we can go and have a drink and find some ladies."

Everyone forced a laugh, except for Favo. He unwillingly gave Ramon the benefit of the doubt, but held his gaze until Ramon lowered his head and walked away. "Cocksucker," Favo muttered after him.

The Hit

Favo wore a faded shirt, open in the front, over khaki trousers with canvas boat shoes without socks. The more formal Captain Dega was dressed in his naval merchant uniform. They arrived at the Trocadero, one of the best cantinas in town, known for its excellent local food, lively music, and the most beautiful señoritas of the evening. The scent of jasmine came in with the moonlight that shone down through the window slats of the cantina onto their table. Favo and Dega, with a couple prostitutes sitting across from them, relaxed in the lounge, enjoying the mariachi band on stage.

Captain Dega leaned in close to his woman with a broad smile. "What will you have to drink?"

"Cerveza." The older of the two women returned his smile.

"If you drink beer, you must be working very hard." Captain Dega chuckled at his own remark.

She tilted her head and shrugged with a dry politeness. For a moment the younger one simply held Favo's gaze. She looked so vulnerable, so ready. Both women were attractive but the younger one with long dark hair and flashing black eyes was beautiful.

"Which one do you want to f***?" Captain Dega said.

Favo wanted to stuff his fist down the Captain's throat for the remark, but instead slowly turned and sent a disgusted look that acknowledged how he felt. The older woman with auburn hair sprinkled with gray sat unnerved before them. There was a marked resemblance between the women. Mother and daughter Favo concluded. Perla, the younger one, looked at Favo and smiled. It was clear from her expression that she understood the difference between the two men. As Captain Dega continued to shoot his mouth off, Perla suppressed her laughter. Her eyes flickered and she caught Favo with a flirtatious stare. "Your friend, he is *muy simpatico, señor,*" she said, a heavy note of sarcasm in her voice.

Favo, focused only on her low-cut blouse, didn't notice the shadow that moved the beaded curtain hanging in the doorway behind him. Perla's eyes widened. A sinister figure emerged, gliding silently behind the crowded tables while steadily observing them. Though she continued to smile and chat away, a brief shudder rippled through her body, her eyes darting through the cantina. Favo, entranced by her lively manner, sat and sipped his drink while making small talk.

Pouncing on a brief pause in the conversation, Perla changed the subject from idle chit-chat to the hot topic of the day, the President of Mexico's new baby grandson.

"Have you heard about it Señor?" Perla smiled.

"No." Favo shook his head. "About what?"

"Presidente Quezon of the Philippine's daughter." Perla's voice rose like out of a dream as she went on to explain. "She is only seventeen when she comes to Mexico and falls in love with our Presidente Cardenas's son. He is eighteen and lives in the palace. She becomes, you know how you say, Señor...with baby? And they marry but before the little chicito is born, the marriage, it falls, no good. After that things are *muy malo* for her Señor, and she is sent back to the Philippines without her baby and how you say it? No more marry."

Favo's eyes were fixated on her compelling beauty, as she continued to speak. "President Quezon begs for them to let his daughter visit her baby but no, they want no part of her. You have no idea, Señor, the hatred they have for each other. I know this because my sister is the nurse who cares for the baby. She sees and hears everything. They would give anything to have the baby back in the Philippines...I mean anything. *Er verdad, Señor.*"

All of this meant nothing to Captain Dega who drummed his fingers, anxious to get back to the freighter. "Why are we listening to this babble? Let's get on with it," he said with a snarl.

Favo said in a burst of anger, "Shut up and go wherever ya gotta go."

The Captain balked, holding his hands up in protest. His eyes flashed side to side as though searching for someone. By now Favo was tired of his horseshit and slammed his palm down hard on the table with a resounding bang! He stood up and pointed a finger at Perla. "Come on, let's go."

"Okay, gringo," Perla stammered, getting to her feet. "I am with you."

She escorted Favo to a room through the back of the hotel overlooking a courtyard.

When they got close to the room, Perla hurried him into an alcove, looking down the hall on each side to make sure they were alone. She gripped Favo's wrist. "That man is not your friend, Señor."

"You're telling me." Favo glanced around obviously upset.

"No," Perla said in a voice edged with desperation. "I mean I see him looking around all the time watching the other man."

"What other man?" He asked, gently shaking Perla by the shoulders. "Who ya talking about?"

Perla's breathing became erratic and Favo could see the panic in her face. "Please, Señor," she said, the skin on her arms prickling with a sudden deep chill. "I know the face of the hombre in the shadows. He is an assassin, Señor...you are in great danger. I would go fast from here Gringo... *muy pronto...ahora...*now."

Perla's words hit him like a sledgehammer. As soon as they

entered the room Favo peered out the darkened window at two men in the distance, descending the broad steps of the veranda into the moonlight. It was Captain Dega and the man Perla referred to as the assassin, everything became clear to him now and his survival instincts kicked in. Favo didn't hesitate. He was a survivor from Delancey Street. He looked at Perla. "Close the door after me and keep it locked. Don't let anyone in until I get back."

Perla opened her mouth then shut it, perhaps unsure about how to say it. "Please be careful, Gringo."

Favo stopped and took a hard look at Perla. "Yeah," he said and disappeared into the darkness.

After silently descending the stairs, Favo made his way up the path and snuck up behind the dark figure. There was a sudden hush in the courtyard. The deadly crack of the assassin's neck echoed in the stillness. He didn't stop to acknowledge life from death and swiftly picked up the assassin's weapon, a stiletto knife. He crept forward with the utmost caution, seeking to overtake the treacherous Captain Dega.

Turning down a dark, quiet street that led to the dock, Favo came up behind the Captain and plunged the stiletto deep into the bottom of his jaw, violently moving it around and around, up though his palate and the mushy gray matter until he got to the thick bone of his skull. He dropped him to the ground dead. Favo took his pistol before returning to the motel. He gave a soft tap on the door. Perla jerked back at the sound, scrambling for the closet. Hearing no answer, Favo entered the room. "Perla?"

She emerged from her hiding place in the closet. "Oh, *Dio mio*," she said, recognizing him. "Ay...I thought you were dead, Gringo."

They stood close, very close. Her scent aroused his senses and Favo flashed a gratifying smile. Her beautiful face responded in kind. He had a plan in mind and asked Perla to keep the room and wait until he returned. He gave her a thousand dollars cash, American money, which was more than she would earn in a year and promised to be back in about ten days. But if he didn't return she was to get on with her life.

The color drained from Perla's face. "Señor, I have never seen so much money."

"Don't worry about it." he measured her with a speculative eye. "You've earned more than that here tonight for saving my life."

"Oh no, Señor," Perla blurted out. "I do nothing."

Favo touched her skin, obsessing over her hands.

"Remember what I said," he moved in closer. "I'll be back."

She looked up. "I pray for it, Señor." She wrapped her arms around his neck and kissed him with a feverish intensity as though she wanted to eat him alive. She clung to his broad shoulders, and Favo kissed her back.

In this moment, this one shimmering moment, Favo knew this was the woman for him. But he had to go. It took him a few seconds to straighten himself out before he walked to the door where he paused and turned. "Oh, incidentally," he said. "That story you told me about your sister and the baby...is it true?"

Perla took a step back, the look in her eyes told him all he needed to know. She lifted a brow, planted her fists on her hips and said unsmiling, "Would I lie to you, Gringo?"

On To San Diego

Favo made his way up the gangplank to the freighter. Near the bridge, he pushed inside past the others, and put the pistol behind the ear of the first officer who stood at the wheel. Knowing no subtle way to ask he said, "Do as I tell ya or you're fuckin' dead."

In simple terms, he explained that the Captain had met his maker and gave the officer a choice: a chance to live and share in the money when the freighter got to San Diego or go like the Captain. It wasn't much of a choice and they settled the deal.

The night was crisp and windless when the freighter got underway. Favo saw officer Ramon from the bridge and boomed, "Hey, Ramon!"

Ramon mounted the steps then blinked in recognition when he saw Favo. "Where is Captain Dega?" He asked.

Favo stood with gun in hand and countered by slapping it

hard across Ramon's face sending him to the deck. He shoved the gun back into his belt and grabbed him by the collar, dragging him over to the railing. With a single heave he threw Ramon overboard, eliminating any further chance of anything else happening.

The rest of the trip to San Diego went as expected. Favo collected the money, paid the crew off, and made plans for his return to Mexico. His mind spun as he made his way back to Mazatlan with more than a hundred thousand dollars secreted under the floorboards of a van he'd purchased. He was sure Perla would be waiting for him when he arrived. The whole situation felt good. His impulse was to involve Perla and her sister in a plan he had devised to kidnap the Presidential family's baby. Of all the pipe dreams he ever had, he believed this one was the most fantastic, but it would depend on Perla to take the initiative.

Favo, on his way back through town toward the motel, caught a glimpse of Perla walking on the beach, her gait that of a young filly. His mood lifted. Favo wondered if the spark that passed between them so recently would still be there. He left the van, walked down to the sand, and quietly stepped up behind Perla, touching her arm. Startled, she whirled around. "Hello, Perla," Favo said in a murmur.

She froze then ran her fingers through her hair. Her chest heaved from the adrenaline fluttering her heart and eased her lips into the slightest of smiles. "Hello, Gringo."

Back in the room, Perla's voice was warm and soft as Favo's fingers opened the bottom button of her blouse. Her bosom rose and she consented with a nod.

After a night of seeing what heaven was like, Favo reclined on a pillow, explaining to her that he'd come up with a plan to kidnap the baby from the Presidential Palace in Mexico City and return it to its mother in the Philippines, possibly for a large sum of money.

"This can only be accomplished," Favo said in a cool detached voice, "With the help of your sister...the baby's nursemaid."

"Tell me more, Gringo." Perla craned her neck to look up at him.

Favo pulled a list off the nightstand and started reading off the options of the plot and analyzing every detail. "From past experience," Favo said, "I know if we try something too complicated, in the end, it usually doesn't work out. We must make this simple for your sister's sake. She's the one that has to carry it out alone, without any other staff members knowing anything about it. She cannot trust anyone. Of course, it's gonna be worth her while."

By the time Favo finished explaining, Perla had been given a clear picture of what the mission entailed, not to mention the extreme gravity if they failed. They were on to something big and Perla invited her mother from next door to join them.

"This is my dream," Perla said balancing herself gingerly on the edge of her chair. "Long ago *mia Madre agui.*" She patted her mother's knee. "Told me and my sister that she could only depart this world in peace if both of us had the means to live a decent life. As you can see, Gringo, we will do anything we have to do to make this possible. My sister will do it Señor." A bitter smile tugged at the corners of Perla's lips. "After all, it is only right that the baby should be with its mother. We will go to Mexico City to see my sister." Perla reassured Favo with a confident nod. "And you will see for yourself."

Handsome and high-spirited, Favo Allan was always one to court the perils of chance. Everyone who knew him agreed that he had all the balls and none of the qualms to go into areas that were off-limits to most other humans. His out-of-bound schemes solemnly entailed every risk. Nothing would prevent Favo from forging ahead with his plan. What lay ahead for them was not only difficult...it was dangerous.

Early the next morning, in windy predawn darkness, Favo, Perla and her mother loaded his van with their belongings and headed for Mexico City. They started the slow trek to the highway, negotiating the street's potholes while heavy rains lashed across the windshield. Once on the highway, the winding route headed east. Favo cranked the wipers as high as they would go to sweep off the relentless rain. Traffic was heavy. Beside the road, a herd of goats clustered beneath a large tree with their caretaker. Favo looked at the herder who seemed not to be bothered by it all and thought, *he's probably happier than any of us.* A break came in the traffic and he pressed his foot down hard on the accelerator jolting the van ahead. Outside of Mexico City, behind a long line of cars, Favo warned himself to concentrate on his driving. He entered a long, deep tunnel, a dark passageway into the city. When he emerged, a sudden gust of wind hit the van and rocked it violently. As another shower of rain blanketed the windshield, he wondered what would it be like to die in a Mexican prison.

Maria, every bit as beautiful as her sister, arrived at the hotel with endless enthusiasm. She hurried to Favo's room where she hugged her mother and sister, Perla.

"You all look wonderful as usual." Her eyes, full of questions, darted to Favo.

"We need to talk," said Perla. "You know our dream of being set for life?"

"*Si*...of course," said Maria continuing to nod.

Perla's hand swept over to Favo and pointed a finger, "Well, this *hombre aqui* may be our answer now. Say hello to Favo Allan."

Maria, who had gained unexpected renown as the most dependable caretaker for the new baby in the Presidential household, turned her smiling face into a stone mountain of concentration.

"Before we talk," Perla said in a tone that reflected the somber moment.

"*Dime Algo,* I have to ask you...are you still caring for the President's new baby grandson?"

Maria paused and looked cautiously around the room. She shrugged and said, "Si." Favo's skin prickled at the gesture.

Perla leaned forward and described Favo's plan in detail. Her tone sharpened the more the information tumbled out. She was so upbeat no one would ever believe just a few weeks before she'd led the life of a prostitute. Maria got the picture immediately and Favo sprang to life when she said, "Just tell me what I have to do and I will do it."

"Here's the plan I have in mind," Favo said and spent the rest of the day going over every detail. After thoroughly rehearsing the plan, he nodded approval that they were ready to swing into action.

The Deed

By a stroke of luck, everyone in the presidential family was away in Guadalajara celebrating a function—everyone, except for the baby. The timing couldn't have been more perfect. Maria put the baby in a sleeper and edged her way out of the room and down towards a back hall that led to an exit door. Once outside the palace grounds, she nonchalantly walked without haste, as instructed, to the end of the block where she stopped under a tree and stepped into a waiting car. They took off, slowly merging into the dense traffic of the avenue, continuing to where Perla and her mother waited. They transferred the baby to their van, and before the kidnapping was even discovered, they were in Mazatlan where they boarded a charter boat Favo had pre-arranged to take them to San Diego. It was as simple as that.

Alarms went out all over Mexico. Almost a thousand agents of the Mexican government searched for the baby. The American Embassy, the FBI, and the Border Patrol undertook additional measures. No strong leads surfaced. No ransom demands were ever made. The meagerness of the information gathered suggested there was very little hope of recovering the baby.

The *La Fortuna* was one of fifty or so fishing vessels working out of Mazatlan. Usually at this time of year, they were all packed with anglers and ready for the season. People from around the world came there to fish. But fishing was not easy and the ocean could be fickle. At the start of the season, a temperature swing of a few degrees pushed the key sport fish out of the range of local boats. Customers were scarce and fuel expensive. Four or five boats had already gone bankrupt in Mazatlan, and if they had another bad year there would be more. The only reason Perla's mother recommended the boat's captain, Manuel Gomez, to Favo was because he occasionally made visits to her. This charter came as a much needed boost for Gomez, as he was on the verge of losing his boat.

The boat ride up the Mexican coast, for the most part, was uneventful. There were two cabins on board, Maria and her mother stayed in one and Perla and Favo in the other. They all took turns watching the baby. Everything continued smoothly until Gomez heard a report over the ship's radio about a missing baby. It didn't take a genius to put two and two together. Gomez called Favo up to the bridge where the radio crackled with the news of the kidnapping. The next thing Favo knew Gomez was talking about the kidnapping with questioning eyes and making statements how he had undercharged them for the trip. Back in Mazatlan, when Favo inquired about the cost to Tijuana, Gomez gave him a price and Favo automatically doubled it, stating that he wanted him to stand by and be ready to go when he arrived. Favo always had it in mind to tell Gomez when they were under way to take them to San Diego instead of Tijuana. When Favo saw Gomez trying to squeeze him, alarms started going off in his brain—not because of the money, but rather that he could no longer be trusted. Favo knew this type. He would go straight to the authorities in hopes of getting the large reward the government offered. Gomez had to go, but first, Favo had to play his cards right. He went along with Gomez's demands for more money, letting him think it wouldn't be a problem.

Once they were off the coast of Tijuana, Favo asked Gomez to put the boat on automatic pilot to go on to San Diego. He let him know that he would pay extra for this and recommended they go to the aft deck to discuss the financial matters. On his way to the deck, Favo grabbed the bat they kept on board for whacking the biggest and most troublesome fish they caught. With a single, mighty swing he rendered Gomez unconscious spread eagle on the deck. Favo proceeded to tie the spare anchor firmly around his neck then punched holes in his stomach with the stiletto to further ensure that his body gasses wouldn't float him back up to the surface when dumped overboard. When they got to San Diego, Favo's distillery connections provided him a van so he could continue on to San Francisco.

Once in San Francisco, Favo searched the want ads and bought a day nursery-care center for Maria and her mother.

He obtained the necessary made-up identification and proof of citizenship papers and gave them fifty thousand dollars to run the new business they always wanted. All of that accomplished, Favo, Perla, and the baby booked passage on a freighter bound for Manila where they would deliver the baby to its mother and the Presidential family.

Time alone with Perla on the voyage was just what Favo needed. Their accommodations, a cabin suite forward, was more than adequate and the food was surprisingly good. Sitting topside, the ocean's mild breeze swept Perla's hair over her shoulders. She flashed a smile of appreciation. "I want to thank you, Gringo," she said. "For what you did for my sister and my mother, you have given them a new life."

"It was all part of the deal." Favo returned her smile. "I just did what I promised."

"I know, Gringo," she said. "That's why you are different... most people don't do what they promise."

Favo let out a long, low whistle. "You got that right. And what about you?"

"Me?"

"Yeah you," Favo said. "I met a few broads in my day and most of them are full of shit too..."

"What do you mean, Gringo?"

"What do I mean? Have ya ever seen a young beautiful girl in love with an old guy that's broke? No! That's because money is everything to most people. When ya got the bucks, it makes ya young and handsome—"

"No with me, Gringo." Perla stirred in her deck chair.

"I know Perla, that's what I'm telling ya...you're one in a million and I'm lucky to be here with ya."

"I'm the lucky one, Gringo," Perla said, the sun clouding her vision. "We all know God is working in our lives, but sometimes we forget not everything for us is good. Like you know, Gringo, how God works in mysterious ways. We don't always know how but sometimes we find it out...like in a miracle...that's what you are Gringo. You are my miracle and that's all I have to say."

With the emotion of the moment bringing them together,

Favo became aroused just looking at her. By the time the freighter landed in Manila, a crowbar couldn't pry them apart. They checked into The Isabella Hotel in the heart of Manila. Under other circumstances they might have enjoyed the spacious accommodations, but the only thing presently on Favo's mind was *how much money should he ask for?*

Before Favo had left San Francisco, he wrote a letter to Lansky who was in Cuba at the Hotel Nacional. The letter explained everything and requested advice on how much he should ask for. Favo didn't trust the phones and wasn't sure about the mail either, especially in Cuba where the government confiscated everything. He had to make sure this letter was personally hand delivered to Lansky, and the only way to do that was to have Perla's mother deliver it. Favo set up the whole trip. To be safe, she took a train from San Francisco to Miami where she contacted Jimmy Blue Eyes who would get the letter to Lansky in Havana. Once the letter was in hand, Favo flew her back to the west coast to be with Maria.

So many ideas and clever plays ran through Favo's mind on how to approach the Presidential family. He knew he had to be careful, after all he was in Manila now with their baby. If El Presidente wanted to, he could just take the baby and do what he wanted with them. Another thing that worried him was the possibility the mother wouldn't recognize the baby, it had been awhile since she had last seen him. Wouldn't that be something? All these thoughts weighed on him, but now it was time to make a serious decision. What to do? What to do?

After a good night's rest, Favo felt better and made his way to the International Wire Service. He wired Lansky that he'd safely arrived in Manila. Two days later he eagerly read his reply. A smile came to his face and he dropped into a vacant chair. "Well, I'll be a son-of-a-bitch." Favo beamed.

"You look happy, Gringo," Perla said. "*Que Pasa?*"

Favo took a deep breath. "No wonder they call Meyer a fuckin' genius." His voice boomed. "He's got more layers than an onion...look at what he wants us to do."

Favo read the wire out loud:

Favo, deliver the package three days from the date of this wire. I'm having the boss of this island call the boss of that island and tell him to expect you so they'll know you're legitimate. Remember it's important. Do not ask for anything. He'll try to give you the moon. Don't take it. Go back in a week and tell him, you want to do there in a major hotel what I do here. A first class casino in a big way, all legal and everything, he can't refuse you. Let me know what happens. We'll send the money and a crew from here to get started when you're ready. We'll be partners again...Meyer.

Perla drew herself up to her full height. "What means this, Gringo?"

"It means we're gonna be millionaires baby," Favo said, unable to contain his excitement. "That's what it means."

The Move

As promised, Batista contacted President Quezon of the Philippines with a message that his baby grandson was safe and sound in Manila with an American named Favo Allan, who would be contacting him shortly to return the baby.

When Favo and Perla arrived at the capitol, they were escorted directly into the Presidential quarters. He walked behind Perla who had the baby in her arms, he could almost keep time with the loud beating of her heart. When President Quezon saw his daughter rush over and tear the baby out of Perla's arms, he visibly struggled with excitement to catch his breath. It took him some time to rebound from the emotion. Once he had his feelings in check, he turned to Favo. "How can I ever repay you for what you've done, *Señor*?"

Favo shrugged, only returning a stare.

"Please," El Presidente said. "Tell me what you want?"

"I don't know, Mr. President."

Presidente Quezon never expected such an answer. Favo took a Cuban cigar from a leather case and offered it to him. "For now, Mr. President, let's just have a Cuban cigar and let me tell you something you should know."

El Presidente lit his cigar, drew in deeply then exhaled smoke that diffused over their heads. "I was separated at birth from my mother," Favo went on to explain with candor. "I know what it's like to grow up without a mother, a baby belongs with its mother. Because of Perla's sister we were in a position to take advantage of the situation and that's what we did...so here we are. She was the baby's nurse and saw how terrible your daughter was treated. No mother should ever go through what you daughter endured. She's a wonderful person I understand."

Favo went on to explain in more detail, and Presidente Quezon took note with a look of admiration. "You are a miracle worker, Señor Favo. Think very carefully what it is that I can do for you. This is favor I cannot let go unrewarded."

Favo, the very sole of discretion, just smiled, remembering that silence was the fence that guarded wisdom.

When the story hit the front pages for all to see, the mood of the country turned jubilant and the people celebrated. Press releases stated the Manila secret police had successfully returned the baby to his rightful place with his mother in the Philippines. Favo knew the confusion of their face-to-face still nagged at Presidente Quezon. He could bide his time when he needed to, but that didn't make the waiting any more comfortable.

Favo and Perla moved into the Manila Hotel as guests of El Presidente. That evening they dined on the balcony of their room, which overlooked Manila Bay. Perla could see Favo was in need of a large dose of tenderness. After a few glasses of wine, the anxiety brought on by the meeting vanished and Favo's self-assurance returned.

"I love you, Gringo," Perla said.

"You wouldn't be pullin' my leg, would you?" Favo asked with a broad smile.

"I pull anything you like, Gringo." A faint flush rose high on Perla's cheeks.

Favo gave her a long meaningful look. He could see her mood was pessimistic, but he wasn't having any of it. He knew she needed encouragement and intended to reassure her and put her background behind him for all time. "You don't think I'm gonna dump you, do ya?"

Perla's eyes remained fixed straight ahead. She wiped a tear away with the back of her hand, audibly cursing the premonitions she'd been plagued with since birth. "I don't think anything, Gringo, but you know what I am, but half the lies they tell about me aren't true," Perla said.

Favo sat there without responding, thinking about what she'd said. Although Perla said she foresaw wonderful times ahead with Favo, she also believed big trouble would come her way. That night, they shared with each other the most intimate details about their lives.

The Offer

The secretary closed the door to the Presidential office, sealing Favo inside with El Presidente. The first thing Favo saw was a magnificent oil painting on an easel. The subject, an attractive young woman in an outdoor tropical setting, her jet-black hair set off her delicate features, all immortalized in a regal pose. The portrait seemed to possess a life of its own. Favo, who knew nothing of art, studied it.

"It's a Gauguin, here on loan," El Presidente said. "If you like it I will buy it for you."

"I never heard of the guy, but someone who paints that good should be famous." Favo walked over and stared at the painting. "She reminds me a little of my Perla. Yeah, I like it."

"Then I'll buy it for you. It's only fifty thousand dollars. Consider it a gift."

Favo waved his finger thoughtfully then threw down his hand. "Naw, forget-about-it," he said and changed the subject. "You asked me what I wanted—there is something, Mr. President, that I believe is in your power to grant me."

Presidente Quezon held up his hand and stepped from behind his desk and went over to his private bar. "I have some rare Napoleon Cognac, that's one hundred years old, I would like to share a glass with you at this time...it's very rare."

He poured the precious liquid into two giant snifters and swirled his around and toasted while Favo raised his glass in return and took a sip, unconsciously comparing it to the hooch Johnny Futto made up in the Bronx. To be honest he couldn't taste any difference, but to sound impressed he said, "Wow, you're right, this is beautiful, very smooth."

The smile on El Presidente's face indicated he was pleased. Favo carefully took his time and positioned himself in front of El President. "Now that I'm in Manila," he said measuring every word. "There is one thing I'd like to do here and that's open a casino in the Manila Hotel."

When Presidente Quezon heard Favo's words his eyes rolled. "A casino? This is all you want? Oh, yes of course this is a simple thing," he said, floored by the meager request. "Of course, we must go through the proper channels, but I can assure you there will be no problems. When do you want to do this?"

"As soon as possible," Favo said in earnest.

"Consider it done. Make your plans, Señor Favo."

"Thank you, Mr. President. You won't regret it. I'm going to set up the most beautiful casino you ever saw."

"Wonderful, let's have another cognac and toast to its success. In the Manila Hotel you say?"

"Yes," Favo hastened to add.

"No problema, Señor Favo."

Favo sat up straight. No words could express what he felt at that moment.

The Beginning of the End

The casino opened to huge public fanfare in the fall of 1938. The style and décor were futuristic and luxurious. Because of Lansky's input, it also boasted a five star gourmet restaurant. In essence, it was an American casino without the lavish floorshows of Cuba. It did however, profit from Lansky's knowledgeable casino partners, Eddie and Dino Cellini who came initially to set up the entire operation. The Cellini brothers were the experts of casino gambling and they brought Tony Rodgers with them to be the casino manager. Their motto was, "Deal a straight game, never cheat." They knew the odds would always be in favor of the house.

Favo and Lansky formed the same partnership they previously had with the San Diego deal. Right from the beginning, big bucks rolled in faster than anyone ever imagined. Within a year they were making millions, most of which went into secret Swiss bank accounts. Favo couldn't be happier, for the first time in his life he felt he'd hit it big, but now, for some reason, he picked up something a little different in Perla's behavior.

"Perla," Favo called out. "Come over and sit by me." She snuggled up against him crossing one leg over the other.

"Don't interrupt me, okay?" Favo debated for a second then went on. He knew Perla still felt beneath others and was embarrassed by the way she spoke. Of course to Favo, this meant nothing. "People today are meeting and mixing more than ever," Favo said as he saw her body move defensively. "I want you to be more involved in meeting people—"

"I cannot change what I am, Gringo."

"Goddamnit, Perla, will ya stop all the bullshit and quit worrying?" Favo said, hit with a sort of inspiration. "As far as I'm concerned that was a lifetime ago and who cares anyway what you were...not me."

"About me." Perla looked at Favo and snapped. "Time changes nothing."

"Whatta ya mean it changes nothing?" Favo protested. "We beat the odds didn't we? Just remember if it weren't for you we wouldn't be here. You know that?"

"I tell you what I know, Gringo," she said with emphasis, meeting his eyes. "I know I love you. That's what I know." Her tension seemed to ease a little.

Favo threw out a challenge. "Then marry me!"

"You just say that now, Gringo," Perla said, shuddering as though hit by a sudden deep chill.

"No, goddamnit, I'm not." Favo glowered. "Sooner or later it's time for us to face reality. We're just a couple a goddamn mutts that belong together."

"If you want, Gringo, I marry you, but a woman like me should no be marry to a man like you." Perla said with one hand pressed against her breast. "But if you want, I do my best to make you happy."

"What, am I talking to a stranger?" Favo said, some testiness creeping into his tone. "I don't want you playing no part, I want you to be my wife for crissake, get it? I love you."

"Marry, no marry." Perla's eyes glittered from cold to hard. "I play no part. You know I die for you, Gringo."

Even though Manila was about eighty percent Catholic, minarets could be seen on top of Mohammed Mosque near Arab Street. Rickshaws barreled down the road, on their way to bring visitors to a Chinese temple with the exquisite name of The Temple of the Heavenly Lotus. Manila was a constant round of gaiety, garden parties, and balls for the international set, but today the great China Sea brought more than cargo to the city. The Japanese army did not march into Manila, they came quietly slipping into the quarter of the city bound by stonewalls, Intramuros—the same Chinese marketplace where Perla had gone to buy exotic silks for her wedding dress.

Something must have gone wrong, she thought. Shattering noises surrounded her on all sides, which quickly became multiple explosions. She heard the sound of gunfire coming closer and people beginning to scream. She bit her lower lip. Japanese troops had entered the crowded avenue packed with people. They were wild-eyed soldiers running, shooting, and bayoneting everyone they came upon. A single thought entered her mind—the pistol Favo always made her carry in her pocketbook. There were six bullets in it and she intended to make every one count. Filipino's were fighting back with anything they could lay their hands on, guns, knives, even sticks, in a cursing, roaring frenzy.

A uniformed figure sprung forward, his sword poised ready to flash down on her, but in that split second Perla raised her pistol and let him have it squarely between the eyes. The force of the bullet hurled him backwards through the air, out the door, and sprawling into the street to kingdom come. She propelled herself into the battle making every shot count, unmindful of the empty click of the seventh round. A Japanese officer with a red sash tied around his forehead caught her unaware and plunged his bayonet full force into her chest. The deathblow slammed her against the wall of a building where she slid down, leaving a blood stained path.

As night closed in on Manila, the streets of the quarter filled with smoke. The smell of death was everywhere. The moon, which had shone so brightly the night before, now hid behind a bank of clouds. It was an awful scene—an absolute hell. The Japanese had taken over the city and occupied all of Manila. Morning found Favo a prisoner in his own hotel, his mind spinning. Time passed, perhaps minutes, maybe hours, before Favo decided to bribe the Japanese officer that stood before him. "Let's talk," Favo said in a flat expressionless voice. "I've got some money... and I'm looking for my wife."

Favo went to his room and retrieved from his safe an envelope full of money. "There's plenty more where that came from," he said, handing it to the Japanese officer.

It was a shot in the dark that definitely hit home. The officer assured him that in the Chinese quarter where Perla had gone there was no hope. "She will certainly be dead," he said. "Orders were to take no prisoners there." Favo slumped to the reality of the situation.

Prison Camp

How alone Favo felt now that everything was gone, including Perla. He had been removed from his hotel, and waited devastated in a stinking Manila prison camp. One glimmer of hope remained. An officer told him that for the right price, he would be able to get him into a prison camp in Tokyo where conditions would be better. Favo agreed and after the right amount of money passed hands, he waited to be transferred to Tokyo from the living hellhole of his prison camp. Days turned into weeks, and weeks turned into months. The thought of Perla kept him going—that's all he thought about. Even though they were from two different worlds, Favo knew he could have shown

Perla a love that was incredibly rich and sweet. Perla had swept him up, she had melted his soul and captured his heart. Little did he know, their love was doomed from the start. There was not one day, one hour that his thoughts were not of her. He tried to smile through his sadness until rage engulfed him. He shook his fist at the sky and screamed, hoping that Perla would somehow magically walk through the door. Reality set in and he finally accepted that she was gone—gone forever was that funny last look of hers that he loved so much. His dreams eroded and he turned inward to himself.

The Japanese officer who took his money had vanished. No word of him, until one day he saw a uniformed figure approaching in the camp yard. "Favo Allan," the officer hailed. "It's been a long time."

Favo struggled to his feet. "Well, if it ain't my old pal."

"The final arrangements have been made. You leave on the Tottori Maru bound for Tokyo tomorrow," he said. "I'm sorry that it took so long."

At first break of sunlight, along with the bronze rising sun, the Tottori Maru sailed into Tokyo harbor. Favo paused for a moment on the forward deck to take in his first sight of Japan. Not since Perla's death had he felt a stirring of optimism and hoped now that things might change for the better.

He spent his first month in solitary confinement at Kempee Tai Tarture prison adjacent to the Imperial Palace grounds in downtown Tokyo. Favo realized Japanese officials were keeping him there until his financial dealings in Switzerland were established. They were all in on the deal, waiting for the money. Treatment there was just above passable and the food barely adequate.

Financial arrangements were completed successfully and Favo was transferred to a military hospital where he spent the next two months. His treatment there wasn't much better than he received at Kempee Tai. He was smart enough to make arrangements with the Swiss bank agent he knew personally to make sure he would recognize his voice and only released money to him via a telephone connection.

Finally, Favo was transferred to Tokyo's main camp, Omori-Ku, as promised. This was the headquarters of Japanese war camps and lay on a sand spit in Tokyo Bay, giving a magnificent view of the city. Billeted in the barracks were mainly American and British airmen. The soldiers kept Favo in a special building where conditions were considered better, but still far from adequate.

On his first day in the prison, Favo stood before the camp commander, Captain Yama-Motto, a sadistic brute, whose throat sagged, jowls hanging forward toward his fat lips.

"You are only alive because you have money," said Yama-Motto's hacked voice. "If your funds are no more, I will personally see to it that things will go badly for you."

Favo's first reaction was to jump over the desk and bite his nose off, but he only clenched his fists.

"You've already taken my millions in Manila." Favo said. "But as long as my friends know I'm alive, they'll keep putting money in the account."

"Don't think this gives you any special privileges, if you don't behave, it will be my pleasure to punish you as I see fit."

"What am I gonna do, escape?" Favo shot him a glance full of anger. "Where am I gonna go?"

He was assigned to a cell with Major Thompson, a British officer. The Major had been the subject of extreme torture, and to Favo's further dismay, he discovered there were many others like him. Favo shrugged off these tragedies for the sake of survival, but pledged to avenge them if and when the time came.

Tales of the commander's horror stories also haunted Favo's prison guards, Kami and Muro. Favo read the shame they wore on their faces for the commander, and he suspected they felt he was a disgrace to their Japanese culture. Favo saw this as a foreshadowing of life in the prison camp to come. He called for Kami and Muro to come to his cell. He plunked down a bundle of cash in Kami's hand, causing Kami to jump back in surprise. "What is this for?" he asked.

"That's for nothin'." Favo shrugged his shoulders with a small smile. "Just for you guys."

Their faces were aghast. "It would be an insult for us to take this money," Muro said. A gleam of sympathy shone in his dark eyes. "What we do for you we do because we like you," he said. "We know you are a good man and see how you help others around us. It would be against our honor to take any money for that." Favo took the money back and never offered them another bribe, but thought, *Where the hell do these guys come from?*

The horrid daily life of prison camp went on, prisoners died, mainly from pneumonia, malaria, and beriberi due to inadequate accommodations and shortages of food and water in cold weather. Favo thought back to what the officer in Manila had told him, that the best POW camps were in Tokyo—now that he was here, he hated to think what the other prison camps were like. The optimism he once felt at his prospects tanked. He also witnessed a multitude of deaths attributed to beatings with sword scabbards, saber belts, belt buckles, bamboo sticks, rifle butts, and kicking. At times prisoners were forced to stand at attention for long periods in cold weather, sometimes naked. The guards poured buckets of ice cold water over their throats and nostrils, letting them freeze to death. The majority of these brutalities were for minor infractions of camp regulations, like failing to salute, being slow or failing to execute orders satisfactorily, accepting foodstuff or cigarettes from Japanese guards they would not name, and sometimes for no reason at all. Favo believed a lot of these incidents occurred because the guards couldn't speak English and the prisoners didn't understand what was wanted of them. The arrival of the monsoon rains added to the severity of the conditions.

Besides all of that, there were the airstrikes to contend with and the Japanese failure to provide protection against them. American planes making airstrikes could never distinguish which barracks were the allied prison camps. Favo always got a kick out of how the prisoners failed to see the irony of cheering their own planes, bombing them. Probably the most exciting moment of Favo's incarceration came when the whole camp saw the first night incendiary raid the B-29 bombers made on Tokyo. The flames from the burning city lit up the night like day and gave everyone confidence that liberation was not far off.

As if that wasn't bad enough for the city of Tokyo, a terrible rumble swelled up from below causing buildings to dance on their foundations. Water mains burst out through broken pavement, gas lines erupted in flames, chimneys tumbled, towers toppled, walls collapsed, and roofs caved in. Many parts of Japan's finest city, lay in ruins. A second great tremor shook the ground. Kami and Muro released Favo and the Major from their cell, just before the building collapsed. As the earth quieted, groans could be heard from all sides of the camp.

"Get shovels," Favo yelled. "Come on, let's start diggin' and get these guys out."

Through the terrible days that followed the earthquake Favo, Kami, and Muro ate only scraps of food to keep their strength up and worked tirelessly digging out many that had been buried alive. Favo made a decision.

"This camp commander ain't gonna give up shit, you know that money I offered you?" Favo shouted out to Muro. "Go find it in the rubble of my cell under the bed and take it to buy all the medical supplies you can get your hands on from the black market. Do it now, boys, as quick as you can."

In almost every quarter of the camp, prisoners shared stories of Favo's escapades and daring following the earthquake.

At the close of the war, the Marines entered the prison camp from the south. The camp's commander decided not to vacate his post. Favo struck a deal with the Marine officer who liberated him to give him ten minutes alone with the commander. Favo, with pistol in hand, led Kami, Muro, and Major Thompson to the commander's office. They entered to see Yama-Motto in the middle of a Hari-Kari ritual but before he could plunge his sword into his stomach Favo kicked it away.

"For sure you ain't robbin' me of that pleasure, ya fuckin' butcher." Favo followed with a swift kick that sent the Commander sprawling across the room, then, with his foot on the Commander's throat, Favo held out the pistol to Major Thompson. "Go ahead...take it," he said. "Put this fat bastard out of his misery."

The Major displayed a smile, the kind of smile that said he wasn't capable. "I can't." He barely uttered the words, then lowered his head.

Favo turned to Commander Yama-Motto who struggled to get up. "Take a look around you piece of shit," he said, "because it's your last."

Without hesitation Favo pulled the trigger, sending a bullet through the lower part of the commander's stomach. He struggled on the floor but it wasn't over. "Now, I'm gonna let ya suffer before I send ya to ya maker, that's what a sick bastard like you deserves." Favo took the sword, bared his teeth, and after lowering the commander's pants, hacked off his penis. Favo shoved it in the commander's mouth and dragged his body out for all to see.

Favo came across the Marine officer and shrugged without apology. "That's the way he'll meet his maker. There's another half a dozen in here like him that need killin'. I'll let you know who they are. I belly shot this son-of-a-bitch just to let him watch me put his prick in his mouth. I let him off easy. He deserved worse."

If the dead could die twice the look on Favo's face said he would have done it.

The Comeback

In post-war Japan, the Allied occupation, under the command of General Douglas Macarthur instituted political, social, and economic reform. The government was democratized and a new constitution and bill of rights were put into effect. Millions of Japanese soldiers and civilians were repatriated from overseas. The devastated country experienced acute shortages of food, housing, clothing, and other goods and services. However, Tokyo remained a beehive of activity. Favo saw opportunities there and told Kami and Muro that he wanted to open a bar in downtown Tokyo. "I wanna call it The Daiquiri Palace, and I want you guys to run it," he said. "We'll be partners fifty-fifty. Daiquiris will go over great here like I saw in Cuba. The important thing is to get it right, I want geisha girls all over the joint. The GIs with money are gonna spend it, and besides, the black market is gonna be big here. We'll all cash in."

Somehow the city settled into equilibrium. Life surged back into Tokyo and the city resonated with a new rhythm. The Daiquiri Palace raked in money hand over fist and turned a much bigger profit than Favo expected. Their success led Favo to inform Kami and Muro that they were expanding into the import-export business now. Before the end of the year, Sunrise Exports grew into a giant operation, far exceeding the success of Favo's casino in Manila. He was now making more money exporting MADE IN JAPAN products to the States than he ever could have imagined.

Back in the States, six men sat at a round table, their ages ranging from mid-fifties to eighty. Each was called by a single first name with a nod of recognition. Meyer Lansky led off the meeting about a Hollywood nightclub owner. Billy Wilkerson, who had a vision to recreate Hollywood's Sunset Strip in Las Vegas on forty acres of land he purchased one mile south of the Last Frontier out on the strip, had run out of funds in the middle of building his first class hotel. The Boys at the table voted by a silent head nod to take it over. Bugsy Siegel, after much politicking, was put in charge of the hotel and called it The Flamingo after his girlfriend, Virginia "Flamingo" Hill.

In an overseas phone conversation, Lansky told Favo that he had nothing to do with putting Siegel at the helm of the new hotel. It was the commission's decision. Their logic was that his Hollywood friends would come to Vegas to see this magnificent hotel. Lansky wanted Favo to come to Las Vegas and bring his Japanese players so he could see everything for himself.

"I'll come, Meyer," Favo said with grim resignation. "But, for sure I ain't meeting no Bugsy fuckin' Siegel for nobody, I'm coming because there's other things I wanna discuss with you."

Sitting in first class on the flight back to the States, Favo reminisced about the many bizarre events in his life over the past ten years. He slipped into a trance, almost sleeping, reflecting on what would have happened if he hadn't met Perla. It still hurt him to think she was gone. Falling in love again felt inconceivable.

Perla had been everything to him. Lost in his recollections, time sped on. *Impossible,* he thought when the stewardess graciously woke him to say they were landing in LA.

Before going on to Las Vegas, Favo had some companies to see in Los Angeles that his Japanese holdings did business with. He figured this would take about three days. This worked out for his Japanese traveling companions, giving them the time they wanted to go shopping at the exclusive stores on Rodeo Drive.

The first thing Favo intended to do was talk to Lansky about the Japanese agendas he'd been pursuing. One was a small inexpensive car that would be ready for export in the near future and the other, which was available now, was Japanese steel. Favo believed Japan was ripe to export steel. Towards the end of the war their grade hadn't been the best but all that changed. They now could match or beat any quality in the world. In spite of how contractors in the states screamed about price, when they bought steel it was only American. If Meyer could reach the right person and change that, the low prices of Japanese steel would not only sweep America, but Canada and Europe as well. A fortune was waiting to be made.

Nikki

Tony Rodgers, wise guy, bon vivant, and Favo's longtime close friend, knew the Flamingo Hotel's first opening was a disaster. He also knew he wouldn't be alive to see the second opening, but made up his mind that his wife, Nikki, should go there no matter what. Nikki, originally from the west coast, left after high school for college in New York City. Eventually graduating with a Master's degree in Art from Columbia University, she enjoyed an illustrious career in the art world.

When Nikki met Tony Rodgers in an elevator in the Supreme Court building, he had just been awarded damages in a slander suit against a major newspaper who claimed he was a known consort of organized crime. The timing was perfect. Handsome, exciting, and charming, he swept her off her feet. They got married and six months later moved out to Tahoe where Tony bought a hotel. With the hotel barely established, Tony was diagnosed with cancer. They struggled together in the fight, but they knew there was no happy ending to be had here.

Nikki, in LA on business, headed to the Beverly Hills Fine Arts Center. She was a striking figure. Many a male head turned as she glided past but she hardly noticed the admiring glances, so intent was she in her purpose. Turning down Rodeo Drive, she experienced a little burst of excitement upon spotting the art gallery. Inside were some of her favorite works of art. She stood for a long moment in front of Gauguin's *Tahitian Women on a Beach,* admiring it's simplistic beauty. It looked so fresh, as if he had created it only yesterday.

A bell rang behind her, signaling the arrival of another customer. A glance told her a man like this wasn't usually found in an art gallery, but he gazed at the Gauguin with an intensity that surprised her. A salesperson approached him asking, "Are you an admirer of Gauguin?"

"Naw...I can't tell ya' a Picasso from a pizza. This one here just brings back some memories to me, that's all."

Nikki stifled a laugh. She couldn't help notice the unique sound of his voice and how his accent was just like Tony's. She didn't want to turn around and spoil the moment.

"We have others in the back...Renoir, Degas, Van Gogh, Cezanne..."

"Don't worry about it, pal. I can't tell ya one from the other, if I did I'd probably be collectin' em."

Nikki closed her eyes, inclined her head, and gave a half-smile.

"You have no idea how much these paintings increase in value." The manager gave him a look of reassurance.

Favo nodded his head, tipping his hat as he walked toward the door. "Tell me about it."

By the time he was back out on Rodeo Drive the idea of a fine art gallery in Tokyo had taken root. *What a winner that would be.*

Lansky made sure that Bugsy wasn't around when he took Favo to visit the construction site of the Flamingo. Favo got right to it,

"I still can't understand how you guys could put a psycho case like Siegel in charge of such a big project like this hotel," he said in a mix of bitterness and affection. "What the hell does he know about running a hotel or anything legitimate for that matter?"

"A lot of people think I put Benny in, but it was all the commission," Lansky said with emphasis. "Bugsy made a passionate plea to them based on his personal ability to attract all of the biggest movie stars, the crème de la crème of Hollywood who'd come, stay, and gamble in Las Vegas. They bought it and put him in charge of the construction and management. I never stepped in between you two guys but I'm afraid on this issue I have to agree with you. We'll see if he delivers."

"When you asked me to invest in The Flamingo," Favo said in a silky voice, "You told me that it'd be the biggest and most beautiful hotel in Las Vegas. Forget Siegel, I thought and said okay only because of you—to me this hotel is chicken feed compared to what I want to talk to you about."

"I'm all ears," Lanksy said.

"Steel!" Favo spelled it out. "S-t-e-e-l."

Lansky sat up, a look of intrigue on his face while Favo told him of his connections with the Japanese steel industry and brought him up to date on their product. After Favo finished, Lansky's head bowed in deep concentration for a long moment. "When your Jap friends start bringing in their steel," Meyer said, "They'll be putting the American distributors here through the wringer. They won't stand for it. You know the deal."

"I know, Meyer," said Favo. "I figured you'd know how to get around that."

"Maybe I do." Lansky sighed. "It's been a few years, but Costello did a lot of business with a certain someone I've got in mind. This guy knows the game. Everyone will have to get a taste, but he could do it if he thinks it's worthwhile."

"Who's the guy?"

"He used to be the Ambassador to England. His name is Joe Kennedy. I don't want to say he'll do it, but there's a good chance he might. Costello did more for him than his mother...he carried him for ten months one time when they ran booze together."

"Who knows, Meyer." Favo gave a quick nod. "Maybe one day ya might be bigger than US Steel...whatta' ya think about that?"

"What do I think? I think it's a long way from Delancey Street."

"Vood den?" Favo responded, mocking the old Jews in their neighborhood and making them both laugh.

Lansky remembered the news he'd been meaning to relate. "You heard about Tony Rodgers?"

"No, what about him?" Favo stopped dead in his tracks.

"Everything was going good for him." Lansky hesitated then his voice suddenly rose. "His hotel, the Ali Baba in Tahoe, and he just got married...then he gets hit with the hammer. They gave him six months...cancer. He knew you were coming and asked me to tell you. Maybe you'll get a chance to go up to Tahoe and see him?"

"For sure." Favo sighed deeply. "What a fuckin' shame...they don't come any better than Tony."

Lansky was the one who'd sent Tony Rodgers over to Manila in the beginning with the Cellini's to be the casino manager. In the two years that Tony spent in Manila he and Favo became close friends.

Favo deplaned in Reno and went straight to the Ali Baba Hotel. Tony greeted him with an enthusiastic, traditional goomba hug. Despite his illness, his fiery personality seemed intact. "You believe this bullshit?" he said. "I dodged a Senate investigation, my casino is up and doing great, I just met and married the greatest goddamn woman anyone could ever hope for and now... just like that, I'm hit with snake eyes." He hesitated for a moment then looked at Favo. "So how you doin'?"

"Okay." Favo chuckled at the change of direction.

"The worst thing," Tony continued, "is Nikki, my wife. Before the ink dries on our marriage license, I'll be gone."

Tony went into detail about Nikki; where she was from, how they met, and above all what a wonderful person she was. "Too bad she ain't here to meet ya, she had to go to LA about some art work. That's what she does...she's an art advisor. I told her when

I go she'll get the hotel and the whole ball-a-wax. She'll be worth a couple, two, three million then. She's still young and—"

"Now, wait a minute," Favo interrupted to set Tony straight. "Lissen a me, Tony, why don't ya use your noodle and sell everything now, why wait? Don't forget this ain't her business," he said. "What does she know about running casinos? Sell the joint now and set her up with a trust account, this way you'll know no matter what she'll always be okay in the future. With all the fuckin' rat bastards around, ya never know."

A curious look came over Tony's face. "I hear ya Favo and that ain't a bad idea," he said. "When I tell people my troubles half of them don't give a shit, and the other half are glad I'm getting what's comin' to me."

"Am I right?" Favo said.

They spent the remainder of the day exchanging stories about the old days. Tony recalled an incident, "Ya remember when Matty Brown wanted two G's from the Dutchman to run a load of his hooch through Fordham."

"Yeah." Favo laughed. "Then after the Dutchman threw a couple a shots at him, Matty got so pissed he raised the price to five G's."

"Yeah, yeah...yeah," Tony laughed then had to gain control of himself because of the pain. "Favo, after I'm gone, do me a favor will ya?"

"Whatta ya mean, after you're gone? Where ya goin'? Ya look pretty good to me. Stop the bullshit, will ya?" Favo shook his head. "Ya sure that croaker ya got knows what he's talkin' about?"

"Ya may be right, but just in case will ya do me a favor?"

"For sure...what's that?"

"After I'm gone, look up my Nikki will ya and see if she's doing all right? I know how ya felt about Perla and who knows if you're ever thinkin' about getting tied up again, but for sure I can see...you and my Nikki might—"

"Why don't ya stop." Favo interrupted, holding up his hands with a grim expression.

"I'm sorry...I don't know what's got into me," Tony said with dread in his voice. "I'm all fucked up."

Favo thought Tony was being melodramatic. He didn't like talk like that. Even though Favo had broken just about every law on the books, he had his own code of morality, especially when it came to respecting another man's woman. *Fat chance of me tying up with a pal of mine's widow,* he thought.

"Sure, Tony," said Favo with a slow and dry smile. "I'll look her up and make sure she's doin' okay...whatever you say. Don't worry about it."

The cancer ravaged on until Favo finally got word back while in Tokyo that Tony was gone. Favo wasn't much for funerals, but he was glad he'd gone to see his old pal before he died.

The Hotel

The initial problem with The Flamingo was Bugsy Siegel. If you didn't know much about him, you'd think he was a nice guy, but he was totally out of his element even before the hotel opened. He had no experience in the field of construction or design, which made the costs rise way over the top because of the constant changes he made. When workers and suppliers got wind of Bugsy's ignorance, they stole material and equipment and resold it back to him over and over. The rising expenditures resulted in furious outbursts, which unnerved construction workers only further delaying the project. In October 1946, Benny "Bugsy" Siegel's assessment of the hotel was premature. He sent invitations out late for a New Year's Eve opening of the grand and beautiful Flamingo Hotel in Las Vegas. The resort's opening was a flop and failed to produce sufficient revenue, which further drained the resources of its investors. By January 1947, the boys ordered Siegel to close the hotel until management could be restructured properly and reopened. It was then the boys discovered that he had skimmed $2.5 million from the outfit to put in a Swiss bank account. "Why the dirty rat," Lansky said, measuring every word. "After all I did for him."

The final straw for Bugsy was when he told Lucky Luciano to go f*** himself at a commission meeting in Havana, Cuba. This was a no-no that Luciano couldn't let slide because it was in front of all the mob bosses of the commission. Only Lansky's pleadings kept Bugsy off the hit list that day. Unfortunately, couple that with the discovery of what Bugsy skimmed from the Flamingo and his fate was sealed.

Frankie Carbo, a friend of Favo's, received the contract. He knew Favo would love to be in on the hit so he approached him in secret, asking Favo if he wanted a piece of the action. "You bet your ass I do." Favo agreed with vivid recollections of his past with Bugsy.

On a balmy June night, two figures came up to the bay window of Bugsy Siegel's home in Beverly Hills. While he relaxed on his living room couch they raised their rifles like a matched set of dancers in a routine and shot him so full of holes he looked like a hunk of Swiss cheese. Then, as quickly as they appeared, they vanished back into the night—never to be discovered.

Second Chance

Nikki's assets included her power of concentration and her ability to put things in order, dealing with the most important things first. Some might call it tunnel vision. On her drive to the Flamingo in Las Vegas with her mother, her mind hummed with focus on the difficult situation she was certain to encounter, even though Bugsy wasn't around anymore.

Benny "Bugsy" Siegel had been one of America's cleverest, shrewdest, and most successful gangsters. He was one of the most feared men in organized crime with a lavish high profile lifestyle and a seemingly endless amount of money to burn. She'd met him through her husband about two years before and although he was brash, opinionated, and dictatorial, they had always enjoyed a good working relationship.

Her mind kept returning to an incident with Bugsy's girlfriend a few years earlier. Tony Rodgers had convinced Bugsy to put a fine-arts collection in the Flamingo hotel as part of the décor. "It'll be an investment where ya can eventually make a lot of money," he'd said. Bugsy wasn't exactly convinced, but he hired Nikki on anyway to curate the collection.

That same day Bugsy's girlfriend, Flamingo, and the Hotel's namesake, called and asked to meet her the next time she was in LA.

"Sorry about all of this with Benny," Flamingo said over a classy LA café lunch. "He's overwhelmed trying to open the hotel and everything."

"It's no problem," Nikki said, enjoying the cool breeze on the outdoor patio. "What can I do to help?"

"*Tahitian Dreams.*" Flamingo tapped the table in pointed emphasis. "Painted by Gauguin in 1896. It's a portrait of a Tahitian woman. The woman is sitting under a tree—"

"I know the painting." Nikki lifted her head boldly.

Flamingo made no response and simply sat staring at her. Nikki knew she had the upper hand for the moment.

"I've described the painting correctly, haven't I?"

Nikki nodded. "You did."

"Can I trust you?"

"You have to trust me." Nikki returned Flamingo's steely gaze.

"I want you to recommend it to Benny. I was looking forward to having that painting."

Nikki realized something then. The reason Benny said to put all the paintings he acquired for the hotel in Flamingo's name was probably because she had forced him to. Flamingo was one smart cookie, realizing one day that these impressionistic masterpieces would be priceless and probably worth more that the hotel itself.

Nikki let out a long, thoughtful sigh. "I can't let you buy that painting."

"Why not?"

"There might be a problem with it."

"Why? Is it a fake?"

"No." Nikki shook her head. "It's real and one of Gauguin's best. But I can't recommend it."

"Well, then would you please explain why?"

"The ownership of that painting is questionable."

Flamingo gave her a questioning look. "How do you know this?"

"It's my business to know these things." Nikki was adamant.

"Why?"

"Because a certain Dr. Gordon bought the painting from Admiral Faraday's wife. Although he was a four star admiral with an impeccable reputation, there is no documentation for the painting and its provenance is disputed."

"So where did he get it from?"

"I'm afraid I can't tell you that and neither can anyone else, now that the admiral is deceased. What we do know is that it disappeared when it was on loan to the President of the Philippines. The conjecture is that the Japanese confiscated it."

"I see." Flamingo nodded with understanding.

Flamingo was thoughtful for a moment then narrowed her eyes. "I suppose you see a possible long legal battle over that, don't you?"

"I have no idea, but there are other paintings."

The grand re-opening of The Flamingo Hotel with Gus Greenbaum, a bona fide hotel manager, at the helm was scheduled for March 1947. Nikki Rodgers knew it would be an exclusive event with all the movers and shakers, including movie celebrities, in attendance. She also knew how close Tony was to Lansky and the people involved with The Flamingo. She wondered how many of his friends would be there. She decided to go to the gala affair with her mother. It would be the first major function she would appear at since Tony had died earlier that year.

For the most part, they drove in silence to Las Vegas. Nikki's mother patting her hand on the steering wheel gave her comfort. The sun was setting by the time they arrived at the lavish entrance of the hotel. Nikki entered the enormous marbled lobby, wondering why the masterpieces she provided weren't hanging on the walls of rococo plaster. Nikki looked around studying it, to her it was as impersonal as a museum but she knew its grandeur fulfilled Bugsy's vision.

She made her way to the reservation desk where she announced herself to the desk clerk.

"Oh, yes. Mrs. Rodgers, Mr. Greenbaum pre-checked you in. He said he'd be pleased to escort you both to the gala this evening, and will meet you at 9 o'clock." The clerk gestured to the nearby bellhop to take their bags.

With quick efficiency, the bellhop led them to their suite on the fourth floor. He turned to her and said, "You're Mrs. Rodgers, right?"

"Yes," she said.

"I worked for Tony years ago. He was the best boss I ever had." He related his memories of Tony with a trace of humility. "If there's anything you need, Mrs. Rodgers, please let me know. I'd be honored to be of service."

She had not mistaken that fanatically respectful gleam in his eye. She had seen it many times before from people that Tony had touched. *Oh, how I miss him,* she thought as she entered her suite.

At that same moment, at the Las Vegas airport, Favo Allan descended the steps of a chartered plane with a contingent of his Japanese gamblers from Tokyo. In the far corners of his mind, the promise he'd made to Tony Rodgers about going to see his widow lingered. He was reluctant, but a promise was a promise.

Arriving at the Flamingo, the initial trickle of guests turned into a steady stream. He took in the grandeur of the hotel. It had obviously been modeled after the spacious resort hotels of Miami Beach but with more gaudy elegance. Its entrance, with its ornately carved and painted ceiling two stories high, left him breathless. Handmade Chinese rugs covered smoked Irish marble floors. Some walls were gilded and others covered with vast murals.

Favo made his way to the bar in the casino. He'd made plans to meet up with Lansky, who was in the kitchen checking out the food. Few people realized that was Lansky's thing—all his establishments served the best food. Favo sipped a glass of Zinfandel, scanning the room and spotting Gus Greenbaum coming into the lounge with a stunning lady on his arm. Another older woman followed behind. He pushed himself up on an elbow to admire her better. *Now that's a beautiful woman,* he thought. *No doubt about it.*

She wore an elegant beige suit that almost matched her coloring. The belted skirt was cut to fit her skintight. Under her jacket, she wore a high-necked blouse of sky blue silk, exactly matching her eyes. The heels of her designer shoes were just the right height to give her legs a graceful turn. Her looks stirred Favo's memory and he couldn't help but notice that she had the gait of a young filly. Not since Perla had he seen a woman that moved him so seductively. The intense desire that had been missing in him for years came rushing back as he watched her.

Gus Greenbaum spotted Favo and steered Nikki and her mother through the crowd over toward him. "Wait till you meet this guy," he said leaning close to Nikki. "He's something else, and a good friend of Tony's." Gus's remark was commonplace to Nikki, she was always hearing that someone or another was a good friend of Tony's. They approached the bar, and Favo stood. Gus greeted him with a warm handshake. "Say hello to Nikki and her mother." He then turned to Nikki and said, "This is Favo Allan."

After what felt like a long moment, Favo's gaze met Nikki's. Her cheeks flushed and every muscle in her body tensed in a wave between disbelief and wonder as she gazed at one of the handsomest men she'd ever seen. Keeping a grip on her emotions, she managed to maintain her outward composure as her hand gracefully slipped into Favo's extended handshake.

Struggling against the sudden overpowering attraction seizing him, all Favo could do was grin back at her like a little kid. Gus, in his new role as host said, "Nikki was married to Tony Rodgers."

Favo shook his head like he'd been blindsided. His jaw dropped and for the first time in his life he was speechless—nothing came out.

Gus couldn't seem to figure out what was happening. "Hey, Favo...are you all right?"

In the lingering silence, Nikki's beautiful blue eyes continued to focus on Favo. Her body remained rigid, but curiosity got the best of her as a smile slowly bloomed. "Are all those stories Tony told me about you true?"

"Ah, I don't know," Favo said, then hesitated adding, "In my life I've done a lot of things—some good and some bad."

He brought her hand up and gave it, a slow, conscious kiss. *This is going to be simple,* he thought. He tried to visualize telling her he loved her. He knew that would come easy. Then asking her to marry him would be like falling off a log. And then making love to her, well, he could hardly wait for that one.

At that moment Gus was called away, but before he left he turned to say, "Thanks for coming, Favo."

Favo, still in a trance, didn't respond.

"Whoa. Favo! You hear me? Thanks for coming," Greenbaum repeated tapping him on the shoulder.

"Believe me, Gus," Favo replied. "You have no idea how happy I am to be here."

"I'm happy, too." Nikki echoed.

It was love at first sight. The air was charged with electricity. Favo continued to gaze at Nikki and asked, "Will you have dinner with me tonight?"

A surge of energy pulsed between them. "I would consider it an honor," Nikki replied, hoping he would never let go of her hand.

Favo's emotions were closing in, "How come nobody ever stole you away?"

"I've been waiting for the right person."

Nikki and Favo had stolen each other's hearts in a mutual seduction. Nikki's mother saw the reciprocal fascination going on between them. "Have you two met before?" she asked.

"No," Favo said with certainty. "An you can kick me to the curb if I'm lyin'. Me and your daughter Nikki here." He paused, taking a steadying breath. "Are at the start of a great relationship."

Nikki's mother turned to see a wide smile of approval on her daughter's face. "You two are crazy, you know that? You just met each other for God's sake...I don't understand."

"What I do understand, Mother, is that the future is ours to see," Nikki said. "In my soul, my heart and my dreams, I believe Favo and I might make a lifetime out of getting to know each other."

It was as simple as that. "You hear what she's sayin' Momma?" Favo said. "End a story."

A Look Back
Suggested Further Reading

Books

Benedetto, John and Patricia Benedetto. *The Shadow of his Smile: Brothers Together in Life and Song*. Benedetto Publishing, 2017.

Bussel, Robert. *Fighting for Total Person Unionism: Harold Gibbons, Ernest Calloway, and Working Class Citizenship*. University of Illinois Press, 2015.

Dundee, Angelo with Bert Randolph Sugar. *My View from the Corner: A Life in Boxing*. New York: McGraw Hill, 2008.

Franco, Joseph and Richard Hammer. *Hoffa's Man: The Rise and Fall of Jimmy Hoffa Witnessed by His Strongest Arm*. Prentice Hall, 1987.

Johnson, John, Jr., Joel Selvin with Dick Cami. *Peppermint Twist: The Mob, The Music, and the Most Famous Dance Club of the '60s*. New York: Thomas Dunne Books, 2012.

Spector, Ronnie with Vince Waldron. *Be My Baby: How I Survived Mascara, Miniskirts and Madness, or My Life as a Fabulous Ronette*. New York: Harmony Books 1990.

Articles

"And Now Everybody Is Doing It; the TWIST." *Life*, November 24, 1961

Getlen, Larry. "A Mob Tale with a Twist." *New York Post*, November 11, 2012

"Instant Fad." *Time*, October 20, 1961

Wolcott, James. "A Twist in Time." *Vanity Fair*, November 2007.

Dick Cami was born in the Bronx, grandson of an Italian immigrant chef who worked for some of the best restaurants and hotels in New York City and, along with a traditional extended Italian family, gave Cami a taste and love for food and life. His musical interests were inherited from his father, a renowned voice teacher and visionary before his time, and his mother a beautiful spirit and gifted, classically trained opera soprano. Cami tried a variety of jobs before a combination of aptitude, opportunity and fate saw him settle into the restaurant business. After an initial stint as a record producer in his early-twenties he was one of the founders of the original New York Peppermint Lounge, the first rock and roll nightclub and home of the Twist. Immediately following that serendipitous success in December, 1961 he opened a second Peppermint Lounge in Miami Beach, Florida. It wasn't that much later until he opened Top of the Home, the fine dining roof top restaurant he operated with partner, Chef Joe Ezbecki, for 26 years in Hollywood, Florida. Simultaneously Cami promoted concerts of classic rock and roll groups, music legends Tony Bennett, Englebert Humperdinck, Dean Martin, Julio Iglesias, various boxers and, at one time, Finbarr Nolan, an Irish touch healer. In later years he owned the chain of fast but fresh Cami seafood restaurants and popular, family oriented restaurants from Scottsdale, Arizona to Key West and eventually back again to the Miami area. He even managed to find time for consulting work with the Teamsters. Love took him to the Pacific Northwest and kept him there where he lives today in Portland, Oregon.

CPSIA information can be obtained
at www.ICGtesting.com
Printed in the USA
LVHW05s1712011018
591987LV00024B/1183/P

9 781941 271322